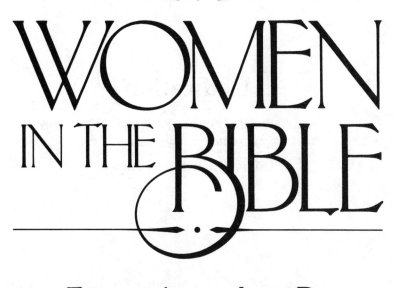

WOMEN IN THE BIBLE

Examples to Live By

by
Sylvia Charles

HENSLEY
PUBLISHING

Dedication

I dedicate this study of women in the Bible to three precious young women in my life, my daughters....

Donna, Laurie, and Nancy

Acknowledgments

I wish to thank all those who have allowed me to use their personal stories as illustrations of Scriptural truths. I pray that their true-life experiences will bless the reader as much as these friends have enriched my life.

I also want to publicly express appreciation to my husband, Don, for his encouragement and support as we have shared the Lord's working out of these teachings in our marriage relationship.

I am, most of all, grateful to my Father in Heaven for sending His Son, Jesus, to die for my sin and give me His Holy Spirit that I may be taught from His Word and then used to share that Word with others.

The Bible version used in this book, unless otherwise noted, is King James Version.

ISBN 1-56322-021-0

Women in the Bible

About Photocopying This Book

Foreword

It was during a quiet time with the Lord a number of years ago that I read, in Luke 17:32, the simple command of Jesus: "Remember Lot's wife." Though I was aware that He was describing the signs of the times just prior to His Second Coming, I was impressed with the fact that Jesus chose this one nameless woman to be remembered out of all history! And, as I realized that I was one of those now living in the end times, I felt compelled to discover why Jesus asked that we remember Lot's wife!

I reread her story in Genesis, trying to put myself in her place. As I did, I saw, anew, the consequences of looking back (for whatever reason) when God is wanting us to move on with Him. I recorded my thoughts, not realizing then that this would be a chapter of my first book, Women in the Word, to be published some years later.

I became so fascinated with "remembering Lot's wife" that I determined to do the same with other Bible women—until I finally completed a study of 64 women named in Scripture. In the process, I began to see that all of these women were but a prelude to the ultimate woman in God's Word—the Bride of Jesus Christ. Thus, the lessons learned from these women in the Bible are part of God's way of preparing us, the Church, as the Bride.

My burden has been that we, who are now living in the days of which Jesus was speaking in Luke 17, need not only to heed the command to "remember Lot's wife," but also to learn from other Bible women.

It is my prayer that every woman who studies Women in the Bible—Examples to Live By will be as blessed as I have been in learning these truths that God would have us apply to our own lives...that we might become a beautiful Bride for Jesus Christ.

"Beloved, now are we the sons of God, and it doth not yet appear what we shall be; but we know that, when he shall appear, we shall be like him; for we shall see him as he is." (I John 3:2)

Table of Contents

Lesson 1
Understanding the Bible

You, as a woman who desires to be in God's Will, are now beginning a study of the women portrayed in God's Word. This will be more than a survey, or even a character study of the women in the Bible, for we will look at these women in Scripture in light of the lessons we can learn from them. Then we'll try to apply these teachings to our own lives—that the Word might be made flesh in us!

Woman was created as the counterpart of man. She was intended to have an intimate relationship with him. Woman is the feminine of man. She is also a symbol for the Church, the Bride of Jesus Christ. And so, as we look at the women in God's Word, we will see ourselves and discover the nature God wants to form in us as He prepares us as a Bride for His Son.

Eve, as the first woman (Genesis) described in the Bible, is but a type of the last "woman" (Revelation), the Bride whose relationship with Jesus will be consummated at the marriage supper of the Lamb. In between are many women from whom we can learn. Some were good examples. Some were not.

Before we actually begin the study of Eve, we will use this first lesson to come into common agreement on the Word of God—what it is, how it came into being, and how we can put our faith in it as being wholly true. If we do not have the same belief in the Word, it will be difficult to discuss the teachings and apply them to our lives.

Bible Versions and Translations

The Bible is one book, one history, one story—*His* story. It's God's written revelation of His plan and will for man. It's a book that is ageless, timeless, and appropriate for each and every person in the world. It's a unique book that brings life to those who read and believe it.

It's a book unlike all others. A progressive, divine revelation which moves from the beginning of time until the end of time. It contains 66 books, was written by 40 authors, and covers a period of about 1600 years! Kings and princes, poets and philosophers, prophets and statesmen, shepherds, doctors, and fishermen were all inspired by the Holy Spirit to write, over a period of several centuries, one story that did not contradict itself. Rather, the story gave one whole and complete message.

It's difficult to know exactly how the Old Testament came into being. There's a strong Jewish tradition that it was Ezra, the scribe, who arranged the canon, although collections of the Pentateuch and some of the Prophets existed long before his time.

The books of the Hebrew canon were arranged in three groups—the Law, the Prophets, and the Writings, which included the "wisdom literature." The 24 books of the Hebrew canon are equivalent to the 39 books of the Greek canon (which we now know as the Old Testament).

Most of the books in our Old Testament are quoted in the New Testament. This suggests that the "Old Testament" Jesus knew was identical to that generally used among the Jews. (About a dozen books are not included in the Protestant Bible. They were not a part of the Jewish Old Testament canon, and were not accepted as genuine and inspired. These are known as the Apocrypha.)

Though we have little early evidence, we can piece together the way the New Testament came into being. The Old Testament was regularly read in early-church services, and it was natural to add a reading from some authentic document about the life and death of Jesus Christ.

At first, the apostles themselves provided a spoken testimony; but after their deaths, the Church needed a written record of what they had said. Their letters were added to the Gospels because they gave guidance on Christian behavior. The Book of Acts was included as a continuation of Luke's Gospel, because it recounted the beginnings of the early Church. The Revelation of John had strong appeal in time of persecution.

Ancient methods of publishing were very different from today's methods. Manuscripts were usually reproduced by a group of scribes writing at the dictation of the chief scribe. Because of the labor involved, the manuscripts were too expensive for general use and, were preserved for use in groups. The form of the manuscript used in the early Church was the papyrus, leather, or parchment scroll, which had been in use for centuries. But there is good reason to believe that quite early in the second century A.D., Christians began using the book form for easy reference. It's from these early scrolls and manuscripts that translators often produce the various versions that we have today.

In the Middle Ages, the Latin Vulgate was the Church's official version. But following the Reformation, there was a desire to translate the Bible into national languages so the common people could understand it. The printing press had also come into being, so Bibles could now be mass produced. It was the German Bible that first contained numbered verses.

In England there were many early attempts to translate parts of the Bible into English. These included Wycliffe, Tyndale, and the Cloverdale editions. Finally, 47 scholars were appointed by King James I to do a translation based on original languages and all available translations at the time. It was the most complete work, and thus, in 1611 it became the authorized version of the Bible.

Since then many other versions have appeared. Some were the work of committees, such as the Revised Standard Version. Others were the work of one man, such as the Living Bible by Ken Taylor, who simply wanted to put Scripture into a language his ten children could understand at the family devotional time. The various versions and translations help shed light on the Scriptures, so it is good to use several when studying the Bible in depth.

All of this is for the purpose of getting out the message, of hearing God clearly and accurately. Even with its many authors and sources, the Bible presents a common theme throughout its pages because the Holy Spirit brooded over the whole process. Though there seems to be a major shifting between the Old and New Testaments, the same God speaks and the same Holy Spirit inspired men. In these fallible men, He planted a seed of faith which would eventually blossom out in its completion in Jesus. And this Jesus, supernaturally conceived, was born into the natural world of problems and sin and became the complete expression of God's Word.

How Can the Word of God be Life?

The kind of life we have on earth, as well as the place of our eternal existence, depends ultimately on one choice that we make: **Will we believe God's Word as true for us—or not?** Our salvation, as well as the depth of our earthly commitment to the Lord, depends on our believing or not believing the Word of God to be wholly true.

We must believe that:
* The Bible is the inspired Word of God.
* It is as true for us today as it was when it was written.
* What the Word says about itself is true.
* God spoke the Word and the heavens and its host came into being.
* This Word is sharp as it divides soul and spirit, as well as the thoughts and intents of the heart.
* The Word endures forever and will not pass away, even though heaven and earth do.
* The Word will not return to God without accomplishing what He wants it to do.
* The Word judges us and reveals our sin.
* Jesus is the Word of God made flesh, even as He came to dwell among men.

To believe God's Word, we must accept that it is true *by faith*. And faith itself comes from hearing the Word! Thus, reading and meditating upon the Word itself builds our faith and gives us the ability to believe the Word as God's Word!

In computer language, if we put "garbage" in, we'll get "garbage" out. If we put trashy literature, junky TV, negative thoughts and idle words into our minds, these things will come out sooner or later in ungodly words and actions. If we put the Word of God into our minds and hearts, the Word of God will come out in actions pleasing to Him.

The one thing that destroys faith is *doubt*. Doubt eventually produces unbelief and makes faith impossible. Satan knows this. He used this tactic successfully with Eve, just as he does when anyone succumbs to his question, "Hath God said...?"

When Satan appeared to Eve in the Garden of Eden in the form of a serpent, he questioned her concerning a command God had given. He tempted her by suggesting that her eyes would be opened and she could become "as God." He even lied, saying God would surely not let her die!

WOMEN IN THE BIBLE

Perhaps these were the thoughts that went through her mind:

...We have much authority now. What's wrong with a little more?

...Adam won't mind when I give him some of this delicious fruit to eat. After all, I ought to be able to make a decision on my own!

. . . The consequences of disobedience can't be that bad. I haven't seen anything terrible happen yet.

Lust, pride, rebellion, the desire for independence—these are some of the things within our nature that Satan uses to tempt us, just as he probably did with Eve. Compare this with the temptation of Jesus in the wilderness following His baptism. Here we see how Satan could find nothing in Jesus with which to tempt Him; no lust, no pride, no rebellion, no desire for independence. Instead, Jesus evidenced victory over Satan by reminding him what God had said through His written Word.

Actually, when we begin to doubt God's Word, we're attempting to become "as God." We're partaking from the forbidden tree, trying to determine for ourselves what is good and what is evil. Jesus, who was God, continued to submit to the wisdom of His Heavenly Father as expressed in the Word and communicated by the Holy Spirit.

Satan, our enemy, wants us to doubt God's Word, thus partaking of his own character of pride and rebellion. The cause of his fall from heaven, in the first place, was because he wanted to "be like the Most High." Satan wants man to rebel also, to assume the position of God, to have the self-obtained knowledge of good and of evil so he can justify his own actions.

God, on the other hand, desires that we allow His Holy Spirit to lead us, for His Spirit is the Spirit of truth and can teach us all things (John 14:17 and 26).

Thus, we have to choose: Will we believe God's Word or Satan's Word? And, if we believe what God says in His Word, are we willing to accept it and obey it no matter what the cost?

Ask the Holy Spirit to guide you as you fill in the main truths from these following Scriptures:

Joshua 1:8 The benefits of continual meditation upon the

Book of the Law are _____

_____

_____

John 15:7 If we abide in Jesus, and His Words abide in us, we

_____

_____

II Timothy 3:16 and 17 _____

_____

_____

4

Scripture is _____

_____

_____

and is profitable for _____

_____

_____

Psalm 119:89 God's Word is _____

_____

_____

Isaiah 55:8-11 God's Word will _____

_____

_____

I Peter 1:23-25 The Word of God _____

_____

_____

II Peter 1:20 and 21 Holy Scripture was written by _____

_____

_____

Revelation 22:18 and 19 If anyone adds to the prophecy of the
Word, God will add to him _____

_____

_____

If he takes away from the words of prophecy, God will ____

_____

_____

John 20:31 The gospel of John was written that _____

_____

_____

Romans 10:17 _____

_____

_____

comes by _____

_____

_____

WOMEN
IN THE BIBLE

Psalm 119:105 The Word is _____

_____

_____

and _____

_____

_____

James 1:22-25 In regard to the Word, we are to _____

_____

_____

_____, not _____

_____

_____

John 12:47 and 48 For those who reject Christ, the _____

_____

_____

will _____

_____

_____

him in the last day.

Revelation 20:4 Those who reigned with Christ were those
who gave their lives for the witness of Jesus and for _____

_____

_____

Lesson 2
Eve

An Example of God's Divine Order for Women

"But I would have you know, that the head of every man is Christ; and the head of the woman is the man; and the head of Christ is God."

I Corinthians 11:3

SETTING THE STAGE

Eve had it made! She not only lived in a beautiful place, enjoyed excellent health, and had all her material needs met, but she was also loved by her husband, and had communion with Almighty God. Eve was a complete, perfect woman. Uniquely created, she was never a child or a daughter; she never knew what it was like *not* to be married.

Unlike any other creature, she was made of bone (not of dust, as was Adam). In fact, she was taken from Adam's side—a place of protection. She was the help meet God provided so man could multiply and replenish the earth.

Scriptures gives this first woman three names:
1. **Woman**—She is called *Woman* "because she was taken out of man" (Genesis 2:23). This is more a generic term than a name, for it shows that she's man's counterpart.
2. **Adam**—She is called *Adam*. "Male and female created he them...and called *their* name Adam"...(Genesis 5:2). This inclusive name implies the ideal for man and wife, that God made them one flesh.
3. **Eve**—She is called *Eve*, "because she was the mother of all living" (Genesis 3:20). This name, which Adam gave her after "the fall," describes her destiny in spiritual history.

In the study of Eve, we will come to understand the divine order that God established subsequent to man's fall. This divine order is in effect all through Scripture. We will see that divine order not only lines up our earthly relationships with the Word of God, but also permits us to become the beautiful, submissive Bride of Jesus Christ.

THE FAILURE OF EVE
(Based on Genesis 2:8 - 5:5)

As the first woman, Eve had no inherited sin. She was created pure and holy. God told both Eve and Adam not to partake of the fruit of one particular tree in the Garden of Eden. It was the tree of the knowledge of good and evil.

Satan, who appeared in the form of a serpent, appealed to Eve's desire to become "as God" as he tempted her to doubt God's Word. Then she not only partook of the fruit herself, but she also gave some to Adam. As a result, they were separated from God and expelled from the Garden.

Their rebellion and disobedience resulted in an awareness of their nakedness, which they tried to cover with fig leaves. But God, knowing that only blood could atone for sin, covered them with animal skins.

Thus, they were "forgiven. "But they still had to live out the consequences of their actions. Adam had to work the cursed ground by the sweat of his brow. Eve as a result of her failure was put under the rule of her husband, and she was given pain in childbirth. From then on, children were born in sin.

LESSONS FROM EVE
The Place of Women in God's Divine Order

Chart 2A

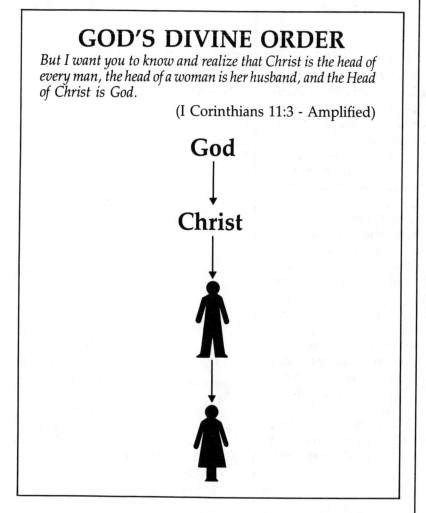

GOD'S DIVINE ORDER

But I want you to know and realize that Christ is the head of every man, the head of a woman is her husband, and the Head of Christ is God.

(I Corinthians 11:3 - Amplified)

God

↓

Christ

God created Adam and Eve in His image and gave them dominion over the whole earth, with the exception of not eating from one particular tree. When Eve yielded to Satan's temptation and caused Adam to disobey as well, they "fell" from the grace of God and were separated from Him through sin. In order to further protect Eve from the wiles of the devil, God put her under the *covering* of her husband. From then on, she would submit to him. Eve, who was taken from Adam's side to stand *with* him, was now required to submit *to* him.

8

We have this *covering* spelled out in I Corinthians 11:3, which says that God is the head of Christ, that Christ is the head of the man, and that man is the head of the woman. In this chain of authority, each one is protected *as he submits* to his head. Only then are all in right relationship to God, who is the overall protector!

I Corinthians 11 goes on to describe how a woman is "covered" in public worship. From this came the demands that women wear long hair or put on a hat or veil when attending church.

Larry Christensen, in his book *The Christian Family*, has another interpretation. He suggests that the word *angelos* in verse 10 can refer to either the loyal spirits of God, or to the rebellious cohorts of Satan (such as in I Corinthians 6:3). Christensen thinks that, because of the context, Paul has the latter in mind. Thus, a woman who is unprotected by her husband's authority is open to evil angelic influences. For this reason she should be "covered' when in worship. Her submission to her husband's authority protects her from Satan's devices.

Our rebellious, sinful nature, however, resists submission. Couple this with pressure from a society that teaches us that we have "rights," and we can see how Satan can easily get to women. He wants us to become like him by completely rebelling against God. But we, who were made in the image of God, are to take on the nature of Jesus—who was fully submissive.

So we must learn to submit to authority not only to be protected from the enemy, but also to become like Jesus. Submission is the place woman has in God's divine order.

For the single woman, submission is a matter of the heart, and God knows whether or not our hearts truly desire to submit.

Satan's Function and Role

Chart 2B

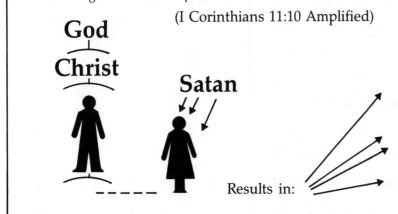

COVERING

Therefore she should be subject to his authority and should have a covering on her head as a token, a symbol, of her submission to authority, that she may show reverence as do the angels and not displease them.

(I Corinthians 11:10 Amplified)

God
|
Christ

Satan

Results in:

Deception—I Timothy 2:13 and 14

Moral Impurity—Genesis 34: 1 and 2

Breakdown of Family Relationships—Genesis 27:5-13

Barrenness—II Samuel 6:20-23

Confusion—I Corinthians 14:34 and 35

Manipulation (Dominating Spirit)—I Kings 21:4-7

Prevention of Husband's Possible Salvation—I Peter 3:1

As we look into Scripture, we find who Satan really is, how he functions, and what role he plays in our lives. We discover that he was, orginally, an angel in the presence of God. But Satan was thrown out of heaven because of his determination to exalt himself and become like the Most High. After his fall, he tried to usurp the authority God gave Adam and Eve when He created them to rule over the earth. Satan did so by causing them to disobey God and, thus, forfeit their position. As a result, Satan assumed the rulership of this world, in addition to his rulership as the "prince of the power of the air" (Ephesians 2:2). Then Satan used cohorts who fell with him to rule over sinful man.

But God defeated Satan by sending Jesus, His own Son, to earth to pay the supreme price for man's sin. According to I John 3:8, as Jesus died upon the cross, He destroyed all of the works of the devil.

When man accepts the atoning work of Jesus' blood, shed to cover man's sin, he is not only "saved" unto eternal life, but is also "saved" from the power of Satan. Thus, Jesus' submission to His Heavenly Father defeated Satan's rebellion and also won—for us—victory over him.

Satan still attempts to deceive, accuse and tempt us. We are tested by how we respond. As Satan comes against us, we respond by how much we know God's Word and obey it concerning divine order, spiritual warfare, and numerous other aspects that we'll cover in future lessons.

The battle between God and Satan is accelerating because Satan knows his time is short. When Jesus comes as King of Kings and Lord of Lords, Satan will be bound for a while. Then, after one last chance to deceive and draw men away from God, Satan will be cast into the lake of fire, where he will be tormented day and night forever and ever.

Satan—Who Is He and Where Did He Come From?

Isaiah 14:12-14 As Lucifer, he fell from heaven because __

_____

_____

John 8:44 From the beginning, he was _____

_____

_____

Matthew 10:28 Satan's power is limited to _____

_____

_____

Revelations 12:9 In the world, Satan is one who _____

_____

_____

Genesis 3:1 and 2 In the Garden, Satan took the form of

_____

10

II Corinthians 11:14 Satan often appears as _____

_____

_____

Job 1:6-12; 2:1-7 Satan is described as _____

_____

_____

II Corinthians 4:4 Satan is called _____

_____

_____

as he _____

_____

_____

lest _____

_____

_____

Mark 4:15 Satan tries to take away _____

_____

_____

Luke 13:16 Satan has the ability to _____

_____

_____

II Corinthians 2:10 and 11 Satan takes advantage of us if

_____

_____

Isaiah 54:16 God created the waster (Satan) to _____

_____

_____

Luke 4:1-13 Satan tempted Jesus by _____

_____

_____

Satan Has Been Defeated

Genesis 3:15 The seed of women (Jesus) would _____

_____

Colossians 2:14 and 15 With Satan, Jesus _____
_____
_____

Hebrews 2:14 Through death, Jesus destroyed _____
_____
_____

I John 3:8 The Son of God was manifested that _____
_____
_____

John 16:11 "The prince of this world" (Satan) is _____
_____
_____

John 16:33 Jesus has overcome _____
which includes _____
_____
_____

Revelations 20:1-10 The future and ultimate fate of Satan is
_____
_____

Our Victory Over Satan
Revelations 12:11 We overcome Satan by _____
_____
_____

II Corinthians 10:3-6 God's mighty weapons will _____
_____
_____

Luke 10:19 Jesus gave His disciples power to _____
_____
_____

Mark 16:17 One of the signs of believers is _____
_____
_____

Ephesians 6:10-18 Our armor in spiritual battle consists of

Jesus and His Bride—Divine Order

Ephesians 5:22-33 parallels the relationship between a husband and wife with that of Jesus and His Bride, the Church. We will consider this in more detail in the next lesson. For now, we will consider the covering that is provided through submission—especially as it is seen in our relationship to Jesus.

I Corinthians 15:45 says, *"And so it is written, The first man Adam was made a living soul; the last Adam was made a quickening spirit."* If Jesus is the last "Adam," then the Church is the last "Eve!" Thus, as we look at Eve, we can gain insight into the relationship the Church is to have with Jesus.

Watchman Nee, in his book, *The Glorious Church,* compares the Church to a type of Eve.

Nee says all that God desired in Adam was to be fulfilled in Christ. In seeing Eve as Adam's wife, we have a picture of the Church as the Bride of Christ. Thus, God's complete purpose is partly achieved through the Church, just as it was partly achieved through Eve.

The first woman was planned before the foundation of the world. So was the second woman. However, while Eve appeared before the "fall," the Church appears after the "fall."

When Christ died, His side was pierced and blood and water flowed from it. The blood signifies redemption; the water signifies life. Therefore, the Church came into being through the death of Christ, just as Eve was taken from Adam's side while he was asleep.

God's purpose in creating the Church is that she may be the help meet of Christ. He desires that the Church rule with Him, as He wants a victorious Church to accompany a victorious Christ. Therefore, God made provisions for the Church to be overcomers in spiritual warfare, as Christ overcame the work of the devil.

Ephesians 5:22-33 Christ has shown His love for the Church by _____

_____

_____

The Church's responsibility is to _____

_____

_____

I Corinthians 6:15-17 If we are joined to Christ, we _____

_____

_____

I Corinthians 15:45-50 Comparisons between Adam and Christ include _____

SUMMARY

In the study of Eve, we begin to see the divine order for man and woman that was established by God subsequent to the "fall" in the Garden of Eden. Divine order, which is in effect throughout Scripture, provides a "covering" for each. This structure not only helps define our earthly relationships, but shows us the position the Church, as the Bride of Christ, is to have with Jesus.

MODERN EXAMPLE

Religious cults are widespread today. Dr. Walter Martin defines a cult as "a group of people gathered about a specific person or person's interpretation of the Bible." A survey of such cults reveals that many were founded by women—women who were deceived because they were out of God's divine order. This appears to be the case in the story of Mary Baker Eddy, founder of the Christian Science movement.

The Christian Science Church (1) denies the doctrine of the Trinity and the diety of Jesus Christ; (2) denies the origin of evil, Satan, and "sin"; (3) does away altogether with the necessity of Jesus' death upon the cross; (4) affirms the nonexistence of sickness and "death," even as it denies that the "body" itself exists!

Like Eve, Mary Baker Eddy was somewhere, somehow tempted to be "as God." In his book, *The Kingdom of the Cults*, Martin says the April, 1889 "Christian Science Journal" reported that Mrs. Eddy allowed the claim that she was equal to Christ as His chosen successor!

Mary Baker Eddy was born in 1821, in a farmhouse in rural New Hampshire. Born into a family of Congregationalists, Mary became deeply interested in religion. As a child, she was often ill and could not regularly attend school. Mary was an avid reader, however, and continued her studies under her mother and older brother.

When she was 22, Mary married George Glover, a neighboring businesman. Seven months later, while Mary was pregnant, George died of yellow fever. This trauma reduced her to an emotional and highly unstable invalid.

Ten years later, against the advice of her father, Mary wed Daniel Patterson, a dentist. Their marriage ended in divorce.

Although she had been plagued with poor health for years, she found temporary help from a highly reputed mental healer, Phineas Parkhurst Quimby. Years of study and meditation convinced Mary that the power of the divine Mind, or "God," could triumph over bodily ailments. In 1875, she published the first edition of "Science and Health." Much of this material was plagiarized from other writers, including Quimby.

During this time, Mary married one of her converts, Asa G. Eddy. In less than five years, he died of a coronary thrombosis. Because of her reputation for being a "healer," Mary tried to conceal the actual cause of his death.

In 1892, when Mary founded the Christian Science Publishing Society, twelve loyal followers established the First Church of Christ, Scientist. It became the mother church of Christian Scientists.

Mary kept firm control of her church, even in her retirement years. Until her death, she inferred that she had authority over men.

As we consider her life story, we find that this woman was rebellious toward a series of men. She was disobedient toward her father. She was without consistent authority from a husband. She took advantage of her teachers, and she established her own church. It would seem that Mary Baker Eddy led an "unsubmitted" life, open to the deception of Satan. We would consider her an "uncovered" woman out of divine order.

WHAT DO YOU THINK?

1. Do your see your husband as your "head," the authority to whom you are to submit? _____

_____

_____

2. How do you allow/or not allow him to be your "head?"

_____

_____

3. What is the result when you assume authority? To your husband? To you? _____

_____

_____

4. If single, who do you look to as your "head"? _____

_____

_____

5. How does the concept of Divine Order help you to better relate to Jesus and to function in His Body? _____

_____

_____

EVALUATE YOURSELF

1. In what ways are you implementing the principles learned from Eve? _____

_____

_____

2. In what ways are you failing to implement the principles learned from Eve? _____

_____

_____

3. What do you need to do to change? _____

_____

_____

4. How will you do it? _____

_____

_____

Lesson 3
Sarah & Queen Vashti

An Example of Submission to Authority

"Wives; submit yourselves unto your own husbands, as unto the Lord."

Ephesians 5:22

SETTING THE STAGE

When women come into Divine Order (as described in I Corinthians 11:3), the questions of submission and authority immediately arise.

Most of us accept that God is the ultimate authority, as we also see that Jesus submitted to God's will. We can also observe how Satan, in his determination to be like the Most High, became the epitome of rebellion against the authority of God. But it's more difficult to recognize *our own* rebellion, and to learn how to submit to God and to one another.

Scripture tells us a lot about submission, both in teaching and in illustration. In this lesson, we will look at two women—Sarah and Queen Vashti. Sarah submitted to Abraham, even when she could have been justified in not doing so. As a result, God protected her. Queen Vashti, on the other hand, refused to do as her husband commanded. As a result, she was deposed from her place in the kingdom.

Using them as examples, we will consider the question of submission to authority. We will look at the position expected of women, as well as lift from Scripture those rare occasions when disobedience to authority is allowed.

THE SUCCESS OF SARAH
(Based on Genesis 11-25; Romans 4:19-21; Hebrews 11:11; I Peter 3:6)

We first meet Sarah as she and Abraham were coming out of Babylonia where God had called them. They were, by faith, following Him, though they knew not "whither they went."

After Abraham's father died in Haran, Abraham took his nephew, Lot, and went into the land of Canaan. Because they found a great famine there, they continued into Egypt. Fearing for his life in this strange country, Abraham sold Sarah into Pharoah's harem. But, the Lord protected her by sending great plagues upon Pharoah until he let her go! Years later, a similar incident occurred with King Abimelech. Again, God protected Sarah for her submission to her husband.

God made a covenant with Abraham, declaring he would be the father of a great nation. It was difficult for him and Sarah to comprehend the fact that they would have "seed," since Sarah was, by now, past the age of childbearing. So, to "help" fulfill God's Word, Sarah gave her handmaid to Abraham, and he had a son by her. Later, he and Sarah had the promised child, Isaac.

Nothing is said about Sarah after Isaac's childhood. We only know that she lived for 127 years and is buried in the Cave of Machpelah along with Abraham, Isaac and Rebekah, and Jacob and Leah.

For the great faith she exemplified in sharing her husband's call and in receiving strength to conceive in old age, she is one of two women named in the "Hall of Faith" in Hebrews 11. Peter also commends Sarah for her submission and obedience. He uses her as an example of one who obeyed her husband, even in calling him "lord."

LESSONS FROM SARAH
Jesus' Submission to God

Can you imagine the ramifications of Jesus' being in full submission to His Father? Jesus *was God*, the part of the Trinity who humbled Himself to indwell human flesh. Jesus *was* before the foundation of the world; He also was involved in the creation of it. Yet, while on earth, He did *nothing* that He didn't submit to His Father. Declaring "not my will, but Thine be done," Jesus was fully submissive—even to His own death on the cross.

We would think that submission to authority was, for Jesus, unnecessary. Yet, Hebrews 5:8 tells us that He learned obedience through the things He suffered. Submission is the way to full obedience to God, with much of it learned through suffering.

Philippians 2:5-11 To be obedient, Jesus _____

_____

_____

Hebrews 5:7-9 Even though He was _____,

Jesus learned obedience by _____

_____

_____

Hebrews 12:1-11 Jesus endured the cross because of _____

_____

_____

John 6:38 Jesus did not come to _____,

but to _____

_____

_____

Luke 6:12 Jesus discovered God's will through _____

18

Luke 4:4, 8 and 12 He reminded Satan of God's will by ____

____

____

Luke 22:39-46 Jesus submitted to His Father when He ____

____

Our Submission to Authority

God's throne is established upon authority. All things were created through it. All the laws of the universe are maintained by it. God is the ultimate authority, even over Satan. Eventually, all must submit to God. Therefore, it behooves us to learn now to submit to His authority, and to those whom He delegates over us.

The key to a truly submissive heart is found in Ephesians 5:22, where wives are told to submit to their husbands *as unto the Lord*. This is a heart attitude, a necessity in submission, if we are to have the proper perspective. It will keep us from disobeying God, even as it gives us the means to submit to man "as unto the Lord."

Four Common Misconceptions on Submission

1. Submission is "blind obedience."

Submission and obedience aren't the same thing. Submission is an attitude of heart; obedience is an act of the will. One can have a submissive heart and not be obedient, just as one can be obedient and not have a submissive heart. Our attitude may be one thing and our action another.

2. In submitting, you become a doormat to the one in authority.

According to Webster, the word "submit" means; to present to others for consideration; to yield to the control of another; to offer as an opinion. These are active directions—to present, to yield, to offer. If we're truly submissive, we will, in the love of the Lord, share what we know and believe, and then accept the decision of the one in authority. Thus, we are protected (covered), though the authority may be dealt with if he is wrong. If, on the other hand, we withhold submitting what we know, we may suffer the consequences.

3. Submission is easier if you have a believing husband.

This is a fantasy of every believing woman who's married to an unbeliever. True, there may be more agreement, especially in spiritual matters, but submission is never easy. Submission is actually death to self, and nobody wants to die. Christian women struggle with submission too—perhaps even more—because they know what's required of them.

4. There's a difference between submitting to an unbelieving husband and a husband who's a believer.

The Word doesn't say so. It simply says, "Wives, submit to

your husbands, as unto the Lord" (Ephesians 5:22). Read I Corinthians 7:13-17 (especially in the Amplified Version) and you'll note that a believing wife never has the option to leave her husband, even if he's an unbeliever. I Peter 3:1 also tells us that wives are to submit to their husbands, even though the husband isn't aware of God's Word.

Where does authority rest? What are the consequences of rebelling against it? (Romans 13:1-7) _____

_____

_____

What is God's will concerning submission? (I Peter 2:13-17)

_____

_____

THE FAILURE OF QUEEN VASHTI
(Based on Esther 1; 2:1, and 17)

Queen Vashti was the wife of Ahasuerus, a king of great wealth and fame, whose kingdom of Persia included 127 provinces and spread from India to Ethiopia.

In the third year of his reign, King Ahasuerus held a great celebration that lasted 180 days. He invited all the nobles and princes of the kingdom to view his vast wealth and the majesty of his empire. During the last week of this event, he gave a party for all who had helped to make it a huge success. On the final day of the revelry, King Ahasuerus commanded that Vashti be brought into the gathering, so that all of the men could behold her beauty. Ordinarily, one of the concubines would have been called in, since it was a breach of custom for a queen to appear where the wine flowed freely. But Ahasuerus, while half drunk, had made a decree, and the command could not be revoked.

Queen Vashti refused to submit to the demand of her husband. She may have been too busy with her own feast that she was holding for the women. She may have been too embarrassed to appear before so many drunken men. She may even have been asserting her will because she was angry with her husband for making such a request. Whatever her reason, she was deposed from her position and her royal estate was given to another.

LESSONS FROM QUEEN VASHTI
When Disobedience to Authority Is Allowed

God raises up authority, just as He puts it down (Psalms 75:6 and 7). All authority comes from Him (John 19:11). It's difficult to discern when we are scripturally allowed to come from under authority, for we are always prone to justify our disobedience. Our "old nature" wants to rebel. Therefore, we must be wary of our feelings when it comes to making a decision to disobey authority. Submission demands death to the "old nature," so it's never attractive to us.

A prime example of acceptable disobedience to authority occurred when Peter and some apostles chose to disobey the

20

priest of the temple by continuing to teach and preach in the name of Jesus (Acts 4:13-20). They chose, instead, to obey God. Even in the Old Testament, we have the example of some Hebrew midwives who spared the lives of boy babies because they feared God more than the Egyptian rulers (Exodus 1:15-21). There may be occasions when we, too, will have to make the choice of whether we will obey man or God.

This is especially true in these last days. We are warned in Scripture, many false teachers will try to deceive us by teaching doctrines that are not of God. Even some husbands are demanding things of their wives which are contrary to God's Word, with the result that wives are being battered.

The question we must answer when considering disobedience to authority is this: ***Am I being required to do something which is explicitly against God's will according to His Word?*** To discover the answer, we must:

1. Know the whole counsel of God, not just a verse out of context. Otherwise, we may misinterpret the truth (Acts 20:27-30); and
2. Have the leading of the Holy Spirit, for He is the spirit of truth and will teach us all things. (John 16:13).
3. Look for *fruit*, especially in a ministry. Gifts and miracles are attractive, but people can do wonderful works in the name of Jesus and still have lives full of iniquity. A tree is known by its fruit as to whether or not it is good. (Matthew 7:21-23).
4. Be involved in a believing church, where correction can be given and received. Fellow Christians may have insight that we don't have (Hebrews 10:25).
5. Ask for a liberal amount of wisdom. We must have a genuine fear of the Lord, for our final accounting will be to Him. He knows our hearts even now (James 1:5).

Rebellion to Authority

Submission is the opposite of rebellion. Lest we disobey authority in rebellion, let's look at the result in the lives of some who did.

Adam and Eve (Genesis 3:1-6, 14-19) _____

_____

_____

Nadab and Abihu (Leviticus 10:1 and 2) _____

_____

_____

Aaron and Miriam (Numbers 12) _____

_____

_____

Korah, Dathan, and Abiram (Numbers 16) _____

_____

_____

Saul (I Samuel 15:1-26) _____ _____

_____

_____

How Is Submission Worked Out Among Believers?

Submission is of God; rebellion is of Satan. There is a contest between these two for our very souls. Will we follow Jesus' way of submission and become a glorious Bride of Christ, or will we rebel and, in doing so, acknowledge that we are of the nature and kingdom of Satan?

We're now making the choices that will determine our ultimate destiny by the way we respond to God's divine order and the authority He delegates over us. This is seen in every area of life, but most appropriately, in the marriage relationship and in the Body of Christ. Ephesians 5:22-33 shows what these "couples" have in common, as it compares Christ and the Church with a husband and wife.

Chart 3A

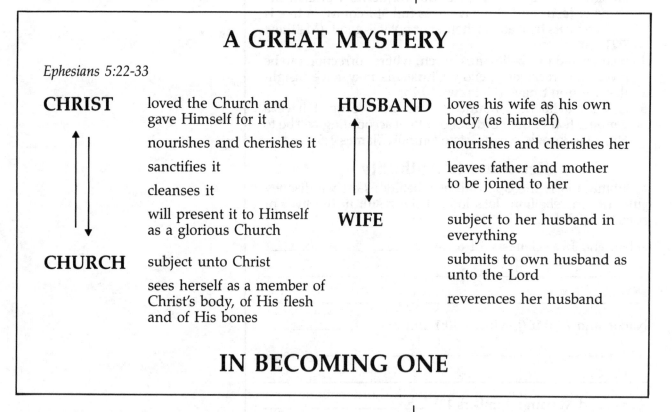

A GREAT MYSTERY

Ephesians 5:22-33

CHRIST	loved the Church and gave Himself for it	**HUSBAND**	loves his wife as his own body (as himself)
	nourishes and cherishes it		nourishes and cherishes her
	sanctifies it		leaves father and mother to be joined to her
	cleanses it		
	will present it to Himself as a glorious Church	**WIFE**	subject to her husband in everything
CHURCH	subject unto Christ		submits to own husband as unto the Lord
	sees herself as a member of Christ's body, of His flesh and of His bones		reverences her husband

IN BECOMING ONE

I Thessalonians 5:12 and 13 What is to be our attitude toward those "over us in the Lord?" _____

_____

_____

Hebrews 13:17 What is required of those in authority? ____

I Timothy 5:17 How are elders to use their authority? _____

_____

I Corinthians 14:33-35 What is woman's role in the Church?

_____

_____

Ephesians 5:32 What is the great mystery concerning Christ and the Church? _____

_____

_____

I Corinthians 12:28 Who sets the ones in various offices in the church? _____

_____

_____

I Peter 5:5 Who is to submit to whom? _____

_____

_____

SUMMARY

Through trust and obedience, Jesus was fully submissive to His "head," God the Father. God's Word commands that wives submit to their husbands (their "head")—even to unbelieving ones, according to I Peter 3:1. Submission, which is often misunderstood, is an attitude of heart, usually demanding a relinquishing of one's rights. Sarah learned the secret of this kind of submission as she did it "as unto the Lord." The question of unsubmissiveness arises as we look at the story of Queen Vashti. Thus, we also consider the times and conditions when it may be necessary to "obey God rather than man."

MODERN EXAMPLE

For months, a battle raged within. Rebellion rose up in every ounce of Bonnie's being, even as the Lord reminded her, once again, of Sarah's submission to Abraham—and that her attitude must agree with her obedience.

Three months earlier, she and her husband Michael moved to California "not knowing whither we went," but under the direction of Michael, who felt that the Lord wanted them to leave Colorado. They felt it was confirmed when Michael found a job. So, before the job began, they made one last trip home for the holidays to see family and friends.

Now they were returning to California, and Bonnie's heart

was full of fear, anger, bitterness, and rebellion, even though she had outwardly "submitted." She did not want to leave the place that had always been her home.

A few days after Michael started his new job and the boys were settled in their new school, Bonnie developed a cough. Within a week, it became so severe that pain shot across her rib cage with nearly every breath. Finally, she went to a doctor. He informed her she had a virus, and the coughing had torn some cartilage in her rib cage. He prescribed codeine to quiet the cough and an antibiotic for the virus.

Bonnie's reaction to the codeine was immediate, with severe vomiting. Mike called the doctor, who took her off the codeine, but said to continue the antibiotic. After about three days, she developed such a stiffness in her neck and joints that the children had to help her out of a chair. Then she started to develop erratic heart palpitations, swelling of her hands and feet, and great discomfort in breathing.

Mike became quite concerned and suggested that she discontinue the medication, but she reasoned that she still needed it for the cough, which had not subsided.

Finally, after four days and nights of pain and sleeplessness, as well as shortness of breath, skin peeling from her body, and continued heart palpitations, Mike took her to a different doctor. He concluded that Bonnie had a rare virus, and he instructed her to continue the medication.

When Michael took her home, she went to bed, crying out to the Lord to either heal her now or take her to be with Him, because she couldn't bear the pain any longer. She was down to her last pill. She looked at the bottle in absolute desperation. Her eyes hurt so bad she couldn't even cry.

Broken at last, she repented and asked the Lord to forgive her for her rebellion and bitterness—especially toward her husband, at whom she had lashed out with angry ravings every chance she got during the last several months. When she finally finished, a great peace settled over her, and she heart the gentle voice of the Lord say, "Don't take that last pill." Questioning if she had really heard correctly, she decided that if, indeed, it was the Lord, she would ask Him to confirm it through Michael. No sooner had she asked this, than Michael came into the room and demanded, "Bonnie, don't take that pill!"

She flushed the pill down the toilet and got back into bed. "Suddenly I understood the meaning of Ephesians 5:22. Submission is an attitude of heart. Though I had outwardly submitted to my husband, I continued to rebel inside. I was to submit to my husband *as unto the Lord*—in my *heart* attitude."

Within 48 hours, Bonnie was completely restored to health. But it was a week later that she realized how the lack of submission to her husband might have cost her her life. She turned on the television just in time to hear a medical report on the particular antibiotic she had been taking. It had been determined that some people severely react to it, even to the point of death from a stroke.

Needless to say, Revelations 3:19 (Amplified) came alive, as she was led to read, "Those whom I (dearly and tenderly) love, I tell their faults and convict and convince and reprove and chasten...(that is), I discipline and instruct them, So be enthusiastic and in earnest and burning with zeal, and repent...changing your mind and *attitude.*"

Bonnie is still learning a lot about a submissive attitude, even as the Lord continues to show her that, in submitting to Michael, she is submitting to Jesus. The husband is the head of the wife, just as Christ is the head of the Chruch. And, as the Church submits to Christ, so also wives should submit to their husbands in everything. Praise the Lord for His chastening love that we might learn His ways, which are far above our own.

WHAT DO YOU THINK?

1. Do you have a submissive heart toward those over you? What if your husband is not sensitive to spiritual matters?

_____

_____

2. What happens when you refuse to submit and do what you want to do? _____

_____

_____

3. How does submitting "as unto the Lord" make submission to man more possible? _____

_____

_____

4. Have you ever chosen to obey God over man? What was the result? _____

_____

_____

5. How does learning submission help us in our relationship with Jesus? _____

_____

_____

EVALUATE YOURSELF

1. In what ways are you implementing the principles learned from Sarah and Queen Vashti? _____

_____

_____

2. In what ways are you failing to implement the principles learned from them? _____

_____

_____

3. What do you need to do to change? _____

WOMEN IN THE BIBLE

_____

_____

4. How will you do it? _____

_____

_____

Lesson 4
Hagar

An Example of Conflict Between Flesh and Spirit

"...Walk in the Spirit, and ye shall not fulfill the lust of the flesh. For the flesh lusteth against the Spirit, and the Spirit against the flesh: and these are contrary the one to the other: so that ye cannot do the things that ye would."

Galatians 5:16 and 17

SETTING THE STAGE

God is Trinity—Father, Son, and Holy Spirit. God made man in His image—a triune being of body, soul, and spirit. He intended to make man His dwelling place, joining His Spirit to man's spirit in order to have fellowship with him and to govern the earth. Because man sinned, God couldn't do this. So, He initiated a plan whereby He would send a Savior to atone for man's sin, so a relationship with man could be restored.

As man accepts Jesus, the One who purchased our redemption with His own blood, he is "born again" by the Spirit who then comes to indwell him. Without this union with God's Spirit, man is only able to function in the power of his own will. Scripture refers to this as *flesh*. It is born out of our *fallen nature*, the *old man*.

Though the Spirit indwells us when we accept Jesus and His atoning work on the cross, we have a continuing battle with our sinful nature, our flesh, which wants to be in control. The strength of the *old man* doesn't die easily, yet God has decreed that it must be crucified. We must let Jesus live His life in us as we learn how to submit our flesh to the will and life of the Holy Spirit.

In calling out a chosen people (whom God would separate unto Himself), He made a covenant with Abraham, declaring that Abraham's seed would inherit all of the promised land. Because Abraham's wife, Sarah, was past the age of childbearing, she couldn't understand how she could bear an heir. Instead of allowing God to bring about His will in His way, she chose the way of self-will, the flesh, and gave her bond-servant, Hagar, to Abraham so that she might bear him a child. This resulted in the birth of Ishmael, a descendent in continuing conflict with Isaac, the promised child later born to Abraham and Sarah.

In Galatians 4:21-31, Paul gives the example of Sarah and Hagar as an allegory—living by the Spirit versus living in bondage to the law (or, by the flesh). We have the same conflict in our lives. Will we be as Sarah, who had freedom to choose the way of the Spirit, or will we, as she did, choose a "Hagar," a way of the flesh?

THE FAILURE OF HAGAR
(Based on Genesis 16 and 17; 21:9-21)

Hagar was the handmaid of Sarah, used by her to bear Abraham a child in order to help fulfill a promise made by God. Thus, in this particular lesson, we label Hagar as "failure," even though she personally, did nothing wrong. In fact, she was fully obedient to her mistress, even when ill-treated by her, and was shown compassion by God.

But if we consider her to be an act of the *flesh* on Sarah's part, we see this as failure, in contrast to God's desire for one to be led by the Spirit.

It's difficult to separate Hagar's story from that of Sarah's. Both their lives are interwoven in the life of Abraham. When Hagar became pregnant by Abraham—at Sarah's arrangement—Sarah became so jealous that Hagar had to leave the household. Hagar fled into the wilderness, where she was found by an angel of the Lord and told to return to her mistress and there bear a son who would be named Ishmael.

Hagar did as the angel commanded, though life must have been miserable, even after her baby was born. For, it was 13 more years before God fulfilled His Word to Abraham and Sarah and gave them the son whom they called Isaac.

As soon as Isaac was weaned, Sarah demanded that Hagar and Ishmael leave. She didn't want him to be an heir with her son, Isaac. So Abraham gave Hagar some bread and water and sent them away.

Again, an angel of the Lord found them out on the desert. He gave them more water and reminded Hagar of the earlier promise that Ishmael, too, would become the father of a great nation—a nation which would be in continual conflict with the people of promise, Isaac's descendants. Thus, the bond-woman, Hagar, had to be cast out. Her son could not be an heir with the son of the free woman. Hagar represented an act of Sarah's flesh, not the means God intended to fulfill His Word.

LESSONS FROM HAGAR
The Trinity

Though there is but one God, He can be known three ways: (1) God, the Father; (2) Jesus, the Son; and (3) Holy Spirit. How God can be three-in-one is a difficult concept for our minds to grasp. (Water is an example of something which can be known in three different forms—liquid, ice, or steam—but the formula remains the same.) Most clearly, we see the three aspects of the Trinity at the baptism of Jesus (Matthew 3:16 and 17). As the Son was baptized, the Father spoke from heaven, and the Spirit descended upon Him.

The Bible reveals God as the only infinite and eternal being, having no beginning and no ending. He is creator and sustainer of all things, the righteous ruler of the universe. He's the source of life, and can be known by revelation. In the Old Testament, God revealed Himself through His prophets. In the New Testament, He revealed Himself through His Son, Jesus Christ. And, we can see Him in the Word:
- Hebrews 11:6 tells us that one comes to God by believing that He *is*.

28

- I Thessalonians 1:9 says that God is living and true.
- I John 4:8 says that God is love. He is also light (I John 1:5), a consuming fire (Hebrews 12:29), a Spirit (John 4:24), gives life (John 5:26), has all knowledge (Psalm 147:5), has all power (Revelation 19:6), and fills the immense universe with His presence (Psalm 139:7).

We know God as our Heavenly Father just as we believe in Jesus and become joint heirs with Him (John 1:12 and 13). Jesus also knows Him as Father (John 6:37).

Christianity differs from all religions, in that the life of the Son of God indwells man. So, we see the Son, the second aspect of God. He is the God-man, Christ Jesus, exalted above all creatures, yet One who humbled Himself to become as man.

Jesus was God, according to John 20:28, Hebrews 1:8, John 17:5, and John 8:51-59. Jesus was also a man, according to Matthew 4:2, John 19:28, John 4:6, John 11:35, and Hebrews 4:15. His two natures, God and man, are bound together in such a way that the two become one, having a single consciousness and will.

The third person of the Trinity is the Holy Spirit. Equal to the Father and Son, He's shown actively engaged in the work of creation along with the other two. In the Old Testament, He came upon men to empower them for a particular service. In the New Testament, after Pentecost, we see the Holy Spirit indwelling man, never to leave him, filling and empowering him. Like God, He is present everywhere (Psalms 139:7-10) and has all power (Luke 1:35).

In Peter's confrontation with Ananias (Acts 5:3 and 4), Peter revealed the deity of the Holy Spirit when he told Ananias that he hadn't lied to men, but to God. The Spirit is revealed as co-equal, co-eternal, and co-existent with the Father and the Son.

Man Is "Triune"—Body, Soul and Spirit

Man is a triune being made in the image of God (Genesis 2:7 and I Thessalonians 5:23). The *body* consists of the five senses by which man contacts the world around him. The *soul* consists of man's mind (intellect), emotions, and will. We recognize this as his personality, the expression of his thoughts and feelings. The *spirit* of man consists of his conscience (which, unless it has been seared, tells man right from wrong), and a moral sense of what is good and evil.

When God made man, He desired to make man His dwelling place. The Holy Spirit would be joined with man's spirit and would rule the soul. Thus, man would be governed by the Spirit of God.

When man "fell," God could no longer live in man because of his sin. But through the death of Jesus, man can be restored as he accepts the atoning work of Jesus' blood for his sin. Until that time, man's spirit remains dormant and he is ruled by his own soul, flesh, outward man, old man, or his carnal nature.

But the conflict isn't over with the salvation experience. As believers, we must then learn how to reckon our old man dead, how to deny the flesh. The release of the spirit comes through brokenness and death to self. As long as self is on the throne, God's Spirit can't rule.

Man's soul, functioning independently from God, becomes strong as man is ruled by his mind, his will, and his emotions.

Some Christians don't understand this and try to live the good life, doing all the right things and many good works. Yet God wants our lives fully yielded to Him, that He might do His work through us. We see this dilemma vividly outlined in Romans 6. And so, we have a conflict between the aspects of our *triune* being.

The Conflict Between the Flesh and the Spirit

The Bible uses various terms to describe man's self as opposed to the spirit within which God desires to dwell. These terms refer to the soul and body of man, the *outward man* that perishes (II Corinthians 4:16).

Chart 4A

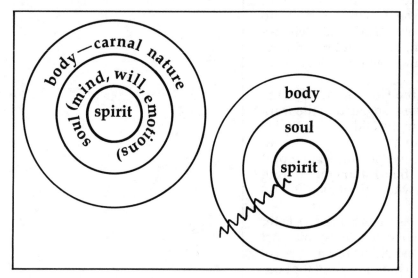

The Natural Man

Ephesians 2:1-3 The natural man is ruled by _____

_____

_____

I Corinthians 2:14 The natural man does not receive _____

_____

_____

They are _____

_____

_____

I Corinthians 1:18 To the natural man, the things of God

_____

_____

_____

30

The Flesh

Galatians 5:16-21 The works of the flesh are _____

_____

_____

John 3:5 and 6 What is born of the flesh is _____

_____

_____

and what is born of the Spirit is _____

_____

_____

I Corinthians 15:50 _____
cannot enter the kingdom of God.

Ephesians 6:12 We wrestle not against _____

_____

_____

but _____

_____

_____

Philippians 3:3 We are to have no confidence in _____

_____

_____

II Peter 2:10-18 Walking after the lusts of the flesh is
described as _____

_____

_____

I John 2:16 The lust of the flesh is _____,

_____

_____

not _____

_____

_____

The Carnal Christian

These are babes, awakened by the Spirit, but not submitted
to the Lordship of Jesus Christ. They are believers in Jesus,
but are ruled by the flesh.

I Corinthians 3:1-3 The carnal Christian _____

_____

_____

Hebrews 4:9-11 Carnal (worldly) Christians cannot claim any permanent victory because _____

_____

_____

Romans 7:13-25 The carnal Christian knows the truth, but is caught in a daily struggle of _____

_____

_____

and allows _____

_____

_____

Romans 8:5-8 Being spiritually-minded brings life; being carnally-minded brings _____

_____

_____

and cannot _____

_____

_____

The New Man

I Corinthians 3:16-25 This man is a dwelling place for _____

_____

_____

Ephesians 3:16 _____

_____

strengthens our inner man.

Galatians 5:22-26 The fruit of the Spirit is _____

_____

_____

Romans 8:1-17 Promises given to those led by the Spirit of God include: _____

_____

_____

_____

32

Our spirit is given us by God to enable us to respond to Him, to enjoy His presence, and to live before Him continuously. Hebrews 4:12 tells us the Word of God is a sharp sword, dividing the soul from the spirit. As we align our lives with God's Word, our soul is separated from the spirit. We no longer give our feelings and reasonings top priority; instead, we submit to the Word of God.

The Holy Spirit also separates the soul from the spirit through His dealings with us. As soon as we are "saved," the Holy Spirit begins to mete out discipline. When we place ourselves unconditionally in God's hand, the Holy Spirit freely works in us, allowing circumstances to come into our lives so that we may be tested and tried. As we learn to submit to the Holy Spirit as a teacher, we learn to differentiate between our thoughts and His leading. We know what He says will always agree with the Word, just as it will probably disagree with our reasoning. God's ways are not our ways, nor our thoughts His thoughts.

So, we have a continual conflict. Will we use "Hagar," (the ways of self-will and the flesh) to bring about our will, or will we allow the Spirit of God to do His will in and through us?

Romans 8:2-5 _____

_____

_____

makes us free from the old law of sin and death.

_____

_____

Romans 8:9 We are not in the flesh, but in the Spirit if ___

_____

_____

Romans 7:5 and 6 The flesh brings _____

_____

_____

Romans 6:4-6 In baptism, _____

_____

_____

Ephesians 4:22-24 We are to put off _____

_____

_____

and put on _____

_____

_____

Colossians 3:8-10 We are to put off _____

_____

_____

and put on _____

_____

_____

Colossians 2:6-11 We are told to _____

_____

_____

II Corinthians 10:2-5 Though we walk _____ ,

_____

_____

we do not _____

_____

_____

For, _____

_____

_____

Matthew 26:41 The Spirit is _____ ,

_____

_____

but the flesh is _____

_____

_____

Romans 7:13-25 The struggle of the two natures is _____

_____

_____

Questions to Consider

What has been crucified with Christ in Galatians 2:20? _____

_____

_____

What does it mean to be "reckoned dead" in Romans 6:11?

_____

_____

What are we to do daily, according to I Corinthians 15:31?

34

What does it mean to take up our cross, as described in Luke 9:23 and 24? _____

_____

_____

What will God not despise, according to Psalm 51:17? _____

_____

Brokenness

To function in the *spirit, self* must be broken. As Roy Hession says in his book, *Calvary Road*, brokenness occurs when that "hard unyielding self which justifies itself, wants its own way, stands up for its rights, and seeks its own glory, at last bows its head to God's will, admits it's wrong, gives up its own way to Jesus, surrenders its rights and discards its own glory...that the Lord Jesus might have all and be all."

Often, it is *self* that tries to live the Christian life. But, as long as *self* is in control, God can do little with anyone. He cannot mature the fruit of the Spirit unless we allow Him to break us. He does this by bringing pressure to bear, and then giving us a choice to make. We can do our thing, as Sarah did when she gave Hagar to Abraham, or we can grow in patience and allow God to do His will in His own time and His own way. This breaks our will and produces fruit in us. Our soulish *old nature* is broken, so that the Spirit may be released.

Jesus, God Himself, became broken. He went to the cross, taking man's sin upon His own body. As a result, God raised Him up to rule at His right hand.

John 12:24 says that a seed must fall to the ground and have its outer shell broken before fruit comes forth. In Luke 20:17 and 18, after Jesus refers to Himself as the cornerstone which the builders rejected, He says that either we fall upon Him for mercy, or He will fall upon us in judgment! Either way, we are broken. How much better it is when we allow the Holy Spirit to do it in us, than to be ground to dust!

SUMMARY

Though the Spirit indwells us as we accept Jesus and the atoning work of His blood, we have a continuing conflict between our flesh, (our old nature) and the Spirit (the new man now within us). Learning how to reckon our *old man* dead and allow Jesus to live in us by the Spirit is difficult and comes only through brokenness.

Like Sarah, we often become impatient and use our own means (Hagars) to bring about His promises to us, instead of allowing God to accomplish His Word in His Way.

MODERN EXAMPLE

Each of us experiences conflicts in our lives, and it is often difficult to discern which is of the flesh and which is of the Spirit. So it was with Ruth Bell Graham. In retrospect, it would seem that she made the right choice!

Ruth was born in China of missionary parents. Her father was a skilled surgeon and superintendent of Tsiangkiang General Hospital. Ruth grew up on a mission compound surrounded by dedicated Christians committed to service in this foreign land. Nurtured in such an atmosphere, it wasn't surprising for Ruth to decide, even at age 12, that she would become a spinster missionary to Tibet.

Though her parents wanted Ruth to go to college, she believed that all she would need in life was a knowledge of the language of Tibet and the Bible. But, her parents overruled and, after a year of postgraduate high school in Korea, Ruth enrolled in Wheaton college, Illinois. Little did she know that when she left her homeland at age 17 she would not return for half a century!

At college young men began to date her, but she always told them that she didn't plan to marry—ever. As Patricia Cornwell writes, in the book *A Time For Remembering*, "Thus far her world had been populated with charming, attentive young gentlemen. In short, what she needed was a man who was as independent, stubborn, and mystifying as she was. Far away, in the rural South, such a person did exist." We know that man to be none other than Billy Graham.

When Ruth and Billy finally met, she was still determined to pursue her goal of becoming a missionary to Tibet. As they continued dating, he argued that he thought a woman's highest call was to be a wife and mother. But, she reminded him that she was an exception.

Finally, Billy suggested that they stop seeing each other while she searched the Scriptures and prayed until she found out just what God's plan for her was. It proved to be a real struggle to give up what she had, for years, believed to be God's will for her life. Her flesh—her mind, emotions, will—all said to pursue her childhood dream of being a missionary to Tibet. But God, evidently, had other plans, and she finally yielded to what now seems to have been His Spirit.

So Ruth Bell became Billy Graham's wife, uniquely designed as his life-companion and mother of their five children. Far from the rooftops of Tibet, she has spent most of their married life in North Carolina. Ruth, who desired to live a lonely, unobtrusive life has instead been observed by millions the world over.

WHAT DO YOU THINK?

1. In what ways do you function "in the flesh," allowing your carnal nature to rule? _____

_____

_____

2. How do you discern the difference between your "flesh" and the "Spirit?" _____

_____

36

3. What are you to do daily, according to I Corinthians 15:31? How is this done? _____

_____

_____

4. What hinders you from being led continually by God's Spirit? _____

_____

_____

EVALUATE YOURSELF

1. In what ways are you implementing the principles learned from Hagar? _____

_____

_____

2. In what ways are you failing to implement the principles learned from Hagar? _____

_____

_____

3. What do you need to do to change? _____

_____

_____

4. How will you do it? _____

_____

_____

WOMEN IN THE BIBLE

Lesson 5
Lot's Wife

An Example of Sanctification

"And the very God of peace sanctify you wholly; and I pray God your whole spirit and soul and body be preserved blameless unto the coming of our Lord Jesus Christ."

I Thessalonians 5:23

SETTING THE STAGE

The process of sanctification involves leaving our worldly life and becoming a holy people, separated unto God. The death of Jesus on the cross provided this sanctification. We can be made righteous because He took our sins upon Himself as a sacrifice for us.

Sanctification is both a one-time experience, as well as an ongoing process. God, alone, is able to keep us from falling and to present us faultless before the presence of His glory (Jude 24). In Jesus' prayer just prior to His crucifixion, He asked the Father to sanctify His followers through His Word. As we align our lives with the Word of God and allow His Holy Spirit to indwell and change us, God performs His work in making us into a holy people, a glorious Church and a beautiful Bride for Jesus Christ.

Jesus, in speaking to His disciples concerning the last days, used Lot's wife as an example of one who chose to look to her past worldly pleasure, rather than be set free and enjoy the life God had prepared for her. As a result, she was turned into a useless pillar of salt.

Surely she's a message for those who are living in the end time of which Jesus was speaking. If we want to be the "salt of the earth," full of savor and useful to God, we must choose not to look back upon past experiences and traditions. Rather, we must allow God to separate us unto Himself. Tnis is our part in the process of sanctification.

THE FAILURE OF LOT'S WIFE

(Based on Genesis 19:15-26; Luke 17:28-33).

All the information we have concerning Lot's wife is actually contained in one short verse of Scripture. "His wife looked back from behind him, and she became a pillar of salt." Yet, of all the women in God's written Word, Jesus says to remember *her!*

To learn more about Lot's wife, we first need to look at the story of Abraham. Lot came with his uncle Abraham out of Ur of Chaldees. First they went to Haran, where Lot's grandfather, Terah, died. Then, God made His covenant with Abraham and the family moved on, into the land He promised.

While they were journeying south, a famine overtook the

land, so Abraham and his family moved into Egypt. After a while, they returned to the land of Canaan where, according to Genesis 13:2, Abraham became very rich in cattle, silver, and gold.

Lot, also, had flocks and herds and tents. In fact, they had too much to continue to dwell together. So Abraham decided they should part company. He gave Lot first choice as to where he wanted to settle. Lot chose the well-watered Jordan valley and left Abraham to dwell on the arid plain.

As Lot traveled east, he pitched his tent toward Sodom. Before long, he was living *in* Sodom, where the inhabitants "were wicked and sinners before the Lord exceedingly" (Genesis 13:14). Lot became a citizen of Sodom, sat at the city's gate in a position of authority, and was treated with honor as a relative of the mighty Abraham, who had delivered the city from an invasion.

Though Lot was regarded as a righteous soul, he evidently closed his eyes to the wickedness of the people and married a woman of Sodom. They had two daughters.

Sodom was such a cesspool of sin that God declared He would destroy it. But because of Abraham's intercession, God agreed to save Lot and his family.

So two angels went to take Lot and his family out of the city before God's judgment fell. Though Lot, his wife and daughters seemed reluctant to leave, the angels admonished them to escape to the mountain without looking back. Again, Lot hesitated. He wanted to go to the little city of Zoar.

As they fled, fire and brimstone fell from heaven and completely destroyed Sodom. Walking behind her husband, Lot's wife turned to look back. She was overtaken with sulphurous vapors and became solidified with salt. She perished as she stood, entombed as a pillar.

Why did she look back? Perhaps she remembered the life of pleasure she was leaving behind and wanted one more glimpse of what she was giving up. Maybe she had so much unresolved guilt and hurt that she was unable to face a new life. Maybe she was angry at God for what was happening.

Whatever the reason, Jesus told us to "remember Lot's wife." In sharing with His disciples concerning the last days (which would be very much like Sodom), Jesus wanted them to know that God could deliver people out of wickedness if they obey and follow Him.

LESSONS FROM LOT'S WIFE
Why Remember Lot's Wife?

We who are living in the last days are living in a society that's becoming more and more like that of Sodom. We need only look at immorality, homosexuality, pornography, violence, drugs, crime, and divorce to know that God's judgment is due us. It's only His mercy that has stayed His wrath thus far.

Jesus wants us to learn from Lot's wife. Instead of looking back, He wants us to look to Him, to listen to His voice, and to move on as He leads by His Spirit. It will be the only way to survive in the days ahead. We are His Bride; He wants us to be ready to reign with Him. He doesn't want us to look back at

40

the old ways of our world. He wants an obedient people, free from worldly entanglements, willing to trust Him completely. As a bride-in-preparation, we need to be free of former loves.

Signs of the Last Days

There are many signs that indicate we are now living in the last days. Let's look at a few:

Luke 21:5-36 _____

_____

_____

I Timothy 4:1-3 _____

_____

_____

II Timothy 3:1-5 _____

_____

_____

Sanctification

In the last lesson, we looked at the conflict between the flesh and the Spirit. We saw how God arranges circumstances in our lives to *break* us—to allow us to be conformed to His image—to see if we will use our natural strength to overcome our problems, or if we will allow God's spirit to flow through us.

God is a *holy* God; He wants a *holy* people. He made man in His image and He wants to take the *world* out of man as He conforms man to His nature. We call this process *sanctification*. It begins and ends with the cross. "But God forbid that I should glory, save in the cross of our Lord Jesus Christ, by whom the world is crucified unto me, and I unto the world" (Galatians 6:14).

The experience of salvation is the beginning of the process of sanctification. When one is *born again*, he repents of his old life and ways, as he accepts the forgiveness that God provides through the atoning work of the blood of Jesus. As a new believer, one then commits his life to the Lord Jesus Christ. The person is *saved* out of the world, as well as *saved* unto eternal life.

Anyone who is truly saved will recognize the continuing need of cleansing and separation. Sanctification occurs at the cross, but the process continues a lifetime as God works out that separation. Though our flesh was crucified with Christ, we must continually *reckon ourselves dead*. Although Satan's works were destroyed, we must continually remind him of that fact.

According to Scripture, the Trinity is involved in the process of sanctification:

God the Father has the power to separate us unto the coming of our Lord Jesus Christ. *"And the very God of peace sanctify you wholly; and I pray God your whole spirit and soul and body be* *preserved blameless unto the coming of our Lord Jesus Christ"* (I Thessalonians 5:23).

God the Son has the power to separate us unto righteousness as a glorious Church. *"Husbands, love your wives, even as Christ loved the church, and gave Himself for it; that he might sanctify and cleanse it with the washing of water by the word, that he might present it to himself a glorious church, not having spot, or wrinkle, or any such thing; but that it should be holy and without blemish"* (Ephesians 5:25-27).

God the Holy Spirit has the power to separate us unto salvation and service. *"But we are bound to give thanks always to God for you, brethren beloved of the Lord, because God hath from the beginning chosen you to salvation through sanctification of the Spirit and belief of the truth"* (II Thessalonians 2:13).

The Word of God also has the power to sanctify us, as it separates us from sin. *"Sanctify them through thy truth; thy word is truth…And for their sakes I sanctify myself, that they also might be sanctified through the truth"* (John 17:17 and 19).

Our Relationship to the World

In Romans 1:17-32, we can see the downward spiral of mankind. How is the worldly man described? _____

_____

_____

II Peter 2, describes false teachers and prophets. How are the ungodly men of the world described? _____

_____

_____

I John 2:15-17 We are not to _____

_____

_____

Leviticus 20:26 God wants us to be _____

_____

_____

I Peter 1:13-17 We are made holy by _____

_____

_____

I Peter 2:9-12 God sees and wants us to _____

_____

_____

Philippians 2:12-15 We are to _____

_____

_____

42

Philippians 3:17-21 The difference between the world and God's people is _____

_____

_____

Colossians 1:20-22 Reconciliation to God is made possible by

_____

_____

Ephesians 5:25-27 The purpose of sanctification is _____

_____

_____

I Thessalonians 3:11-13 God will _____

_____

_____

Revelation 21:7 and 8 Those who are not made holy are ____

_____

_____

II Timothy 2:19-23 Sanctification includes _____

_____

_____

Titus 2:11-15 We are to live _____

_____

_____

Romans 8:17 and 18 The hope of holy people is _____

_____

_____

II Corinthians 7:1 As recipients of the promises, we _____

_____

_____

John 17:17 and 18 Though we are to be sanctified, we are

_____

_____

Acts 26:17 and 18 We are sanctified by _____

_____

_____

I Corinthians 6:11 We are _____

WOMEN IN THE BIBLE

_____

_____

What are your attitudes, desires, or goals toward the *world*?

_____

_____

What is your attitude toward your *past*? _____

_____

_____

Becoming Free of the Past

To become free of the past, we need to deal with both the good things that always seem better than what we have now, as well as the sin and hurts that keep us in bondage.

We need to put our past into proper perspective and accept all that has happened to bring us where we are now. Add to this list other things that we can't afford to do such as; (1) remind our husbands of the "better" homes we had where we used to live, (2) keep from becoming involved in a new church because it isn't like the one we used to be in, (3) rest in the glory of a special accomplishment instead of taking on a new project, (4) continue in such close relationship with friends of the past that we have no time to cultivate new friendships.

Not only must we recognize a tendency to wish to live in the good things of the past, but we must deal with any unresolved hurt, guilt or unforgiveness that would keep us from going on to what the Lord has for us now. Though we initially received forgiveness by the cleansing of Jesus' blood at the moment of our salvation, we find a continuing need of that cleansing so that we can be healed.

Sometimes we hang onto past hurts because we blame other people and situations when, in fact, we need to look at our wrong responses and confess those as sin. As we do that and submit ourselves to the Holy Spirit for instruction and correction, we can experience true restoration.

The healing of most past hurts hinges upon an act of the will—to repent, to forgive and to allow God to heal. His power is available to us; we must *will* to be open to it. As we have already discovered, we can't depend upon our feelings, which are of the flesh.

In Matthew 18:21-35, Jesus tells of a king who forgave a servant a large debt. This same servant then went out and demanded that a fellow servant pay his entire debt to him, or he would put him in prison. When the king heard what had happened, he reminded the first servant how he had been forgiven and questioned him as to why he hadn't had the same compassion. The king then delivered the servant to the tormenters until his whole debt was paid.

Jesus concluded the story by saying, "So likewise shall my heavenly Father do also unto you, if ye from your hearts forgive not every one his brother their trespasses." Can it be that our unforgiveness of people in the past has been the cause

44

of hurts by which we have been tormented through the years?

II Corinthians 2:10 and 11 If we do not forgive _____

_____

_____

Isaiah 43:25(LB); Hebrews 8:12 If we forgive, _____

_____

_____

Isaiah 26:13 and 14 As to other lords that have had dominion over us, God can _____

_____

_____

We must not only forgive past hurts, but we must also renounce our old lives, so we may live new lives in Christ. This is *reckoning dead* the flesh. Jesus said, in Luke 14:26, *"If any man come to me, and hate not his father, and mother, and wife, and children, and brethren, and sisters, yea, and his own life, he cannot be my disciple."* We find the same idea expressed in Genesis 2:24, where the man is admonished to *leave* his father and mother so that he can become one flesh with his wife.

We can see this vividly in the story of Joseph, who had many reasons to recall his past. He could not only have been unforgiving toward his brothers, who sold him into Egypt, but he could also have been hurt by all the experiences he suffered in the new land—the trickery of Potiphar's wife that landed him in prison, the two-year forgetfulness of the butler who could have won his freedom, and the discouragement of wondering if God, too, had forsaken him.

But, what was Joseph's reaction when he was finally reunited with his brothers? He said, *"...ye thought evil against me; but God meant it unto good."* Joseph could forgive and go on, because he *knew* that God was in control and he trusted Him—no matter what happened.

SUMMARY

God is holy, and wants a holy people. Man was made in God's image, but "fell" and allowed the spirit of the god of this world (Satan) to rule over him. God provides a way back to Himself through Jesus Christ. He also wants to conform us to His nature, so that we may be a fit bride for His Son, Jesus Christ. This process of separating man from the world unto Himself is called "sanctification." Jesus used Lot's wife as an example of one who looked back, and asked that we remember her—even as we allow God to separate us from the world.

MODERN EXAMPLE

Evelyn Christenson, in her book *Lord Change Me* tells how the Lord answered her prayer to do just that. She realized that God wasn't as interested in her praying for Him to change her husband, her children, or others, as He was in sanctifying her own life.

An able Bible teacher and author, she also liked to "teach" at home whenever she could. But her 18-year-old daughter, Jan, came to resent this. One night at the dinner table Jan asked that her mother never again talk about her "philosophies." Evelyn was hurt. After the family meal she went to her bedroom to cry. She picked up her Bible and read I Peter 3:1 and 2 which instructs a woman to be a good example to her husband so he can be won *without a word*. The Lord spoke to Evelyn's heart and she decided to apply this Scriptural principle to her relationship with her daughter.

It wasn't an easy task. Evelyn had to die to her old nature many times. It was especially hard not to give advice and comments when Jan enrolled in the very college where Evelyn and her husband had met.

After eight months of silence on certain subjects, Evelyn had occasion to eat a meal with Jan and her date on the college campus. She was stunned to hear Jan telling her friend that "my mother believes this" or "my mother thinks that." God Himself brought to Jan's mind many things which Evelyn really did think and believe. At the same time, He was conforming Evelyn to His own nature. Through these circumstances, He was teaching Evelyn to trust in Him, to have faith in His Word, to exhibit patience toward Jan, and to develop self-control in always having to be the "teacher"—a few of the character qualities which may not have matured had she continued in her old way. When she later received a birthday card from Jan signed, "To my mother who says so much in silence," Evelyn was thrilled.

Several years later God confirmed the work in her. One day her daughter Nancy told her how much she appreciated her for being such a good *example*. Evelyn was changed from a woman of many words to one learning to live "without a word," by the sanctifying process of the Holy Spirit as she submitted to God's Word and prayed, "Lord, change *me*."

WHAT DO YOU THINK?

1. How does remembering Lots wife change your life? ____

_____

_____

2. How is God separating you from the hold of this world? What part do you have in the process? _____

_____

_____

3. How does your reading and meditating upon God's Word sanctify you? _____

_____

_____

4. Are there other ways by which you are being set apart or conformed to the nature of God (ex., losing your desire for worldly pleasures you used to enjoy)? _____

46

_____

_____

5. What is (or should be) your relationship to the world?

_____

_____

6. Are you free of your past? If not, how can you become so?

_____

_____

EVALUATE YOURSELF

1. In what ways are you implementing the principles learned from Lot's wife? _____

_____

_____

2. In what ways are you failing to implement the principles learned from Lot's wife? _____

_____

_____

3. What do you need to do to change? _____

_____

_____

4. How will you do it? _____

_____

_____

Lesson 6
Rebekah

An Example of Idolatry

"Thou shalt have no other gods before me."

Exodus 20:3

"Little children, keep yourselves from idols."

I John 5:21

SETTING THE STAGE

The definition of idolatry, as quoted from J. R. Miller's *"Devotional Hours in the Bible:"*

"Anything which we keep in our hearts in the place which God ought to have is an idol, whether it be an image of wood or stone or gold, or whether it be money, or desire for fame, or love of pleasure, or some secret sin which we will not give up. If God does not really occupy the highest place in our hearts, controlling all, something else does. And that something else is an idol."

We recognize the statues and images worshipped by pagans as idols. We observe the way some people allow their lives to revolve around possessions, television programs, leisure-time activities, and we call these idols. We see people almost worshipping a religious leader, becoming devastated when he "falls." But we are often unaware of the way *we* put people, even family members, on pedestals and expect them to fulfill our needs and satisfy our deepest desires.

This was true for Rebekah. She put Jacob in a position of idolatry. She continually favored him over others, including his twin brother Esau, her husband, Isaac, and even God.

God is a jealous God, according to His Word (Exodus 20:5). He has given us His all, and He wants us to seek Him with our *whole* heart (Psalm 119:2), to put our expectation in Him—not man or idols (I John 5:21).

THE FAILURE OF REBEKAH

(Based on Genesis 22-28; 49:31; Romans 9:6-16)

Sometime after Sarah died, Abraham instructed a servant to go to the country of his ancestry and bring back a wife for his son, Isaac. He didn't want Isaac marrying any of the Canaanite girls.

Reassured that God would send an angel before Him, the servant set off for Mesopotamia. He prayed that the right girl would be at a well where he would stop, and she would respond in a certain way. When all this happened, he lost no time in telling her why he had come. After meeting her family and sharing his mission with them, the servant returned to Canaan with her.

Isaac happened to be in the field when the caravan bringing Rebekah arrived. Immediately, he invited her into his mother's tent and "took Rebekah, and she became his wife, and he loved her."

Rebekah was barren, but eventually, after Isaac called on the Lord in her behalf, she became pregnant. Upon feeling a struggle within her womb, she learned from the Lord that she would bear twins, and that the elder child would serve the younger.

With the birth of sons Esau and Jacob, the family became divided. Rebekah showed partiality toward Jacob, while Isaac favored Esau. Eventually, Esau sold his birthright to Jacob for a bowl of stew. And Rebekah later schemed so Jacob would receive what should have been Esau's blessing from his father, Isaac. In the end, Isaac had been deceived, Esau was angry, Rebekah was hurt, and Jacob had to flee for his life. Rebekah, who had put Jacob in a position of idolatry, never saw him again.

Thus, we see that idols are not only graven images or things. We can put people in idolatrous positions, too. We try to conform them to our image instead of God's, even as we look to them to meet our needs. When they fail us, we both are hurt. Rebekah would know.

LESSONS FROM REBEKAH
What is Idolatry?

The first two of the ten commandments God gave to Moses dealt expressly with idolatry. Exodus 20:3-5(NIV) says, *"You shall have no other gods before me. You shall not make for yourself an idol in the form of anything in heaven above or in the earth beneath or in the waters below. You shall not bow down to them or worship them; for I, the Lord your God, am a jealous God, punishing the children for the sin of the fathers to the third and fourth generation of those who hate me..."*

When Jesus was asked which was the greatest commandment of all, He replied, *"The most important one is this: 'Hear, O Israel, the Lord your God, the Lord is one. Love the Lord your God with all your heart and with all your soul and with all your mind and with all your strength.'"* (Mark 12:29 and 30 NIV) God wants our total allegiance.

Simply stated, idolatry is any love, affection, or worship which rightfully belongs to God but is given to someone or something else. This may include a person, a possession, a ministry, a church, a job, a teaching—anything that demands our attention above God Himself. God has exclusive right to us, as we accept the covenant He made through the shed blood of Jesus Christ.

Satan is always behind the scenes, wanting the glory that rightfully belongs to God. His main tactic is to offer man substitutes, so that love and affection, or trust and loyalty are directed to persons and things other than God, and thus, indirectly to himself.

Idolatry in the Bible

From the very beginning, idolatry has been a problem between man and God. It was the cause of man's fall. When Adam and Eve ate of the forbidden fruit, they succumbed to the temptation to be "as God," and have the knowledge of good and evil. They put their wisdom above God's.

50

The whole history of Israel is a chronicle of God trying to win the exclusive allegiance of His chosen people for Himself. Instead, they kept turning to other substitutes. Time and time again, they looked to other gods, their own resources, or to the help of other nations. And time and time again God, in His mercy, attempted to bring them back to Him through His Word and His prophets.

Finally, God's only recourse was to remove them from their land and force them to submit to their enemies. Later, He brought back a remnant who seemed to have learned their lesson.

However, by the time God visited His people (as Jesus) His own did not even recognize Him! They had become so legalistic they were now leary of accepting anyone who claimed to be God! They had gone to the opposite extreme. They were now so involved in keeping the letter of the law, that their hearts were far from God. They were guilty of substituting *religion* for *God*. Religion, itself, had become their idol.

God gave Jesus as a sacrifice for sin that man might again have a relationship with Him; that He might have first place in man's heart.

The Book of I John, a description and exhortation of God's *agape* love, ends with a simple command. *"Little children, keep yourselves from idols."* John knew that idolatry is the one thing which keeps us from knowing and receiving the love of God.

Exodus 34:10-14; Exodus 20:3-5 God's command to His people was to _____

_____

_____

Leviticus 26:1-13 The blessings of obedience are contingent upon _____

_____

_____

which includes _____

_____

_____

Deuteronomy 7:25 and 26 Concerning idols and our homes,

_____

_____

Deuteronomy 11:16 We are not to worship _____

_____

_____

Romans 1:8-23 Part of the downward spiral of the reprobate man begins with _____

_____

WOMEN IN THE BIBLE

I Corinthians 5:11 We must not associate with _____

_____

_____

I Corinthians 10:14 We are to _____

_____

I Corinthians 10:19-21 We are not to fellowship with _____

_____

_____

We cannot be partakers of the Lord's Table and _____

_____

_____

II Corinthians 6:15-17 We, who are the temple of God, have no agreement with _____

_____

_____

We are to _____

_____

_____

Philippians 3:19 One's God can be _____

_____

_____

Colossians 3:5 and 6 Idolatry (which is _____),

_____

_____

is one part of our old nature that we are to _____

_____

_____

I Thessalonians 1:9 One can turn from idols to _____

_____

_____

Ezekiel 14:1-8 From those who have idols, God wants _____

_____

_____

52

How God Deals with Idolators

In a brief survey of Scripture, we find several significant events in which God dealt with idolatry. Here are a few:

(1) *The golden calf* (Exodus 32:1-8). At the very time God was giving the ten commandments to Moses, the Israelites were begging Aaron for other gods. Aaron complied and asked the people to give him the gold jewelry they had brought out of Egypt. He melted the gold and formed a golden calf, then built an altar before it and proclaimed a feast unto the Lord. When the Lord saw them worshipping this golden calf, He angrily commanded Moses to go down from the mountain. His wrath was so great He wanted to consume His own people. Moses interceded on their behalf, and instead of destroying them, the Lord sent a plague upon the people.

(2) *The brazen serpent* (Numbers 21:8 and 9; II Kings 18:1-4) While the Israelites were in the wilderness, God had Moses make a serpent of brass and set it upon a pole. If anyone was bitten by a serpent he could look upon the brass serpent and live. The brazen serpent was a "type" of Christ. It brought Israel a form of deliverance.(See also John 3:14) Yet, instead of the Israelites being drawn closer to Yahweh, their Deliverer, over the years they permitted this point of contact itself to become an object of their devotion. Hezekiah, recognizing this for the idol worship it was, destroyed the brazen serpent Moses had made along with the groves and other images.

(3) *Serving Baal in the time of the Judges* (Judges 6:25-32; 10:6-16; 17:1-13; 18:30 and 31) Baal was not the name of one god, but the name of the presiding deity of any one locality. Because the worship of Baal was much the same everywhere in Canaan, in time "Baal" came to represent the idea of one god. The Baalim were the gods of the land, owning and controlling it. The increase of crops, fruit, and cattle was under their control. Some were over specific cities; others were worshipped in "high places" in general. In the time of the judges, there were altars to Baal everywhere. Even the priests had been corrupted by idolatry. It was a time when there was no king in Israel, and everyone did what was right in his own eyes.

(4) *Idolatry in the time of the kings* (I Kings 11:1-8; 12:28-32; 14:22-24; 18:20-40) Though Solomon was given great wisdom, his many wives eventually turned his heart after other gods. His sons, Rehoboam and Jeroboam, continued to tolerate and encourage idolatry. By the time of Ahab and Jezebel, the worship of Jehovah was almost supplanted by that of Baal. The struggle between Baalism and Judaism came to a head on Mt. Carmel when the prophet Elijah met the priests of Baal and slew 450 of them. The cult quickly recuperated, however, and prospered until crushed by Jehu. Jezebel gave the worship of Baal new momentum. When she was overthrown, the temple of Baal at Jerusalem was destroyed and the chief priest was killed before the altar. Before long, however, there was another revival of the worship of Baal. Josiah again destroyed the temple of Baal and caused the public worship of the god to cease for a time. Prophets of Israel,

especially Jeremiah, often denounced Baal worship.

(5) *Idolatry in the scattering of God's people* (II Kings 17:5-23; II Kings 23:24-27) God allowed the King of Assyria to carry the Israelites out of their own land because they had sinned against Him by worshipping other gods. And though Josiah brought reform to Judah, God also removed them from the land and allowed them to be carried into captivity in Babylonia because of their idolatry. Ezekiel 16 tells us how God felt about His beautiful bride, Jerusalem, who became a "prostitute" as she gave herself to other gods.

(6) *Idolatry in New Testament times* (Matthew 6:24; Acts 15:29; I Corinthians 8:1-13; 10:14; Revelation 9:20; 13:12-14)

There are few references to idolatry in the New Testament, other than warnings against it. The Maccabean war resulted in the Jews becoming fanatically opposed to the idolatry of Old Testament times. They were not now tempted to worship images or gods other than Jehovah. Jesus, however, warned them that to make possessions central in life is also idolatry. Christians in apostolic times, many of whom were converted from paganism, were repeatedly warned in the epistles to be on guard against idolatry. They were also advised on certain practices, such as eating meats which had first been offered to idols. In Revelation, the last book of the Bible, John predicts a time of idolatrous apostasy in the last days, when the Beast and his image will be accorded divine honors.

SUMMARY

God is a jealous God who desires that we worship Him alone. We must seek Him with our *whole* heart. Idolatry is any love, affection, or worship which rightly belongs to God, but is given to someone or something else. This may include possesions, a ministry, a job, a teaching—anything which demands our attention and allegiance above God Himself. God denounces idolatry from Genesis to Revelation. For Rebekah, idolatry came in the form of her son.

MODERN EXAMPLE

Cathy and Rob, products of the rebellious 60's, were settling down into "the establishment" with a family of their own. Still searching for the answer to their emptiness within, they decided to accept an invitation to attend a neighborhood church. Soon they were regular participants at the Sunday worship services, where they heard the Gospel preached. God's Word began to take root in their hearts and Cathy accepted Jesus as her Savior.

But the more they got involved, the more they became aware of friction in the church. They didn't understand what was happening, only that so-called Christians seemed to be fighting one another. So they searched for another church and found one through an advertisement in the weekly paper.

On their first visit to the new church, they knew they had found what they were looking for! The people were caring and the pastor seemed very interested in them. Relieved to be out of a tense situation and into a loving fellowship, they began to involve themselves in all the functions of the new congregation.

As an added blessing, Rob found Jesus and began to share Cathy's commitment. Both of them grew in relationship with each other and to the Lord. They were especially fond of the pastor and enjoyed many good times with him, even as they looked to him for all their spiritual needs.

Several months later, they were attending a church picnic when they noticed the pastor being particularly attentive to his secretary. But they shrugged it off, deciding that they were talking business. In the months ahead, other little things disturbed Cathy and Rob, but they kept justifying whatever happened. Besides, they were trying not to be judgmental—especially toward the pastor who taught them not to be so.

Then one day, on a visit to the church office, Cathy saw first hand what she been trying to deny. The pastor and his secretary were involved in more than a business relationship. With a heavy heart, she shared what she had observed with Rob that evening. Angry, he wouldn't accept it. He simply couldn't believe that the pastor who had led him to the Lord and baptized him could be having an adulterous affair.

It wasn't long, however, before things came into the open and the pastor resigned to marry his secretary and go into other work. Reeling with the rest of the congregation, Cathy and Rob were devastated. They didn't feel like staying with the church, but neither did they feel like getting involved anywhere else.

First, they blamed the leadership for allowing things to get this far. Then, they blamed the pastor for succumbing to temptation. Next, they blamed God for letting it all happen. Everyone else was blamed. They felt justified in being innocent victims in the whole situation.

It wasn't until much time and teaching later that they realized their own sin. They had set both churches and pastors on pedestals, allowing them to replace God. Without a graven image in sight, they had fallen into the age-old trap of idolatry.

WHAT DO YOU THINK?

1. What "idols" do you have in your life? (What gets more of your attention than your time with the Lord?) _____

_____

_____

2. Are you willing to put your home, your job, your family, your possessions, everything in a lesser priority than your relationship to God? _____

_____

_____

3. How do you make "idols" out of people? _____

_____

_____

4. Do you have anything in your home which gives recognition to another god? (such as occult items, statues of Buddha or Tiki gods) _____

_____

_____

EVALUATE YOURSELF
1. In what ways are you implementing the principles learned from Rebekah? _____

_____

_____

2. In what ways are you failing to implement the principles learned from Rebekah? _____

_____

_____

3. What do you need to do to change? _____

_____

_____

4. How will you do it? _____

_____

_____

Lesson 7
Leah & Rachel

An Example of Covenants

"But this shall be the covenant that I will make with the house of Israel; after those days, saith the Lord, I will put my law in their inward parts, and write it in their hearts; and will be their God, and they shall be my people."

Jeremiah 31:33

SETTING THE STAGE

Jacob had two wives, Leah and Rachel. In their parallel stories we can see the contrast between a covenant relationship and a commitment based upon feelings, soulish desires, lust. As we consider these, our own eyes should be opened as to what it means to have a covenant relationship with God and/or another person.

After working for Rachel's father for seven years in order to marry Rachel, Jacob was tricked into taking her elder sister, Leah, as his wife. He then had to work another seven years for Rachel. Though Jacob was loyal to them both, he obviously preferred Rachel.

This, of course, left Leah the undesired wife. But as she put her trust in God and fulfilled her marriage vow, God blessed her with six sons whose names were given to half of the twelve tribes of Israel. She was also allowed to enter the Promised Land with Jacob and was buried with him.

Rachel, on the other hand, seemed to relate to her husband, others, and God primarily according to her feelings. She strove with Leah, envying Leah's motherhood. She was angry toward Jacob for not giving her children. She deceived her father as she took his idols. The latter leads us to believe that she was not fully committed to God. She seems to have had no true covenant relationship with anyone.

Jeremiah 31:32 says that God is a husband to His people. He wants to have a covenant relationship with us. He wants us to respond with whole-hearted commitment, not unreliable feelings of the moment. The contrast in relationships can be seen in Leah and Rachel. Leah fulfilled her covenant with both her husband and God despite the negative feelings she probably had—especially toward a husband who didn't love her. Rachel, on the other hand, allowed her commitment to them both to fluctuate according to how she felt at the time.

THE SUCCESS OF LEAH
(Based on Genesis 28-35)

To compare the relationship of Leah and Jacob with that of Rachel and Jacob, we must first review the story which includes them both.

After Jacob cheated his brother, Esau, out of his blessing and birthright, he was sent to his mother's homeland to find a wife. On the way, Jacob had a dream in which he saw angels ascending and descending a ladder that reached from earth to heaven. From above this ladder, Jacob heard God's voice reminding him of the covenant He had made with Jacob's grandfather, Abraham, and Jacob's father, Isaac. Then, God spoke to Jacob about passing this covenant to him. God promised to bless Jacob's descendants and give him a land for his inheritance. In return, Jacob made a vow unto the Lord that, if God would be with him, he would recognize God as *his* God.

Jacob traveled on, until he came to a place where some sheep were waiting to be watered. While asking the shepherds the whereabouts of his uncle Laban, Laban's daughter Rachel arrived with his sheep. Jacob thought Rachel was beautiful and ran to uncover the well so that her sheep could get water. Impulsively, he bent over and kissed her. It was love at first sight!

Rachel took Jacob home to meet her father, Laban. After staying with the family and working a while, Jacob asked for Rachel's hand in marriage. Laban agreed that Jacob could have Rachel after seven years of work.

The day finally came. Laban invited guests to celebrate the happy occasion. When evening came, he took his daughter into Jacob's tent, and they were joined as husband and wife. But the real surprise came the next morning when Jacob discovered that his bride was not Rachel, but her older, not-so-beautiful sister, Leah. The custom was that the elder daughter be given in marriage first, but this had not been the agreement with Laban. Jacob was furious. He lost no time in finding his new father-in-law, who then agreed to give him Rachel—for an additional seven years of hard labor—following the bridal week he was committed to spend with Leah.

Adding to the already contentious situation, Leah began to bear Jacob children, while Rachel remained barren. Unloved by her husband, Leah put her trust in the Lord. With the birth of each son, her relationship with God grew. When her first child was born, she named him "Reuben," believing that God had noticed her predicament.

She hoped it would cause her husband to love her. At Simeon's birth, she recognized that God had given her a second son to make up for the love her husband would not give her. When Levi, her third-born, was named, she said, "Now this time will my husband be joined unto me, because I have borne him three sons." It didn't happen; she still did not have Jacob's real affection even after Judah, their fourth son, was born. Even so, she was true to her covenant as a wife. She put her trust in God to help her fulfill this covenant, declaring at the birth of Judah, "Now I will praise the Lord!"

Leah had no more children for a while. During this time Rachel bore Jacob a son, as did two of their handmaids. Later, Leah had two more sons, as well as a daughter. Never once do we hear of Jacob giving Leah the affection and love she so desired. Yet, she is the one recognized as the covenant wife of Jacob, buried beside him in the cave of Macpelah along with Abraham and Sarah, and Isaac and Rebekah. God honored her whole-hearted commitment to Him and to Jacob despite her feelings.

58

THE FAILURE OF RACHEL
(Based on Genesis 29-31; 35:16-19)

As noted in the previous story, Jacob actually met Rachel first. And, he seems to have fallen for her immediately because of her beauty. Within a short time, he made arrangements to marry her.

Contrary to Leah, Rachel swings from one feeling to another. Though Scripture does not say so, we can imagine that she was very angry when her father gave Leah to Jacob on the night she and Jacob had hoped would be their wedding night. Genesis 30:8 tells us that from that time on, she was in a fierce contest with her sister, especially when Leah began to have children and she did not. This caused angry scenes between Rachel and Jacob. She blamed him for her barrenness.

Finally, when God opened her womb and she did have a child, she didn't express gratitude. Her only remark was that now God could give her another son.

Envious of her sister, sometimes angry with Jacob, Rachel also lied to her father. When Jacob's family left Padamaram, she hid her father's idols under her seat, and lied to Jacob that she didn't have them. That she took the idols illustrates her lack of whole-hearted commitment to God.

Most poignant of all, is Rachel's death during the birth of her second son, Benjamin; the most-loved wife of Jacob was never allowed to enter the Promised Land. Feelings can not enter in—God's promises come through faith, and a covenant relationship with Him.

LESSONS FROM LEAH AND RACHEL
Covenant

Simply said, a covenant is an agreement between two parties. God is a covenant-maker. He desires a covenant relationship with His people.

However, in order for fallen man to have this kind of relationship with God, God not only had to bind Himself to a covenant, but also found it necessary to help man keep his end of it. Thus, the covenant between God and man demands that God will never leave nor forsake us, even as He undertakes to keep us true to Him. God wants to draw us to Himself, to render us entirely dependent upon Him, so that He can fill us and have "oneness," like husband and wife.

God has made two major covenants with man—the old and the new. They indicate two stages in God's dealings with man and two ways man has been able to respond to God.

In the Old Covenant, man had the opportunity to show what he could do by obeying many rules and laws. That covenant ended in man's unfaithfulness and failure. He simply couldn't keep the law.

In the second, or New Covenant, God shows what He can do with man, unfaithful and weak as man is, when *He* does all the work in keeping the covenant. This, of course, depends upon man's willingness to accept what God offers (Jesus' sacrifice for man's sin, thus allowing God to indwell man). When man enters the covenant on God's terms, God provides everything.

WOMEN IN THE BIBLE

Covenant Throughout Scripture

Genesis 9:1-17 The first mention of a covenant is with Noah. After God destroyed all life on earth, except Noah and his family who were in the Ark, He promised that He would never again destroy the earth with flood waters. The token of this covenant is the rainbow.

Genesis 12:2 and 3; 15:18; 17:1-22 Here, God made a covenant with Abraham, as He called out a people unto Himself. He promised to make Abraham and his seed a great nation. Furthermore, God promised He would bless those who blessed this nation and curse those who cursed it. The sign of this covenant was circumcision. Abraham's response was to obey God in faith.

Genesis 26:3-5 The covenant was renewed with Abraham's son, Isaac.

Genesis 28:13-22 The covenant was again renewed with Isaac's son, Jacob.

Exodus 19:5 and 6 At Mt. Sinai, God told Moses that, if the people would obey His voice and keep His covenant, they would be a special treasure unto Him. They would be a kingdom of priests, a holy nation.

Deuteronomy 7:9 We are reminded of God's faithfulness in keeping the covenant. With those who love Him and keep His commandments, He will keep His covenant a thousand generations.

Psalm 89:3,4,28 and 34 In this Psalm, David reminds us of the covenant God renewed through him. (See II Samuel 7:8-16 as to how this was done.)

Jeremiah 31:31-34 God foresaw the need of a new covenant. His people were unable to keep the old one by means of the law. Through the prophet Jeremiah, He told of the new covenant He would make. It would not be like the first one, dependent upon man's outward obedience. This time, He would write the law upon man's heart.

Ezekiel 16:59 and 60 Again, through the prophet Ezekiel, we have the promise that God would remember the old covenant, which had been broken, and would make a new, everlasting covenant.

I Corinthians 11:23-28 On the same night Jesus was betrayed, He instituted the "Lord's Supper" with His disciples. At this time, He revealed the New Covenant. He took the cup and told his disciples the new covenant would be made through His blood. Jesus said for His followers to remember His broken body and shed blood as they observe this supper in remembrance of Him.

Hebrews 8:6-13 Here we are reminded that Jesus is the mediator of a better covenant, one which was established on better promises. With the coming of the second covenant, the first passed away.

Hebrews 9 and 10 These two chapters describe the differences between the Old and New Covenants. They tell us of the failures of the old and the benefits of the new. In summary, the first covenant included a physical tabernacle where God's laws for sacrifice could be carried out. Jesus came as High-Priest of a better system. He went into the greater, perfect tabernacle in heaven where, once and for all, He took blood into the Holy of Holies and sprinkled it upon the mercy seat.

60

This time it wasn't the blood of goats and calves that atoned for sin, but His very own blood which He shed at Calvary when He purchased our salvation.

Thus, as we accept the atonement of Jesus' shed blood, He comes into our hearts, where the New Covenant is written. Hebrews 10:16 (LB) says, *"This is the agreement (covenant) I will make with the people of Israel, though they broke their first agreement; I will write my laws into their minds so that they will always know my will, and I will put my laws in their hearts, so that they will want to obey them."* This, then, is the difference between the Old and New Covenants, or, as we know them, the Old and New Testaments.

The Marriage Covenant

In our study of covenants, we see that man cannot keep his part of a covenant without God's help. Thus, a husband and wife need the help of God to truly fulfill a covenant between them. Marriages which don't include God in partnership can't experience covenant in the truest sense. As a result, many of these marriages fail.

The need for God's help is evident when we note that a loving husband-wife relationship demands death to selfish desires on the part of each person. This is only possible when one's "rights" are given to God. Thus, in a true covenant relationship, all "rights" are given to God. He gives the ability to love sacrificially.

The marriage covenant is entered into by making "vows." In the Old Testament, these vows were considered sacred and binding (Deuteronomy 23:23), Ecclesiastes 5:4 and 5 says, *"When thou vowest a vow unto God, defer not to pay it; for he hath no pleasure in fools; pay that which thou hast vowed. Better it is that thou shouldest not vow, than that thou shouldest vow and not pay."* In the New Testament, Jesus mentions vows only to condemn their abuse. (Mark 7:10-13).

In God's sight, as marriage vows are exchanged, husband and wife become one flesh. And what God has joined together, no man is to put asunder. Paul reinforces this in I Corinthians 7:39. He says that marriage vows bind husband and wife and only death parts them.

Faith Versus Feelings

The way to enjoy the promises of a covenant relationship is to claim them by faith. As a covenant people, we walk by faith in God, not by sight (what we see or feel). Let's look at some of these promises in Scripture and see how they're obtained.

Ephesians 2:8 and 9 We are saved through _____,

_____

_____

Not _____

_____

_____

John 12:48 We are judged by _____,

_____

_____

not feelings of worth.

Matthew 5:44 We are to respond to others in _____

_____

_____

not in _____

_____

_____

I Peter 3:9 We are called to _____

_____

_____

in spite of how we feel.

Proverb 14:12 Ways that seem right are _____

_____

_____

Isaiah 55:8 and 9 Our thoughts and feelings are _____

_____

_____

SUMMARY

One of the themes that runs through Scripture is that of *covenant*. God is a covenant-making God. He wants His people to have a covenant relationship with Him. The first Covenant was superseded by a New Covenant, when Jesus was sacrificed for our sins.

Marriage is a type of covenant agreement. Through it we can learn the commitment God desires. We find an example of this in Leah and Jacob's marriage, as compared to that of Rachel and Jacob, whose marriage was founded on the feelings they had for one another.

MODERN EXAMPLE

David Roever was a young man sent to Vietnam soon after he married his high school sweetheart. While at war, a grenade exploded in his hand, blowing off half of his face, as well as much flesh from the rest of his body.

After immediate treatment in Asia, he was flown back to the States along with other seriously injured servicemen. He was the only one of that group to survive.

He gives credit for this to his wife, who overcame her own feelings and initial shock to stand by him throughout many operations and years of recuperation—including much skin-grafting, artificial parts and hair implantation. Even now, his appearance is a bit unusual.

In contrast, he tells of one wife who, when she saw her mutilated husband, threw her wedding ring on the hospital bed and walked out declaring that she would be too embarrassed to be seen with him again.

With the support and encouragement of his loving wife, David not only made a comeback physically, but he has been greatly used of God to speak to thousands of teen-agers concerning vital subjects—drugs, sex, suicide, fear, loyalty, commitment. Spellbound, they listen to him as a man of authority on these subjects. They also laugh with him as he tells humorous stories about himself.

David often ends his program by playing the piano, with a thumb and finger on one hand and some knuckles on the other, while the young people reflect upon what he has said. Without a doubt, many of them wonder at the commitment of a very special wife and the marriage vow which was, to her, a lifetime commitment.

WHAT DO YOU THINK?

1. Do you see yourself in a covenant-relationship with God? If so, how is this worked out? _____

   _____

   _____

2. If you are married, do you see your relationship with your husband as that of a covenant? Or, is your marriage based on the "feelings" you have for one another? _____

   _____

   _____

3. How do you come into a covenant relationship with God?

   _____

   _____

4. How do you come into a covenant relationship with your husband? _____

   _____

   _____

EVALUATE YOURSELF

1. In what ways are you implementing the principles learned from Leah and Rachel? _____

   _____

   _____

2. In what ways are you failing to implement the principles learned from them? _____

   _____

   _____

3. What do you need to do to change? _____

_____

_____

4. How will you do it? _____

_____

_____

Lesson 8
Dinah, &
Potiphar's Wife

An Example of Sin—Repentance

"For the wages of sin is death, but the gift of God is eternal life through Jesus Christ our Lord."

Romans 6:23

SETTING THE STAGE

When God made man in His image and placed him in the Garden of Eden, He warned him not to eat the fruit of the tree of the knowledge of good and evil, saying that if he did, he would surely die. When man yielded to Satan's temptation, he died spiritually. As a result he could no longer fellowship with God. With his new knowledge, man attempted to cover his nakedness with fig leaves. But, this didn't cover sin. According to God's plan, only shed blood atones for sin (Hebrews 9:22b). So God, Himself, provided animal skins to literally cover Adam and Eve's bodies and symbolically cover their sin (by inferring, of course, that blood had been shed).

Throughout the Old Testament animal sacrifice, with its many rules and regulations, atoned for sin. This became a burdensome system. God eventually sent His own Son, Jesus, as the perfect Lamb to be sacrificed once and for all for sin. As man accepts this work of atonement, the blood of Jesus cleanses him from sin and he is forgiven. He then becomes a child of God and joint-heir with Jesus.

Through this salvation experience, man is forgiven all past sin and promised eternal life with God. However, as long as man lives in this world, he has the continuing freedom to sin. These daily sins continue to separate him from God until he repents of them and once again claims the restoring power of the blood of Jesus.

Man tends to make light of sin. Lust, as shown in the life of Dinah, or lying, as described in the story of Potiphar's wife, may seem like small sins when compared to witchcraft or murder. But in God's sight, sin is sin. It separates us from God. He provided the way back through Jesus. He wants us to accept the work of the cross and repent of our sin, so He can continue to forgive us and restore fellowship with us.

THE FAILURE OF DINAH

(Based on Genesis 34)

Dinah was the only daughter of Jacob and Leah. Perhaps she was spoiled, being the only sister of twelve brothers. Perhaps she was just curious as to what was happening with other girls her age. Whatever the reason, one day Dinah stole away from her father's drab tents to wander into the city.

While she was there, Shechem, son of Hamor the Hivite, prince of the country, saw her. And though Dinah probably never intended to get involved, he "lay with her and he defiled her."

This seduction brought sin and shame to Dinah, but the young prince offered reparation to her father, as required by Hebrew law (Deuteronomy 22:28 and 29). This included marriage, as well as payment. Shechem, much taken with Dinah, demanded that his father make the arrangements.

So, Hamor went to Jacob and his sons to discuss the matter of marriage between Shechem and Dinah. Jacob became very angry, but his sons seemed to agree that the marriage should take place. Jacob's sons proposed that Dinah could marry the young man on the condition that all the male Shechemites submit to the rite of circumcision. The agreement was made.

On the third day after the circumcision, when the pain was bad and the men had difficulty moving about, two of Jacob's sons attacked and killed all the males in the city, including the young prince and his father. They rescued Dinah from Shechem's house and returned her to her home. Then Jacob's sons plundered the city because their sister had been dishonored there. They took the flocks, the herds, and everything they could lay their hands on, both inside the city and outside in the fields. They also took all the women and children.

Though Jacob was unhappy with what his sons had done, this tragedy reminded him of his vow to God. He and his family surrendered their strange gods and purified themselves once again. For their crime, Simeon and Levi received a curse instead of a blessng at the time of Jacob's death. After the massacre, we hear no more of Dinah.

Lust

Though we could name other sins, such as rebellion or fornication, the *root* of Dinah's problem seems to be lust. Her lust for adventure opened the door to Shechem's sexual lust toward her. She left the protection and discipline of her father's house for the ways of the world which seemed so enticing.

Be definition, lust is desire, intense longing, craving. We usually associate it with sexual desire, but one can lust for many things. Lust has its roots in dissatisfaction. It always wants something it doesn't have. Lust always seeks to get what it wants and usually attracts those of the same spirit, as happened in this story.

Let's look at what Scripture says concerning lust and how we're to deal with it.

II Peter 1:4 The corruption that is in the world has come through _____

_____

_____

I John 2:15-17 Not of the Father, but of the world is _____

_____

James 1:14 and 15 When lust conceives, it _____

_____

_____

Matthew 5:28 Lust causes one to _____

_____

_____

Ephesians 4:22 We're to put off our former manner of living, which is corrupt due to _____

_____

_____

We can deal with lust in the following ways:

Galatians 5:24 _____

_____

_____

Colossians 3:5 _____

_____

_____

Titus 2:11 and 12 _____

_____

_____

II Timothy 2:22 _____

_____

_____

Galatians 5:16 _____

_____

_____

THE FAILURE OF POTIPHAR'S WIFE

(Based on Genesis 39)

When Joseph arrived in Egypt as a captive of the Ishmaelite traders, he was purchased by Potiphar, captain of Pharoah's guard. The Lord blessed Joseph in this household. Everything he did succeeded. Soon Joseph was put in charge of Potiphar's whole household and all of his business affairs.

One day, when Potiphar's wife was alone with handsome young Joseph, she suggested that he come sleep with her. Joseph refused. But she continued to make her suggestions every day. One day, when they were in the house alone, she grabbed him and demanded that he sleep with her. He tore himself away. As he did his jacket slipped off and she was left holding it while he fled from the house. Unable to accept his rejection, she began to scream. As other men came running to see what was wrong, she cried hysterically, "Joseph tried to rape me, but when I screamed, he ran and forgot to take his jacket." When her husband came home that night, she told him the same story.

When Potiphar heard his wife's story, he threw Joseph into prison and left him there for several years.

Lying

We can see several sins in the story of Potiphar's wife and this incident with Joseph, but, the one we will consider is lying.

What happened to Potiphar's wife as a result of her lying? We can imagine that she may have spent some sleepless nights knowing that, because of her lie, Joseph was in prison. Or, if she had told many lies before, her conscience may have become so seared that she had little guilt. We don't know if Potiphar's wife saw lying as a sin. But we have God's Word which tells us that lying is an abomination to God, and that all liars will someday find themselves in the lake of fire.

Many of us don't realize we lie. We may not tell big, obvious ones, but what about the little "white lies," the way we just let people think something is true when it isn't? Potiphar's wife used Joseph's coat to imply that he had attempted to lay with her.

Whether we simply refrain from the truth, or whether we lie outright, we aren't walking in God's way of light and truth. Eventually we can even deceive ourselves to the point that we don't recognize truth itself. This is the fearful result of lying.

Let's see what God's Word says concerning lying.

John 8:44 Lying originates with _____

_____

_____

II Thessalonians 2:10 Man can perish because _____

_____

_____

Proverb 6:16-19 Lying is _____

_____

_____

I John 2:4 If one says that he knows Christ, but _____

_____

_____

he is a liar.

Proverb 19:5 _____

_____

will be punished, and a liar will _____

_____

_____

Proverb 12:22 The Lord detests _____

_____

_____

Revelation 21:8 and 27 The destiny of liars is _____

_____

_____

LESSONS FROM DINAH AND POTIPHAR'S WIFE

Sin

We are living in a time when sin no longer has much meaning. Some who believe sin to be a fact, continue with little thought of its penalty. Yet, we can see the results of its reality all around us.

On the other hand, God makes much of sin. He said, *"The soul that sinneth, it shall die"* (Ezekiel 18:20), and, *"The wages of sin is death"* (Romans 6:23). The presence of sin cannot be escaped in this life, but it can be overcome by the power of God.

The origin of sin is one of the mysteries of the Bible. It is first noted in the heart of Satan. He was a created being, perfect until iniquity was found in him. (Ezekiel 28:11-19). Satan fell from perfection when he exerted his will above God's will. This is sin.

To some, sin is a weakness of the flesh. To others, it's the absence of good. The latest theory seems to be that sin is a disease to be treated by science, because man is inherently good—only sick. God declares that sin is:

I John 3:4 _____

_____

_____

Romans 3:23 _____

_____

_____

Isaiah 1:2-4 _____

_____

_____

I John 5:10 _____

Isaiah 53:6 _____

_____

I John 5:17 _____

_____

The Blood of Jesus

Blood is a strange and mysterious substance. The Bible doesn't tell us the chemical composition of the red or white corpuscles, but it does tell us that the *life* of every living creature is in its blood (Leviticus 17:11).

When God made man in His image, He breathed His own spiritual life into him. That life was held in the substance which we call blood. When man dies, life leaves the blood.

Before we can see how the blood of Jesus atones for sin, we need to understand some things that are unique about His blood. We are indebted to Dr. William Standish Reed of the Christian Medical Foundation of Tampa, Florida for enlightenment concerning the sinlessness of Jesus Christ, because of the fact that all of His blood was from God!

Luke 1:31 specifically states that the conception of Jesus took place in Mary's *womb*. Therefore, His was a supernatural conception. Normal human conception doesn't take place there. Rather, the uniting of the male sperm and female ovum takes place in the fallopian tube of the female. Neither the sperm nor the ovum have blood in and of themselves, only the ability to create blood of the new life as it comes into being. Furthermore, the placenta which forms keeps the mother's blood from passing into that of the fetus.

Therefore, since Jesus' body was wonderfully fashioned in Mary's womb, He was sinless; none of the Adamic blood entered His being. Thus could Jesus, the only-begotten Son of God, declare, "I am the LIFE!"

What does Scripture say concerning Jesus' Blood?

Colossians 1:12-14 _____

_____

_____

Ephesians 1:6 and 7 _____

_____

_____

Acts 20:28 _____

_____

_____

I Corinthians 11:23-25 _____

_____

_____

John 19:31-34 _____

_____

_____

Romans 3:23-25 _____

_____

_____

Romans 5:6-11 _____

_____

_____

Hebrews 9:12-14 _____

_____

_____

Hebrews 10:10-19 _____

_____

_____

Hebrews 13:12 _____

_____

_____

I Peter 1:19-21 _____

_____

_____

Salvation

By one man, sin entered the world (Romans 5:12). And, when Adam sinned, his seed became corrupt. Man is, therefore, born in sin (Psalm 51:5). All have sinned (Romans 3:23) and all are condemned to die (John 3:18 and Romans 6:23). We know that, through the blood of Jesus, God has made provision for the atonement of our sin. But what is our part in receiving deliverance from the bondage of sin and the gift of eternal life?

(1) **We need to recognize our sin and repent of it.** Salvation is not automatic. One has to *do* God's Word to *acquire* it. Since He tells us that *all* have sinned, we know that we are sinners. Acts 17:30 (NIV) says that God commands all people everywhere to repent. Repenting means feeling remorse. We must be sorry enough for our sin that we are willing to turn in a new direction.

(2) **We need to confess our sins to God and, sometimes, to others.** I John 1:7 (NIV) says, *"If we confess our sins, he is faithful and just and will forgive us our sins and purify us from all unrighteousness."* When we have God's forgiveness, we have salvation. There are times when we also need to receive forgiveness from others.

(3) **We must believe in the Lord Jesus Christ.** The 16th chapter of Acts tells the story of Paul and Silas in jail. Following an earthquake which opened the jail doors and loosed everyone's bonds, the jailer became frightened and asked them, "Sirs, what must I do to be saved?" The reply was that he should believe in the Lord Jesus Christ. One must have faith to believe that Jesus did what the Word says He did, or the promises can't be claimed.

As one believes in Jesus, he then desires to confess this belief before others. (The Philippian jailer did, and his whole household was saved.) Jesus says, in Matthew 10:32, (NIV) *"Whoever acknowledges me before men, I will also acknowledge him before my Father in heaven. But whoever disowns me before men, I will disown him before my Father in heaven."*

(4) **We should submit to water baptism.** After the jailer and his family believed, they were baptized, signifying that they are now dead in their sin and risen to walk in newness of life. Romans 6:4 (NIV) tells us, *"We were therefore buried with him through baptism into death in order that, just as Christ was raised from the dead through the glory of the Father, we too may live a new life."*

These steps fulfill all that is implied as our part in John 3:16. *"For God so loved the world that he gave his one and only Son, that whoever believes in him shall not perish but have eternal life."* This is our salvation.

SUMMARY

Man is a sinner. In fact, *all* have sinned and come short of the glory of God. Sin separates man from God, but God provided a way back for man. The blood of Jesus Christ made atonement for our sin. God wants us to repent and confess our sin, as we accept what Jesus did for us upon the cross. When we do that, He can forgive us and restore us to right relationship with Him. Though we know of neither of these two women's "salvation," a study of Dinah teaches us about the sin of lust. Potiphar's wife portrays the sin of lying.

MODERN EXAMPLE

Author of the popular radio series, "Unshackled," Eugenia Price has written hundreds of stories of people who were "saved" under the ministry of Pacific Garden Mission on Skid Row in Chicago. But, it's in her book, *The Burden is Light,* that she tells the story of her own conversion to Jesus Christ.

Eugenia (or Genie, as she calls herself), was born into an upper middle class Christian family in Charleston, West Virginia. She attended church most of her growing-up years, mainly at the insistence of her mother who directed the church choir. Although she was a very bright girl in school, Genie admits she hardly ever listened to a sermon. The world was a great attraction to her, and she began smoking at age 14.

Eugenia went on to college where, after taking a course in Comparative Religion, she determined that she was an atheist. She pursued a major in English so that she could write, but later changed to a pre-dental course in order to have a more lucrative career as did her father, a dentist. She was, in fact, the only woman accepted in Northwestern Dental School in Chicago the year she entered. She made honor grades for three years until she became bored. She then entered the University of Chicago to study philosophy and more writing courses.

She discovered, much to her dismay, that she really had nothing to say as a writer. So she wrote commercials for beer and cigarette sponsors. During this time, as she continued to smoke and drink heavily, she became very overweight. At age 33, she was considered successful by the world's standards, but her heart was extremely burdened.

On a vacation to her parent's home, she had a dream which she had had several times before. Because a childhood friend always appeared in this dream she decided to call and find out where she was. Though they hadn't seen each other since they were teen-agers, Ellen happened also to be in town on vacation, so Genie invited her over for a visit.

But Eugenia was in for a big surprise. Ellen, who had also been very worldly, now declined to smoke or drink. Furthermore, she claimed to now have Jesus as the center of her life and said she didn't care to do any of the former things.

Eugenia had a difficult time accepting Ellen's testimony. She had long ago decided that there was no such thing as sin, therefore, no need of a Savior.

Still, the visit opened doors to a continuing relationship with Ellen. She invited Genie to visit her in New York. Eugenia did, though she wouldn't stay at the household of Christians where Ellen lived. Instead she rented a hotel room nearby. It was in this room that she picked up a Gideon Bible and, for the first time, really read the Word of God. Finally, Ellen persuaded her to go hear Dr. Samuel Shoemaker. For the first time in 18 years, Genie found herself in church. The sermon, "The Grace of Jesus Christ," put Eugenia under real conviction, and she began to walk toward the altar at the end of the service. But half-way there, she turned and ran back to the hotel and entered the bar.

When Ellen found her, they talked and talked. Finally, feeling that nothing was coming of the conversation, Ellen got up to leave. But when she saw Eugenia panic, she turned and confronted her, once more, with God's plan of salvation. Eugenia fell into a big chair by the window and sobbed. Ellen didn't move, but after a time of letting her cry, calmly told Eugenia that she thought the most wonderful thing that could happen was for the old Genie Price to die so that a new one could be born.

In the lengthy silence that followed, Eugenia recognized herself for the sinner that she was and accepted the grace of the Lord Jesus Christ. No fanfare—not even an audible prayer—but, from that moment on Eugenia Price's life was not the same. She was translated from the kingdom of darkness to the kingdom of God's dear Son, Jesus. From a heaviness of body and soul, the yoke became easy and the burden light.

WOMEN
IN THE BIBLE

WHAT DO YOU THINK?

1. Have you ever repented from and confessed your sins, accepted the atoning work of the blood of Jesus Christ, and received God's forgiveness? If so, when and where did you first do this? _____

_____

_____

2. If you haven't done the above (and thus been born again, according to John 3:3-16), do you now desire to do this? (If so, share this with someone.) _____

_____

_____

3. After your salvation experience, what do you do about the sins you continue to commit? _____

_____

_____

4. Do you *know* God's forgiveness? How? _____

_____

_____

EVALUATE YOURSELF

1. In what ways are you implementing the principles learned from Dinah and Potiphar's wife? _____

_____

_____

2. In what ways are you failing to implement the principles learned from them? _____

_____

_____

3. What do you need to do to change? _____

_____

_____

4. How will you do it? _____

_____

_____

74

Lesson 9
Jochebed, Miriam & Zipporah

WOMEN IN THE BIBLE

An Example of Parental Responsibility—Praise—Circumcision

"Train up a child in the way he should go: and when he is old, he will not depart from it."

Proverb 22:6

"By him therefore let us offer the sacrifice of praise to God continually, that is, the fruit of our lips giving thanks to his name."

Hebrews 13:15

"In whom also ye are circumcised with the circumcision made without hands, in putting off the body of the sins of the flesh by the circumcision of Christ."

Colossians 2:11

SETTING THE STAGE

Moses is known as the great deliverer of the Hebrew people. He took them from bondage in Egypt, through a wandering in the wilderness, and into sight of the Promised Land. As we look at his story and writings in Exodus, Leviticus, Numbers and Deuteronomy, we can see how God used him as a leader. It was to Moses that God gave the Law. He allowed him to be an intercessor for the people. God also gave Moses the plans for the tabernacle, and rules and regulations concerning sacrifices, to pass on to the people. God arranged that he spend the first 40 years of his life in Pharoah's palace and the second 40 years tending sheep on the back side of the desert, uniquely training him for these tasks.

Three women stand out as having had an influence upon Moses—his mother, Jochebed; his sister, Miriam; and his wife, Zipporah. As we consider these women in the life of Moses, we will look at three different subjects. With Jochebed, we see the responsibility of parents for their children. She took her responsibility under very difficult circumstances. With Miriam, we will consider the subject of praise. She helped Moses teach their people the ways of God, particularly the need to praise Him. With Zipporah, we will look at the matter of circumcision. She, who circumcised her son reluctantly, points out our need to allow spiritual circumcision to take place in our own hearts.

THE SUCCESS OF JOCHEBED
(Based on Exodus 1; 2:1-11; 6:20; Numbers 26:59; and Hebrews 11:23)

Jochebed is referred to as a daughter of Levi, who married a man of the house of Levi. Wed to her nephew Amram, she was both his wife and aunt—a situation not uncommon in those days.

Three children were born to Amram and Jochebed. All of them were chosen by the Lord for the task of leading His people out of Egypt and into the Promised Land.

The oldest child was Miriam, a gifted musician and poetess who led the women in praise. The eldest son was Aaron, Israel's first high priest and spokesman for Moses. The youngest of the three was Moses, one of the greatest leaders the world has ever known.

Jochebed is introduced to us in the first chapter of Exodus as a concerned Hebrew mother living in Egypt. At that time the Hebrew population had greatly multiplied. Pharoah was afraid the Jews would soon outnumber the Egyptians and take over the nation. Thus, he declared that all newborn Hebrew boys were to be thrown into the Nile. How heavy Jochebed's heart must have been, for she was awaiting the birth of her third child. What would happen if the midwife told her that she had borne a boy?

At last, she did bear a son. When Jochebed saw the baby she saw that he was a goodly child. She was determined to fight for his life. She hid him in a secret place where he couldn't be seen or heard until she was unable to conceal him any longer. Then she made a basket of papyrus reeds and placed it in the river among the bulrushes. She asked 10-year-old Miriam to stand near and watch the baby.

At her usual time, the daughter of Pharoah came to the river to bathe. She and her maidens saw the cradle/basket with little Moses tucked inside. The princess had compassion on him and determined to find a Hebrew nursemaid. She even decided to call the child Moses, which meant "drawn out of the water."

As soon as Miriam saw what was happening, she approached the Pharoah's daughter and asked if she could get the child a nursemaid. And so, Jochebed was paid to be her child's private nurse!

Though we aren't told, it doesn't appear that she was alive to see how her children were used of God. Even so, we can assume she was probably the chief influence in their preparation for the great tasks God had planned.

LESSON FROM JOCHEBED
The Responsibility of Parents for Children

Though Jochebed had some influence upon her son while he was small, she had to give him over to be raised in a pagan environment. She trusted God to teach him the way; He spared him at birth. We find a similar situation with Hannah and Samuel. After receiving him as an answer to prayer, she gave him to Eli for his upbringing (and Eli had done a terrible job in raising his own sons). Likewise we, as parents, often wonder what influence we have in a society that has much influence over our children. Our responsibility is to teach them as well as we can while we have them, then commit them to the Lord for His training. Isaiah 54:13 is a good verse to claim. *"And all thy children shall be taught of the Lord; and great*

76

shall be the peace of thy children." His ways are not our ways. God knows exactly what our children need. He can do a much better job of drawing them to Himself than we can.

Teaching children the faith of their fathers was one of the Hebrew parents' chief obligation. It was Moses, who later received God's laws, who commanded parents to *"teach them diligently unto thy children, and talk of them when thou sittest in thine house, and when thou walkest by the way, and when thou liest down, and when thou risest up. And thou shalt bind them for a sign upon thine head, and they shall be as frontlets between thine eyes. And thou shalt write them upon the posts of they house, and thy gates"* (Deuteronomy 6:7-9).

Though God has His way of teaching our children when we commit them to Him, He also gives us instruction on discipline and training in His Word.

THE SUCCESS OF MIRIAM
(Based on Exodus 2:7-10; 15:20 and 21; Numbers 20:1; and 26:59)

Miriam was the eldest child of Amram and Jochebed, and sister of both Aaron and Moses. We never read of her having a husband, though she lived well into adulthood.

We have already seen, in the story of Jochebed, the part she played in getting Moses' own mother to be his nurse after the Pharoah's daughter found him in the river.

Though Miriam failed at another time of her life(when she and Aaron rebelled against the authority of Moses), this lesson will consider her role as a leader of praise among God's people.

Miriam is called a prophetess and is identified as the sister of Aaron (a prophetess is one raised up by God and inspired by His Spirit to proclaim the will and purpose of God.)

We first see Miriam in action at the Red Sea, proclaiming and singing about the power and faithfulness of God. God had caused the waters to roll back and allow the Israelites to pass through on dry ground while the pursuing Egyptians were drowned as the waters came crashing down upon them. When they were safely on the other side, Miriam led God's people in a time of praise to Him.

Miriam knew God was worthy of praise. She had experienced His supernatural acts among His people both before and after leaving Egypt. He protected them during the terrible plagues. He delivered them from Pharoah's army by rolling back the waters of the Red Sea so they could escape. He provided all their physical needs, including food, as they traversed the wilderness. As a prophetess, she knew God's desire to communicate with His people. In gratitude and thanksgiving, Miriam encouraged the people to respond to the Lord, not only for His mercy and blessings, but just to acknowledge Him as God. She took a timbrel in hand and sang and danced before the Lord, worshipping Him in praise. In song, she recalled His mighty acts, and the women joined her in joyful ministry unto the Lord.

LESSON FROM MIRIAM
Praise

Psalm 100:2 and 4 admonish us to *"serve the Lord with glad-*

ness; come before his presence with singing...enter into his gates with thanksgiving, and into his courts with praise." We enter into true worship by, first, thanking God for what He has done. Then we are able to praise Him for who He is.

If we look at the following Scripture, we'll note that praise is always *active*. We can't just *think* praise, as we think prayer or think of the things we're thankful for.

Praise demands the sacrifice of ourselves. Hebrews 13:15 tells us to *"offer the sacrifice of praise to God, continually, that is, the fruit of our lips giving thanks to his name."* We must give of our lips, our time, our energy. God enjoys our praise. He commands it. We're always blessed as a result of it.

Like Miriam, we can dance, sing, and play musical instruments before the Lord. Psalm 150 enumerates some of the latter as the timbrel, stringed instruments, organ, and cymbals.

Psalm 47 reminds us to *sing* praises as well! *"Sing praises to God, sing praises: sing praises unto our King, sing praises. For God is the King of all the earth: sing ye praises with understanding."* There are several Scriptures concerning dancing in praise as well. Psalm 149:3 says, *"Let them praise his name in the dance..."* Of course, we know that it must be an act of true worship and not an act of the flesh.

God is restoring praise in the Church in these end times. It's a part of worship that has often been neglected. Man has frequently become a spectator and often finds it more comfortable to participate passively in worship services. God wants us to start praising Him now, since that is what we're going to do in eternity. All through the Book of Revelation, we find elders, beasts, and others, praising the Lord. In fact, John says a voice came out of the throne commanding, *"Praise our God, all ye his servants, and ye that fear him both small and great"* (Revelation 19:5).

THE FAILURE OF ZIPPORAH
(Based on Exodus 2:21 and 22; 4:24-26; 18:1-6)

Moses met Zipporah when he fled into Midian after killing an Egyptian. She and her sisters were at a well and Moses kept some shepherds from disturbing them. When they went home and told their father what had happened, he let Moses stay with the family and work in Midian. Thus it was that Jethro, the priest of Midian, gave Moses his oldest daughter, Zipporah, in marriage. Moses and Zipporah had two sons, Gershom and Eliezer.

Zipporah was a Midianite descended from Abraham and *Keturah*, the wife Abraham had after Sarah died, and thus, not of the covenant people. She didn't share the same spiritual values as Moses. To keep peace, Moses compromised with his unbelieving wife and withheld circumcision from his son. The Lord intervened and, as a sign of divine displeasure, struck Moses with a mortal disease. Conscience-stricken, Zipporah yielded and circumcised the child, while Moses lay on the ground. She took the body's foreskin and threw it down before Moses saying, "Surely a bloody husband art thou to me!"

When Moses was restored to health, relations between him

and Zipporah were strained. He went on, alone, to Egypt. Zipporah and the two boys went back to her home in Midian. We don't hear of her again until Moses is already leading the Israelites through the wilderness. She and the boys accompany Jethro to see him. Moses welcomed them, but we don't know if they stayed. Exodus 18:27 only mentions Jethro's departure. We never hear of Zipporah again.

Thus, the only Biblical knowledge we have about the relationship of Moses and Zipporah concerns the matter of circumcision.

LESSON FROM ZIPPORAH
Circumcision

Circumcision is the physical act of cutting away the foreskin of the male. It is a rite of the covenant God made with Abraham (Genesis 17:10-14).

Though circumcision was probably practiced among other peoples, the Bible describes it as distinctively Jewish and divinely instituted by God as a sign of the covenant between Him and His people.

Circumcision is always related to the fulfillment of God's purpose and promise. It was a reminder of the covenant. It was also an act of preparation for what God wanted to do in that covenant relationship. Let's look at some specific examples.

Exodus 12:44 Only the circumcised could _____

_____

_____

Joshua 5:3 Before the Israelites could partake of the Passover at Gilgal prior to entering the Promised Land, Joshua _____

_____

_____

Luke 2:21 As with all Jewish infant boys on the eighth day of life, Jesus _____

_____

_____

Acts 15:1-29 One of the major controversies in the early Church had to do with the matter of circumcision. The result of the council at Jerusalem was _____

_____

_____

Galatians 6:15 Paul reiterates this significant conclusion here, when he says _____

_____

_____

The law was a task master designed to bring man to Christ so he could be justified through faith. Thus, in Romans 2:28 and 29, Paul says, *"For he is not a Jew, which is one outwardly; neither is that circumcision, which is outward in the flesh; But he is a Jew, which is one inwardly; and circumcision is that of the heart, in the spirit; and not in the letter, whose praise is not of men, but of God."* God, in His great wisdom and creativity, has a way of using literal physical acts as types of spiritual truths. Circumcision, though an act of the flesh, also has spiritual meaning throughout Scripture. It is this spiritual application to which we now turn.

Significantly, it was to Moses that God first gave the insight of the spiritual circumcision. In Deuteronomy 10:16, Moses says *"Circumcise, therefore, the foreskin of your heart, and be no more stiffnecked."* Moses, who had been reluctant to physically circumcise his own son, knew that man could also have a barrier towards God in his heart. It's our flesh, our old nature, that keeps our hearts hard and unavailable to God.

Moses also knew that our lips need to be "circumcised" in order to speak God's words and not our own.

Exodus 6:30 Moses said he couldn't speak to Pharoah because

_____

_____

Deuteronomy 30:6 God will circumcise the heart to _____

_____

_____

Jeremiah 6:10 Jeremiah says that the ear _____

_____

_____

Ezekiel 44:9 To truly worship God, one must be _____

_____

_____

How, then, do we obtain this circumcision of hearts, ears, and lips?

Spiritual circumcision, as part of the process of sanctification (separation unto God), is both a one time act, and an ongoing process. We not only turn to God, but we also turn away from sin.

We must daily reckon our flesh crucified. Just as the ordinance of physical circumcision necessitates shedding blood, so it is that through the blood of Jesus our flesh is cut away.

As we become new creatures in Christ, we want to follow God's Word. Though the "old man" is symbolically buried in water baptism, we continue to need to reckon him dead in our conflict between the flesh and the spirit. God wants a holy people. He wants the foreskins of our hearts to be circumcised, so that He can reign in us. I Corinthians 15:50 reminds us that flesh and blood cannot enter the kingdom of God.

80

God called Moses to be the leader of His people and expected him to be an example. He dealt with Moses concerning the lack of circumcision of his son. Though Zipporah submitted outwardly, seeing that it was done, she vented her anger toward God as she ridiculed her husband. It is likely that, as a result, her hard heart kept her from a further relationship with either God or her husband.

Match the following to complete the proverbs concerning the relationships parents are to have with their children.

Chart 9A

Proverb 10:1
A wise son brings joy to his father,

Proverb 23:13
Do not withhold discipline from a child;

Proverb 20:11
Even a child is known by his actions

Hebrews 12:11
No discipline seems pleasant at the time, but painful.

Proverb 29:17
Discipline your son, and he will give you peace;

Proverb 22:6
Train up a child in the way he should go,

Proverb 13:24
He who spares the rod hates his son,

Proverb 17:25
A foolish son brings grief to his father

Proverb 22:15
Folly is bound up in the heart of a child,

Proverb 19:18
Discipline your son, for in that there is hope,

Proverb 14:1
The wise woman builds her house,

Proverb 29:15
The rod of correction imparts wisdom,

he will bring delight to your soul.

but he who loves him is careful to discipline him.

but a child left to itself disgraces his mother.

but a foolish son grief to his mother.

but with her own hands the foolish one tears hers down.

and bitterness to the one who bore him.

and when he is old he will not turn from it.

do not be a willing party to his death.

but the rod of discipline will drive it far from him.

Later on, however, it produces a harvest of righteousness and peace for those who have been trained by it.

by whether his conduct is pure and right.

if you punish him with the rod, he will not die.

SUMMARY

In this lesson, we look at the three women in the life of Moses. His mother, Jochebed; his sister, Miriam; and his wife, Zipporah, each provide a brief teaching in a different area. As we note the parent that Jochebed seemed to be, we consider the responsibility of parents in raising their children in the fear of the Lord. From Miriam, we look at the praise and its place in the life of a believer. With Zipporah, we try to understand what is meant Scripturally by "circumcision of the heart."

MODERN EXAMPLE

Perhaps one of the most influential mothers in modern history is Susanna Wesley, a mother who personally tutored her 19 children. One of them wrote over 6,000 hymns which modern man can use in praise to God!

Susanna was married to Samuel Wesley, a rector of a parish in England. An author as well, he was a poor manager of money and had to spend various periods of time in debtor's prison for non-payment of bills. As a result, much of the care of the family rested upon Susanna, an energetic woman with high standards.

She refused to compromise her ideals. She taught her children not only basic education, but spiritual values as well. She insisted, for instance, that each one master the alphabet in a certain length of time. She demanded courtesy, self-discipline, and rigorous study. Her children proved to be exceptional achievers. It is said that she spent a specific amount of quality time with each child each week—all this in a day when there were none of the conveniences of our modern homes.

These 19 children had such great influence upon our world that credit for the following can be traced directly, or indirectly, back to them—the Methodist Church, the YMCA, the Salvation Army, orphanages, and many well-known hymns. Her sons, John and Charles, are perhaps the most famous of her children.

Together, they worked for revival in the Church of England and, in the process, founded a movement which resulted in the Methodist Church. John wrote several books on such subjects as grammar, history, and biographies. Though an older brother, Samuel, also wrote a number of well-known hymns, Charles Wesley is the author of over 6,000 hymns, among which are "O, For a Thousand Tongues to Sing," "Jesus, Lover of My Soul," and "Hark, the Herald Angels Sing."

In a day when home schooling is on the rise, parents would do well to look to the example of Susanna Wesley.

WHAT DO YOU THINK?

1. Are you raising your children in the fear of the Lord and according to His Word? If so, how do you do this? If not, where can you begin? _____

_____

_____

82

2. What do you do about the influences over your children that you know are against the principles of God and His Word? _____

_____

_____

3. What is involved in praise? Do you participate in regular times of praise to the Lord? _____

_____

_____

4. How have you allowed your heart to be circumcised? __

_____

_____

5. What keeps one's heart from becoming hard? _____

_____

_____

EVALUATE YOURSELF

1. In what ways are you implementing the principles learned from Jochebed, Miriam, and Zipporah? _____

_____

_____

2. In what ways are you failing to implement the principles learned from them? _____

_____

_____

3. What do you need to do to change? _____

_____

_____

4. How will you do it? _____

_____

_____

Lesson 10
Tamar & Rahab

An Example of Mercy—Grace

"Let us therefore come boldly unto the throne of grace, that we may obtain mercy, and find grace to help in time of need."
Hebrews 4:16

SETTING THE STAGE

Who can comprehend the everlasting mercy and amazing grace of God? In no way can we, in our filthy rags of unrighteousness, come into the presence of a holy, righteous God except by the mercy and grace which ultimately comes through Jesus Christ.

Tamar's righteousness came through the Levirate marriage law, which declared that if a woman's husband died, his brother would become her husband (Deuteronomy 25:5). Because this commandment wasn't kept, God, in His mercy, provided for her.

Rahab believed in the God of the Israelite spies she helped to escape. In the process, God bestowed His grace upon her and her family, and saved them. Her works were a result of faith which God, in His mercy, gave her through her belief.

These two women represent sinners who committed sexual sins requiring the death sentence. Yet, both are included in the genealogy of Jesus Christ (who becomes our righteousness when we believe in Him). Thus, both can be called successful because of what *God* did. Without God's mercy and grace through Jesus Christ, we along with Tamar and Rahab, would be lost forever.

THE SUCCESS OF TAMAR

(Based on Genesis 38:6-30; Ruth 4:12; Matthew 1:3)

Tamar was a Canaanite woman who married into the family of Judah (the fourth son of Jacob and Leah). First she married Er, the oldest son of Judah and Shuah (also a Canaanite). We don't know what Er did to displease God, but God slew him. Tamar didn't remain a widow long. In accordance with the Levirate marriage law, she was given to the next son, Onan, so that she could raise up seed for her dead husband. But Onan intentionally failed to fulfill his responsibility, so God slew him too. The third son of Judah, Shelah, should have become Tamar's next husband, but he was too young. Judah suggested that Tamar return to her father's household until Shelah came of age.

Years later, Judah's wife Shuah died. When Judah had recovered from his grief, he went to visit a friend. Tamar heard of his trip and covertly saw Judah and Shelah. She realized Shelah was by now of age and Tamar had no intention of giving her to him, so she resorted to tricking her father-in-law in order to save the family from extinction.

Tamar disguised herself as a harlot and sat in an open place where she could be approached.

Judah happened by and, not knowing who she was, made a bargain with her. For a one-time relationship with her, he would give her a kid from his flock. Until he sent it he would leave her his identification seal, walking stick and bracelets as a pledge. Tamar agreed. Judah slept with her, and she became pregnant.

Sometime later, Judah sent the goat by his friend, in order to get his pledge back. But the friend could never find the prostitute, and returned to Judah empty-handed.

About three months later Judah heard that his daughter-in-law, Tamar, was pregnant. He assumed it was a result of prostitution. He became so angry that he demanded that she be brought out and burned, not realizing, of course, that he was the man responsible for her condition!

When the men came to get her, Tamar sent a message to Judah, along with his bracelets, seal and stick. "The man who owns this identification seal, bracelets and walking stick is the father of my child. Do you recognize them?" Needless to say, Judah was deeply chagrined. He admitted he had refused her his third son in marriage and said Tamar was actually more righteous than he.

In due time, Tamar bore *twin sons* Pharez and Zarah, in a breach birth. So it was that, through Pharez (the "second twin" which came out first), Tamar became an ancestor of Jesus. It could only happen by the mercy and grace of God. Her success was wholly dependent upon Him.

THE SUCCESS OF RAHAB
(Based on Joshua 2; 6:17-25; Matthew 1:5; Hebrews 11:31; James 2:25)

Soon after Joshua became the leader of the Hebrew people, he sent two men into Jericho as spies. They ended up at the house of Rahab, a known harlot of the city. It was from these travelers, no doubt, that she came to learn the facts of the Exodus and of the miracle at the Red Sea. When they sought cover, she provided it. She had come to realize that their God must be the "God in heaven above and in the earth beneath." She then helped plan their protection and escape.

First, Rahab took the men up to the flat roof of her house and told them to cover themselves completely with a pile of flax which she had laid out to dry. Then, when their pursuers knocked at her door, she met them with the plausible excuse that the men had been there, but that they had left. She even let them search the house, but they found no one.

In return for aiding the spies in their escape, Rahab received the promise that, when they returned along with Joshua and his army, she and her family would be spared. The spies assured her that she would be dealt with kindly and truly. Rahab let them down a scarlet rope and awaited her own deliverance.

The actual fall of Jericho came about in a most unusual way. God told Joshua to order the people to march around the city once a day for six days. Then, on the seventh day, they were to march around it seven times without saying one word. At the end of the seventh time, they were to sound a ram's horn and blast a trumpet. This would be the signal for people to give a shout of victory. When they did, the entire wall of the city fell flat. They burned and plundered it.

Joshua, true to his word, saved Rahab and her whole household. The Israelites took them in to live with them.

Rahab is mentioned three times in the New Testament. In Matthew 1:5, we find that she is one of the ancestors of Jesus. Hebrews 11:31 commends her for her faith. James 2:25 recognizes her as one justified by works.

LESSONS FROM TAMAR AND RAHAB
The Grace and Mercy of God

Grace and *Mercy*. These words raise concepts which man cannot fully understand because human understanding can't grasp the nature of God. For God is mercy, and mercy expressed is His grace!

The main Hebrew word for *mercy* is *hhesed*. In the Old Testament, the world *hhesed* is translated by three main synonyms: mercy, loving kindness, and kindness. This word describes a strong, personal desire to do the good which is, in itself, a loving kindness.

The Greek word for the same concept is translated *grace*. Thus, *grace* is used predominantly in the New Testament. *Grace* is usually defined as *unmerited favor*, especially the favor bestowed upon sinners through Jesus Christ. In other words, *grace* is *mercy accomplished*. Perhaps this can be more clearly seen in Hebrews 4:16 (Amplified) *"Let us then fearlessly and confidently and boldy draw near to the throne of grace…the throne of God's unmerited favor (to us sinners); that we may receive mercy (for our failures) and find grace to help in good time for every need…appropriate help and well-timed help, coming just when we need it."*

Mercy can be described as:

Jeremiah 33:11 _____

_____

_____

Psalm 25:6 _____

_____

_____

I Peter 1:3 _____

_____

_____

Lamentations 3:22 and 23 _____

_____

_____

Psalm 103:8 _____

_____

Psalm 103:17 _____

_____

Psalm 94:18 _____

_____

Micah 7:18 _____

_____

Romans 9:15-21 _____

_____

Psalm 108:4 _____

_____

Concerning mercy, God commands:

Zechariah 7:9 _____

_____

Micah 6:8 _____

_____

Hosea 12:6 _____

_____

Colossians 3:12 _____

_____

Proverb 3:3 _____

_____

Luke 6:36 _____

_____

Matthew 9:13 _____

_____

_____

Jude 21 _____

_____

_____

What do we learn about grace from these Scriptures?

Romans 6:14 _____

_____

_____

Romans 11:5 and 6 _____

_____

_____

Galatians 2:21 _____

_____

_____

Titus 3:5 _____

_____

_____

Romans 5:20 _____

_____

_____

Ephesians 2:8 and 9 _____

_____

_____

In the light of God's grace, what should our attitude be toward God, ourselves, others?

I Peter 3:16-18 _____

_____

_____

II Timothy 2:1 and 2 _____

_____

_____

WOMEN IN THE BIBLE

Colossians 4:6 _____

_____

_____

II Corinthians 9:8 and 14 _____

_____

_____

Revelation 22:21 _____

_____

_____

How do you see the mercy and grace of God apparent in the lives of:

Noah (Genesis 6:5-8) _____

_____

_____

Abraham (Romans 4:1-21) _____

_____

_____

Joseph (Genesis 50:15-21) _____

_____

_____

Moses (Exodus 2:1-10) _____

_____

_____

David (II Samuel 11; 12:13; I Chronicles 21:7-13; I Samuel 13:14) _____

_____

_____

Peter (Luke 22:54-62; John 21: 15-19; Acts 2:14-40) _____

_____

_____

Cheap Grace

A term often used to distinguish between true grace and grace which man takes lightly is *"cheap"* grace. Essentially, it means that one accepts the work of the atoning blood of Jesus on the cross, but goes on living as he always had, thus making *cheap* the price that Jesus paid for sin.

Luke 14:26 tells us, *"If any man come to me, and hates not...his*

90

own life, he cannot be my disciple." One cannot just say he believes in Jesus; he must do the Word and hate sin enough to leave it. Thus, we must do, as exhorted in Colossians 3:1-10 (See LB), and put away the evil desires lurking within us and have nothing to do with sexual sin, impurity, lust and shameful desires. We must not worship the good things of life.

We must throw away all anger, hatred, cursing, and dirty language for we are living a brand new life, trying constantly to be more and more like Christ who created this new life within us.

What does God say about the following? Do you hate them enough to do something about them, lest you take the grace of God cheaply?

Anger—Matthew 5:22; Psalm 37:8; Ephesians 4:26

Criticism—Matthew 7:1 and 2; Romans 2:1

Pride—I Peter 5:5; Proverbs 16:5 and 18; Luke 16:15

Desire for attention—Matthew 23:5-11

Unbelief—Revelation 21:8; Matthew 17:20; Hebrews 3:12, 4:6

Disobedience—I Samuel 15:22; John 14:23

Disrespect for authority—I Peter 5:5; Acts 5:29

Envy—I Peter 2:1; James 3:16; I Corinthians 3:3

Love of money—I Timothy 6:6,9 and 10

Hypocrisy—Matthew 23:28; Matthew 24:51; I Peter 2:1

Impatience—I Thessalonians 5:14

Lukewarmness—Revelation 3:16

Ingratitude—Romans 1:21-24, I Thessalonians 5:18

Bitterness—II Timothy 3:1-5; Matthew 18:34 and 35; Hebrews 12:14 and 15

People-pleasing—Galatians 1:10; James 1:8; Matthew 10:28

Scoffing—II Peter 3:3; Psalm 1:1

Self-pity—Hebrews 12:10-14

Talkativeness—Ephesians 5:6; James 3:8; Matthew 12:36 and 37

Worry—Matthew 6:32; Philippians 4:6

Sexual Sin

Since it was in the area of sexual sin that the mercy of God was extended to both Tamar and Rahab, let's briefly consider what Scripture says concerning this.

In our day, its' becoming increasingly difficult to distinguish men from women—both in outward appearance and in the roles they assume. More and more, we're living in a unisex society with women demanding equal rights and men abdicating their authority and responsibility. Even the Christian home, with its traditional values, is under great attack from Satan.

According to Galatians 3:28 *"There is neither Jew nor Greek, there is neither bond nor free, there is neither male nor female; for ye are all one in Christ Jesus."* Thus, in a spiritual sense, when we're born again, we aren't reborn male and female. Our spirits, which aren't sexual in nature, are made alive with God's Spirit.

This is further confirmed in Mark 12:18-25, where Jesus reminds us there is no marriage in heaven.

But when God created the earth, He made us male and female. He blessed the first couple and told them to be fruitful and multiply; He made provision for this. God spelled out the difference between man and his "helpmeet," who was to submit to him as he toiled for a living. She would bear the pain of childbirth, though, in God's sight, they were one flesh.

The Bible continues to say much on the relationship between the sexes. Let's now look at a few relationships which He declares to be sin:

Incest *"No one is to approach any close relative to have sexual relations. I am the Lord"* (Leviticus 18:6 NIV).

Homosexuality *"Do not lie with a man as one lie with a woman; that is detestable"* (Leviticus 18:22 NIV). *"Because of this (believing a lie), God gave them over to shameful lusts. Even their women exchanged natural relations for unnatural ones. In the same way, the men also abandoned natural relations with women and were inflamed with lust for one another. Men committed indecent acts with other men, and received in themselves the due penalty for their persuasion"* (Romans 1:26 and 27 NIV).

Prostitution *"You must not bring the earnings of a female prostitute or of a male prostitute into the house of the Lord your God to pay any vow, because the Lord your God detests them both"* (Deuteronomy 23:18 NIV).

Fornication *"To avoid fornication, let every man have his own wife, and let every woman have her own husband"* (I Corinthians 7:2). *"Flee fornication. Every sin that a man doeth is without the body; but he that committeth fornication, sinneth against his own body"* (I Corinthians 6:18).

Adultery *"If a man is found sleeping with another man's wife, both the man who slept with her and the woman must die"* (Deuteronomy 22:22 NIV). *"Ye have heard that it was said by them of old time, 'Thou shalt not commit adultery;' But I (Jesus) say unto you, That whosoever looketh on a woman to lust after her hath committed adultery with her already in his heart"* (Matthew 5: 27 and 28).

Dress *"A woman must not wear men's clothing, nor a man wear women's clothing, for the Lord your God detests anyone who does this"* (Deuteronomy 22:5 NIV). *"I also want women to dress modestly, with decency and propriety, not with braided hair or gold or pearls or expensive clothes, but with good deeds, appropriate for women who profess to worship God"* (I Timothy 2:9 and 10 NIV).

SUMMARY

In no way can we, as sinners, come into the presence of a holy, righteous God. Yet because God loved us, He provided a way of righteousness for us by His mercy and His grace. The ultimate demonstration of God's love and mercy to us was in the sacrifice of His Son, Jesus Christ. His death for our sin is God's grace.

Two women, Tamar and Rahab, represent sinners upon the dunghill of life. They committed sexual sins which, in God's law, demanded death. Yet both, through the mercy of God, became a part of the lineage of Jesus. Without God's mercy and grace through Jesus Christ, we, along with Tamar and Rahab, would be lost forever.

MODERN EXAMPLE

Cookie Rodriguiz was born in a very poor ghetto in a small town in Puerto Rico. Her mother was a mere girl of 13. Her 17-year-old father had committed suicide prior to her birth. Thus, she was essentially raised by her maternal grandmother, who took her to New York when she was 12 years old.

After their money ran out, life became even more difficult. Soon Cookie found herself involved in gangs. Tiny, but spunky, she fought for her very existence. She became involved in drugs, drinking, and illicit sex. By age 15 she was considered incorrigible and spent time in reformatories, jails and state hospitals.

While mainlining heroin, she became pregnant.

As her need for drugs continued, Cookie became heavily involved in shoplifting and prostitution. The streets of New York were her home.

During her different confinements, people would try to help Cookie, but she had become very hardened. Finally, a friend took her to Teen Challenge, a street ministry founded by David Wilkerson. After a while there, she was taken to a youth rally in Pittsburg where David Wilkerson was a speaker. While sitting in the crowd, Cookie watched other young people go forward to accept Jesus and look to Him for their healing and deliverance. Suddenly, her whole life flashed before her eyes—all the poverty, the hurts, the misery. Then she became aware of a loving Presence enveloping her. Tears began to roll down her cheeks. God, in His amazing grace, was reaching down to save a tough little "wretch" like Cookie.

In His enduring mercy He used her to found a ministry through which He would touch many other girls just like her. Cookie Rodriguiz later founded the ministry called "New Life for Girls."

WHAT DO YOU THINK?

1. Do you recognize God's mercy toward you? (Think of a specific instance.) _____

_____

_____

2. In what ways do you take the grace of God lightly? What can you do to keep this from happening? _____

_____

_____

3. Have you participated in any of the sexual sins which God's Word so plainly forbids? If so, how have you dealt with this? _____

_____

_____

EVAULATE YOURSELF

1. In what ways are you implementing the principles learned from Tamar and Rahab? _____

_____

_____

2. In what ways are you failing to implement the principles
   learned from them? _____

_____

_____

3. What do you need to do to change? _____

_____

_____

4. How will you do it? _____

_____

_____

Lesson 11
Deborah

An Example of the Holy Spirit

"But the Comforter, which is the Holy Ghost, whom the Father will send in my name, he shall teach you all things, and bring all things to your remembrance, whatsoever I have said unto you."

John 14:26

SETTING THE STAGE

Deborah was one of the early judges and a prophetess of the nation of Israel. A courageous woman, she, along with her captain, Barak, led God's people into war against Sisera and his mighty army. As she prophesied before the battle began, her nation was delivered from the enemy and Sisera was killed at the hand of another woman. She was given supernatural knowledge and wisdom, and was able to truly prophesy the way Israel's enemy was defeated.

Throughout the Old Testament, the Holy Spirit, as part of the Trinity, gave specific gifts to specific people for specific situations.

In the New Testament we discover His nature and purpose more fully. After Jesus' death, resurrection, and ascension, the Holy Spirit was sent to empower Believers as God's witnesses, as well as to be their teacher, comforter, and guide.

While Jesus now intercedes for His church, the Holy Spirit is endowing her with gifts to help her do the work Jesus left her to do until the time she is united with Him at the Marriage Supper of the Lamb. The Holy Spirit also has the job of preparing the Church as a Bride fit for Jesus. The Holy Spirit and His gifts are available to all who have received God's fullness and power and yield themselves to His guidance.

In this lesson, we will look at Deborah, a woman who was given supernatural wisdom and knowledge so she could prophesy. We will also look at the One who gives these gifts— the Holy Spirit—His nature and work, His spiritual gifts, and how we can receive them.

THE SUCCESS OF DEBORAH
(Based on Judges 4 and 5; Hebrews 11:32-34)

We know nothing of the background of Deborah except that she was the wife of Lapidoth. Their home was in the hill country of Ephraim. The palm tree under which Deborah ruled must have been a landmark, because palms were rare in Palestine in that time.

Deborah was the fourth of the judges of Israel. She was raised up by God to deliver His people from the bondage their idolatry had brought upon them at a time when everyone tried to do what was right in his own eyes.

Her prominence as a ruler is rather remarkable. She was the

only woman to hold this position. All Israel was under her jurisdiction. She dispensed justice from under a palm tree. After the victory over their enemy, she ruled a peaceful land for 40 years.

Deborah was one of several women named in Scripture who were given a prophetic gift of being able to discern the mind and purpose of God and then pass it on to others.

Deborah did more than prophesy. She aroused her nation from its lethargy and despair. Day after day, she excited those who gathered to hear her words of divine wisdom. With certainty she told them of their deliverance from the enemy— if only they would rise up and fight.

One day, Deborah sent for Barak, captain of the soldiers. She told him God had shown her that he should lead their army against Sisera, a mighty man of war, who had terrorized Israel for years. Barak hesitated, but finally decided to do it if Deborah would go with him.

The odds were great against Deborah and Barak. They had only 10,000 men to fight Sisera's 100,000 men and 900 iron chariots. But Deborah knew that God was on their side.

God threw the enemy into a panic. Sisera's troops died by the sword. Not a man of them was left. Only Sisera escaped, but he was later killed by a woman (just as Deborah said would happen). Jael, wife of an ally, took him into her home when he appeared at her door seeking refuge. She recognized him and pounded a peg through his temples as he slept. So, God subdued the enemy, and Deborah gained fame as a great warrior.

The last glimpse we have of Deborah is as "a mother in Israel" (Judges 5:7). Deborah, who as far as we know, had never borne children of her own, became as a mother to all Israel. She cared for God's people as she trusted in Him and received the gifts He sent through His Holy Spirit.

LESSONS FROM DEBORAH
The Holy Spirit

In an earlier lesson, we discovered that the Holy Spirit is the third person of the Godhead (the Trinity of Father, Son, and Holy Spirit). In this lesson, we will look in more depth at who the Holy Spirit is, what His function is, and how He can be part of our lives.

Because we are living in the last days, the Holy Spirit seems to have a more prominent place than ever before. So it should be. According to the prophet Joel, whom Peter quoted on the Day of Pentecost, "...it shall come to pass in the last days, saith God, I will pour out of my Spirit upon all flesh" (Joel 2:28; Acts 2:17).

Titles and Adjectives Given to the Holy Spirit (KJV)

Genesis 1:2 _____

_____

_____

Genesis 6:3 _____

_____

Isaiah 61:1 _____

_____

Matthew 10:20 _____

_____

John 14:16 and 26 _____

_____

John 14:17 _____

_____

Acts 5:3 and 4 _____

_____

Romans 1:4 _____

_____

Romans 8:2 _____

_____

Galatians 4:6 _____

_____

Hebrews 9:14 _____

_____

Revelation 19:10 _____

_____

Matthew 28:19 The Godhead, the Trinity, is composed of

_____

Attributes of the Holy Spirit (KJV)

Psalm 139:7-12 The Holy Spirit is _____

_____

_____

Luke 1:35 The Holy Spirit is the _____

_____

_____

I Corinthians 2:11 The Holy Spirit _____

_____

_____

I Corinthians 12:4 The same Spirit gives _____

_____

_____

II Corinthians 13:14 We can know God by His _____,

_____

_____

Jesus by _____

_____

_____

and the Holy Spirit by _____

_____

_____

Romans 14:17 In the Holy Spirit, there is _____

_____

_____

Galatians 5:22 and 23 The fruit of the Spirit is _____

_____

_____

Functions of the Holy Spirit (KJV)

John 3:1-8 What is the role of the Spirit when one is *born again?*

_____

_____

98

Acts 2:4 What did the Spirit do when, on the day of Pentecost, the people were filled with the Holy Spirit? _____

_____

_____

John 14:16 God gives us the Holy Spirit as _____,

_____

_____

to _____

_____

_____

John 14:17 The Holy Spirit, as _____

_____

_____

can _____

_____

_____

Thus, we will _____

_____

_____

John 14:26 The _____

_____

_____

will send us the Holy Spirit in the name of _____,

_____

_____

so that _____

_____

_____

John 16:7 One of the conditions for the Comforter to come,

was _____

_____

_____

John 16:8-11 When the Holy Spirit comes, He _____

_____

_____

WOMEN IN THE BIBLE

John 16:13 What two things will the Holy Spirit, as the Spirit of Truth, do when he comes? _____

_____

_____

Acts 9:31 Churches can experience the Holy Spirit in _____

_____

_____

Romans 8:16 The Holy Spirit _____

_____

_____

confirming to us that _____

_____

_____

Romans 8:26 What two things does this verse say the Holy Spirit can do? _____

_____

_____

How is the second one done? _____

_____

_____

Romans 8:27 What two things does this verse tell us the Spirit does? _____

_____

_____

Romans 15:16 One of the jobs of the Holy Spirit is to _____

_____

_____

I Corinthians 2:10 What two things does this verse tell us that the Holy Spirit does? _____

_____

_____

I Corinthians 12:3 Only by the Holy Spirit can _____

_____

_____

I Corinthians 12:7-13 The gifts which the Spirit gives to man

include _____

_____

_____

II Thessalonians 2:13 Again, we are told that one of the jobs of the Holy Spirit is _____

_____

_____

Hebrews 10:15-17 The Holy Spirit is a _____

_____

_____

that _____

_____

_____

I John 4:1-4 How can one know the Spirit of God from the spirit of the antichrist? _____

_____

_____

I John 2:20 and 27 The anointing of the Spirit will _____

_____

_____

The Holy Spirit in the Old Testament

In Genesis, the Holy Spirit is actively engaged in creation, along with the Father and the Son. In the Old Testament, the Spirit came upon men to empower them for service; when they were disobedient, He departed from them. He was "poured out" and made available to every man, only after Jesus' ascension back into heaven. Let's look at some of the ways the Holy Spirit was at work during Old Testament times.

Genesis 1:2 In creation, The Spirit of God _____

_____

_____

Exodus 31:1-6 God filled Bezaleel with His Spirit so that _____

_____

_____

I Chronicles 28:12 David received the pattern for the temple by

_____

_____

_____

Psalm 51:10 and 11 David knew that he needed to be cleansed of his sin so he asked God to _____

_____

_____

II Peter 1:21 The prophets of the Old Testament spoke as they were _____

_____

_____

Isaiah 61:1-3 Isaiah recognized that the Spirit of God was upon him to _____

_____

_____

Joel 2:28 Joel foretold of the Spirit _____

_____

_____

Micah 3:8 Micah was empowered by _____

_____

_____

Zechariah 4:6 Zechariah heard the Lord say that he could not do things by his own might and power, but only by _____

_____

_____

The Holy Spirit in the Life of Jesus

Luke 1:35 Jesus was conceived in Mary's womb by _____

_____

_____

Luke 3:22 When John the Baptist baptized Jesus, we find the Trinity come together. As *Jesus* is baptized, a *voice from heaven* (the Father) says that, in Jesus, He was well pleased. When this was spoken, a dove descended upon Jesus, representing

_____

_____

Luke 3:16 and 17 Though John the Baptist baptized Jesus in water, he recognized that Jesus would be the one to baptize others with _____

_____

_____

102

Luke 4:14 Following His temptation in the wilderness, Jesus returned to Galilee in ———————————————

————————————————————————————————

and ————————————————————————————

————————————————————————————————

————————————————————————————————

John 3:34 God did not give Jesus the Spirit ————————

————————————————————————————————

————————————————————————————————

Therefore, He whom God had sent was able to speak the words of God.

The Day of Pentecost

To know what happened on the Day of Pentecost, we must turn to the Book of Acts. But before we do, let us see what *Pentecost*, itself, is all about.

The Israelites were commanded to appear three times a year, before God in the Holy Temple in Jerusalem. The occasions were the *Passover*, celebrating the deliverance from Egypt and symbolized by eating unleavened bread and offering the Passover lamb; *Pentecost*, or the Feast of Weeks, typified by offering two wave loaves made of newly harvested wheat; and the *Feast of Tabernacles*, symbolized by the booths, commemorating Israel's wandering through the wilderness and entrance into the land of promise.

The word *Pentecost* is Greek, meaning *fifty*. It was so designated because it was observed on the 50th day after the Passover Sabbath. Leviticus 23:15-17 gives instruction concerning the observance of this feast in the Old Testament times.

For centuries, Isreal was an agricultural people, depending upon the produce of the land for her sustenance. Pentecost was the Feast of the ingathering of the firstfruits of the wheat harvest, a thanksgiving festival during which Israel expressed her dependence on God for harvest and daily bread.

Pentecost was a popular holiday, falling in early summer when the cloudless skies were blue and the weather warm. Jews streamed from every part of the country to Jerusalem to appear before their God. Visitors came from abroad for this special occasion.

In time, when the Jews were dispersed among the nations, Pentecost lost its primary importance as a harvest festival and became known as the "Feast of Giving of the Law." Ancient rabbis, by careful calculation, came to the conclusion that God gave the law to Moses on the Day of Pentecost.

Fifteen hundred years passed after God commanded His people, through Moses, to observe the Feast of Weeks. Much happened in that time. Prophets came and went, all foretelling the coming of a Savior to redeem Israel from sin. At last He came, was crucified, and rose again, before ascending back into Heaven. Just before He ascended, He commanded His disciples to wait in Jerusalem until they received the Holy Spirit. They waited 49 days after His resurrection, just as the Jews wait 49 days from Passover to Pentecost.

At the end of this time, the Holy Spirit was poured out upon those gathered in the Upper Room. All the disciples began to preach with new power. Three thousand Jews and some Gentile proselytes accepted Christ when Peter preached The Church was born.

From this we see the meaning of the two wave-loaves of bread baked with leaven. The church of Christ, of which both Jews and Gentiles are members, is not without sin. It contains leaven, the Biblical symbol of sin, which reminds us not to look for perfection in the Church, but in the perfection of the Son of God, who was without sin.

The 3,000 believers were the spiritual firstfruits of the church of Jesus Christ, a Church composed of Jewish and Gentile believers, and purchased by the blood of the Lamb.

On the Day of Pentecost the apostles, being filled with the Holy Spirit, spoke in many and various tongues, witnessing to others about Jesus Christ.

That day, the church received power to evangelize the world. It was a spiritual phenomenon issuing forth in joyful ecstasy amd miracle-working power, resulting in conviction of sin, repentance towards God, and faith in Jesus Christ as Lord.

Acts 1:8 Jesus said that when the Holy Spirit came _____

_____

_____

Acts 2:1-8 The evidence of the outpouring of the Holy Spirit, on the Day of Pentecost, was _____

_____

_____

Acts 2:14-40 As a result, Peter _____,

_____

_____

and _____

_____

_____

Acts 2:38 and 39 The gift of the Holy Spirit is received when

_____

_____

_____

The Gifts of the Holy Spirit
There are four lists of gifts covered in Scripture:
I Corinthians 12:7-11 One group is known as the "manifesta-

104

tional" gifts. Verse 7 says that to each person is given the manifestation of the Holy Spirit.

Ephesians 4:11 and 12 The gifts of "ministries" allow the Church to function for the edification of the Body of Christ.

Romans 12:5-13 These gifts represent those given according to the grace given us of God that we may love and serve one another.

I Corinthians 12:27 and 28 God gave these gifts so that order may be established in the Church.

The first group includes the gifts specifically given by the Spirit as manifestations of the Spirit. They are specifically for empowering the Body of Christ for God's work in this world—especially in winning others to Him, since spiritual warfare is also waged against God's enemy, Satan. The Spirit gives faith, healing, miracles, prophecy, discernment of spirits, tongues, and interpretation of tongues. All of these gifts were essential in ministry as the Church began to function on the day of Pentecost. They are no less useful in the latter days of the Church.

How Can We Receive the Holy Spirit and His Gifts?

If the Word of God is just as true today as it was for the people of Jesus' day, then we can receive the Holy Spirit even as they did.

Acts 2:37 and 38 says that at the end of his anointed preaching, Peter exhorted the people to _____

_____

_____

This experience is called salvation. One must be saved in order to receive the Holy Spirit and His gifts. Furthermore, he must be sincere in desiring this gift. Acts 8 gives the story of Simon, a sorcerer, who wanted the gifts of the Holy Spirit. He even came to believe in Jesus and was baptized. But when it was discovered that he wanted to purchase the Holy Spirit for the miracles he could then do, he was refused because his heart wasn't right with God. The Holy Spirit wouldn't benefit such a bitter man.

Acts 8:14-17 Those in Samaria who had received the Word received the Holy Spirit when _____

_____

_____

Acts 10:44-48 When Peter preached to the Gentiles, _____

_____

_____

They hadn't even been baptized as yet, but they knew the Holy Spirit had been given because _____

_____

_____

Acts 19:1-6 When Paul went to Ephesus, he asked the disci-

WOMEN IN THE BIBLE

ples there if they had received the Holy Spirit since they had believed. When they replied _____

_____

_____

he asked them unto what they had been baptized. They replied, _____

_____

_____

Then Paul told them _____

_____

_____

After they were baptized, Paul _____

_____

_____

and the Holy Spirit _____

_____

_____

Luke 11:5-13 The Holy Spirit is given when _____

_____

_____

I Corinthians 13:8-10 Until the perfect (Jesus) comes, we can expect _____

_____

_____

I Corinthians 14:26-40 It is expected that believers have the fullness of the Holy Spirit because some of the exhortations concerning worship are _____

_____

_____

SUMMARY

Deborah was one of several persons in the Old Testament who was apparently endued by God with the anointing of the Holy Spirit for certain tasks. As a judge in Israel, she was given special knowledge and wisdom to defeat the enemy. On the Day of Pentecost, God poured out the Holy Spirit, filling people with power and giving them spiritual gifts. The Comforter and Spirit of Truth which Jesus promised them had come to do his work and will remain until Jesus returns.

MODERN EXAMPLE

On one of their several trips into Russia, John and Doris Haladay

106

stood at the window of their 18th floor hotel room in Moscow, looking out over the array of massive apartment buildings. Their spirits lifted as they spotted the colorful onion-shaped domes of a tiny red brick church.

They held hands and prayed for the millions in that Godless state of Communism. Suddenly, the Holy Spirit spoke to Doris, "Go quickly toward those church spires. Go now!" She told John how she felt. The compulsion was too strong to resist.

They dressed, ate a hurried breakfast, and packed their handbags with Bibles and other materials God had allowed them to bring into the country. (John was head of Global Outreach.)

It was cold as they walked through alleys rutted and filled with stagnant, putrid water. Containers overflowing with garbage lined the way. The tiny church, so clearly seen from their room, was now hidden in the maze of buildings, garages, fences, and back alleys.

They asked several people for directions to the church, but no one seemed to know. Finally, a young man in a breakfast shop pointed out the direction he thought they should go. Within a few minutes they came to a corner fence of an old church cemetery. While passing a heap of unevenly-stacked cement blocks, they were startled by a low muffled greeting in Russian. They stopped and looked at an elderly man. As John approached, the man motioned for Doris to join him. In Russian, the man told John that God had shown him, in a vision the previous night, that he was to come at daybreak look at the cross and wait. He had come to this very spot because it was the only place where he could see the cross on the church.

"Then," he continued, "I saw the cross that your wife is wearing around her neck and I realized that *it* may be the cross I'm to look for. No one wears crosses in public here. You must be Christians—and the answer to the vision. You must be carrying God's Word, which we need so desperately. Is it not true?"

When John excitedly told Doris what the man had said, they all hugged and wept. They assured the man that they did have Bibles in his language. Deeply moved, he told them where a secret body of believers would be meeting that evening. John and Doris met with them, sharing the Bibles and listening to testimonies of how God had worked among them even though they had had no complete Scriptures since the Communist revolution.

The Holy Spirit had not only guided John and Doris through words of wisdom and knowledge, but He had given a vision to an old man as well.

WHAT DO YOU THINK?

1. Do you know the three persons of the Trinity? _____

_____

_____

How are they unique? _____

_____

_____

How are they alike? _____

_____

_____

2. When did you come to know Jesus? The Holy Spirit?

_____

_____

3. How have you observed the Holy Spirit at work in your own life or in others? _____

_____

_____

4. Have you ever received and/or functioned in any of the gifts of the Spirit? _____

_____

_____

EVALUATE YOURSELF

1. In what ways are you implementing the principles learned from Deborah? _____

_____

_____

2. In what ways are you failing to implement the principles learned from Deborah?_____

_____

_____

3. What do you need to do to change? _____

_____

_____

4. How will you do it? _____

_____

_____

Lesson 12
Delilah & Abigail

An Example of Spiritual Warfare

"For the weapons of our warfare are not carnal, but mighty through God to the pulling down of strongholds; casting down imaginations, and every high thing that exalteth itself against the knowledge of God, and bringing into captivity every thought to the obedience of Christ."

II Corinthians 10:4 and 5

SETTING THE STAGE

We're involved in a spiritual battle whether we recognize it or not. Satan, the present "god of this world," tries to blind our eyes to his very existence, as well as keep us from knowing the salvation and deliverance we can have in the Lord Jesus Christ.

When we are *born again,* and thus transferred from the power of darkness into the kingdom of God's Son, we have available the infilling and power of the Holy Spirit to do battle against Satan and his host. With the authority that comes from Jesus (who destroyed all the works of the devil), we can have victory over Satan. Jesus is now interceding for us, but we must stand clothed in the full armor of God, resisting Satan as he attacks our bodies, our families, our friends, our churches, and our society.

We're given specific weapons to wage warfare against prinicpalities and powers, rulers of darkness, and spiritual wickedness in high places. Satan, on the other hand, likes nothing better than to get us into fleshly battles with each other.

As we look at the story of Samson and Delilah, we can see how Delilah, as a type of Satan, wore Samson down until he simply give in just as Satan does us.

In Abigail we find a peacemaker, one who used the means she had at her disposal to stave off a battle and bring peace into the situation.

THE COUNTERFEIT SUCCESS OF DELILAH

(Based on Judges 16:4-21)

Samson fell in love with a girl named Delilah. The Philistines wanted to capture Samson, so they bribed Delilah to find out what made Samson so strong. They wanted to know how to overpower him and put him in chains.

Delilah began to nag. First, she begged Samson to tell her why he was so strong. He replied that he would become weak if he were tied with seven raw-leather bowstrings.

So while he slept, she tied him up. But when she cried out that the enemy had come, he got up immediately and snapped the bowstrings.

Delilah accused him of deceiving her. She asked him again, what made him so strong. This time, he told her that the ropes needed to be brand new.

Sure enough, as he slept again, she tied him with new ropes. But once more, he broke them when he was awakened.

Delilah persisted. Complaining that he had mocked her, she begged some more. This time he told her to weave his hair into her loom. Needless to say, she was exasperated when he woke up as strong as ever, and even walked away wearing the pin and the loom.

Now Delilah accused him of not loving her. She continued nagging for several days until, finally, Samson couldn't stand it any longer and told her his secret—his strength was in his long hair.

The next time he slept, she had his hair cut off, and Samson did, indeed, become weak. Thus he was captured by the Philistines, who gouged out his eyes, thinking a blind Samson was safer than a sighted Samson.

Delilah's continual nagging wore Samson down until he gave in to her. This is a picture of the success Satan has by persistently tempting us, wearing us down until we, too, give in to him.

THE SUCCESS OF ABIGAIL
(Based on I Samuel 25:1-42; II Samuel 3:3)

David and his soldiers were in the wilderness of Paran where there lived a wealthy man named Nabal. When David heard that Nabal was shearing his sheep, he sent ten of his men to ask him for a contribution—something not uncommon.

But, Nabal was angry at such a request and told them so. When the soldiers told David of Nabal's refusal, he became angry and set off with 400 men to kill Nabal and his men.

Meanwhile, one of Nabal's men learned what was happening and told Nabal's wife, Abigail. He also told her David's men had actually protected Nabal's men and sheep.

Without telling her husband, Abigail hurriedly gathered 200 loaves of bread, two barrels of grain, 100 raisin cakes, and 200 fig cakes and packed them all onto donkeys. She set off to meet David before he got near their property.

When Abigail saw David and his men, she dismounted and bowed before him. She then took the blame for her husband's bad temper. She also confronted David, telling him that taking vengeance on Nabal would be inappropriate. In talking to her, David realized the cost of his action should he, indeed, murder Nabal; he left without doing a thing.

Abigail returned home where she found Nabal in the midst of a party. Aware that he was very drunk, she didn't tell him where she had been until the next morning. He suffered a stroke and died several days later.

When David heard that Nabal was dead, he praised the Lord for His punishment of Nabal, and that Abigail had kept him from committing a terrible sin. Abigail staved off a battle by using non-military weapons. Instead of arming herself with weapons of destruction, she gave gifts to her husband's enemy, at the same time confronting this enemy with the consequences of the sin which he intended to commit. Abigail was victorious with unconventional weapons. God further rewarded her by allowing her to become the wife of King David.

LESSONS FROM DELILAH AND ABIGAIL
Satan's tactics

Delilah used persistent nagging to wear Samson down until he became vexed and gave in to her. This is one of Satan's tactics against us. He has others as well. Let's look at some of the ways he tries to defeat Christians. Jesus exhorted His followers to be "wise as serpents"—which means at least as wise as Satan, who was once identified as a serpent.

Satan seems to have at least three main modes of attack. If one doesn't succeed, he tries another. The three ways he comes against us are as (1) a tempter (2) a deceiver and (3) an accuser.

The first time he came to mankind, he came as a *tempter*. In the form of a serpent, he tempted Eve by questioning her concerning what God had said. Satan also tempted Jesus in the wilderness. Paul recognized this role of Satan. He said in I Thessalonians 3:5, *"For this cause, when I could no longer forbear, I sent to know your faith, lest by some means the tempter have tempted you, and our labor be in vain."*

Many are harmed by the adversary when he comes as the *deceiver*. This is a more subtle tactic than temptation. Paul referred to this means in II Corinthians 11:14 and 15, when he said, *"And no marvel, for Satan himself is transformed into an angel of light. Therefore it is no great thing if his ministers also be transformed as the ministers of righteousness; whose end shall be according to their works."*

Paul taught that false pastors will even appear as true ones. So Satan, himself, can masquerade as a true angel of God. Though a person may overcome the tempter with the confession of God's Word (as Jesus did), he needs the *whole counsel of God* to detect deception.

The third, and strongest form of attack, is that of the *accuser*. Such was Delilah, who allowed the enemy to work through her. Satan accuses the believer to God, and accuses God to the believer. He accuses Christians to each other, and the believer to himself. Soon, the Christian is overcome with condemnation, guilt, discouragement, and unbelief, and Satan has that person right where he wants him. For, he comes as a thief to steal, to kill, and to destroy.

As we consider these tactics of Satan, we must also realize that Isaiah 54:16 says *"God sent the waster to destroy!"* God sometimes allows Satan to tempt, to deceive, to accuse, in order to test us—as He did Job. He determines if we do His Word and fight the spiritual battles with the weapons He has provided. When we're rightly related to Christ Jesus and are endued with the power of the Holy Spirit, we have victory over Satan, no matter how he comes against us.

Spiritual Warfare

In Ephesians 5, we have the main Scripture which describes

the relationship the Church is to have as Jesus' Bride. This great mystery is compared to the relationship between a husband and wife.

In Ephesians 6, we're given the command to *"be strong in the Lord, and the power of His might,"* as we put on the whole armor of God. Though Satan's works have been destroyed, he's still allowed to go about as a roaring lion, seeking to devour whatever he can—particularly the Church, because of her relationship to Jesus.

The Church is involved in a spiritual battle as Satan tries to deceive her into thinking the victory hasn't been won. God has provided protection and weapons. It's up to the Church to avail herself of them.

Battlegrounds

Physical—Not all illnesses are attacks of Satan, but some are. No doubt he would like to disable the "temple of the Holy Spirit."

Moral—Satan will tempt us to break God's moral laws and then delude us into justifying our actions. Thus we'll disobey His Word and see no need of repentance.

Beliefs—We are warned of "seducing spirits and doctrines of demons," and are admonished to test the spirits and beware of false prophets.

Children—When out from under the covering of believing parents, children are particularly vulnerable to attacks of Satan.

Places and things—Because of association with the occult, buildings and artifacts have been known to display supernatural demonic activity. (Thus, "haunted houses", amulets, etc.)

Our Protection

We've already seen (in a previous lesson) how the blood of Jesus is our protection. When we have a proper relationship with Him, we'll put on the whole armor of God which is, essentially, Jesus Himself! Ephesians 6:10-18 describes this armor in detail.

Girdle of Truth—Jesus, as Truth, keeps us from deception and false accusations.

Breastplate of righteousness—Only God's righteousness, which we have through Jesus, can protect us. Our righteousness is like filthy rags and makes us vulnerable to Satan.

Sandals of the Gospel of Peace—We must be in readiness to make the gospel known.

Shield of Faith—We need a constant, unflinching attitude of faith to ward off the fiery darts of unbelief that Satan directs toward us to discredit what Jesus has accomplished for us.

Helmet of Salvation—Our protection through Jesus is the price He paid for our sin. Because of our salvation, Satan should have nothing in us, especially in our minds which is where our doubts begin. All of Satan's works were destroyed at the cross.

Sword of the Spirit—This is the only offensive weapon. It's the Word of God. When we're fully clothed, we're to simply stand; the battle is the Lord's! However, there are other weapons mentioned in Scripture which help us stand in the victory that is ours through Jesus. Let us now turn to some of these.

Weapons of Spiritual Warfare

Ephesians 6:12 tells us that the reason we put on the whole armor of God is because *"we wrestle not against flesh and blood, but against principalities, against powers, against the rulers of the darkness of this world, against spiritual wickedness in high places."* In other words, an unseen war is raging in the heavens.

The heavens represent three distinct areas. Paul speaks of being caught up to the third heaven (II Corinthians 12:2). If there's a third, there must be a first and second. We can consider the first heaven as the atmosphere around the earth. The second heaven is above the first. It's the heavenly sphere in which Satan, the prince of the power of the air (Ephesians 2:2), has his domain. The third heaven is the place of God's abode.

Ephesians 2:6 says, *"God raised us up with Christ and seated us with Him in the heavenly realms in Christ Jesus."* Thus we, as believers, are seated with Christ on His throne. The second heaven is under our authority. It has become our footstool, for we have the same authority over the devil that Christ has. We've been given power over satanic principalities and powers in the heavenlies as well. We claim the victory Christ Jesus accomplished for us by reminding Satan and his host what Jesus has done. Someday Satan will be thrown in the lake of fire (Revelation 20:10). Until that time he will continue to harass Christians. Believers must remind Satan who they are, and who he is!

II Corinthians 10:3-5 (LB) reminds us: *"It is true that I am an ordinary weak human being, but I don't use human plans and methods to win my battles. I use God's mighty weapons, not those made by men, to knock down the devil's strongholds. These weapons can break down every proud argument against God and every wall that can be built to keep men from finding him. With these weapons I can capture rebels and bring them back to God, and change them into men whose heart's desire is obedience to Christ."*

The Sword of the Spirit, which is the Word of God (Ephesians 6:17; Hebrews 4:12; Luke 4:4-8, and 12) We find in Hebrews 4:12, that the Word of God is likened to a sword. It's what divides the soul from the Spirit. It sifts the purposes and thoughts of the heart. There's nothing quite like the Word of God, proclaimed in the power of the Holy Spirit, to force the enemy into the open and reveal him for who he is. We know that Jesus used this weapon as the means to defeat Satan in the wilderness. He simply quoted God's Word for every temptation Satan offered.

The blood of the Lamb and the word of our testimony (Revelation 12:11). As we affirm the work of Jesus' blood over our sin, Satan is reminded that all of his own works have been destroyed by the shedding of Jesus' blood. We can also claim the testimony of Isaiah 54:17, that no weapon formed against us will prosper, as we testify to what Jesus has done in our lives.

Praise to the Lord (II Chronicles 20:22). Jehoshaphat, King of Judah, became fearful when he had to lead the people into battle against their enemy. So he called a fast. The Lord spoke and said, *"Be not afraid nor dismayed by reason of this great multitude; for the battle is not yours, but God's."* Then God told him to appoint *singers* to go out before the army, singing

"Praise the Lord, for his mercy endureth forever." When they began to sing and to praise, the *Lord* set ambushes against the children of Ammon, Moab, and mount Seir, which were come against Judah; and they were smitten. Psalm 22:3 tells us God inhabits the praise of Israel (His people). When we praise the Lord, He defeats the Enemy. The battle is His.

Praying in the Spirit (Ephesians 6:18). When we consider the whole armor of God, we often overlook one of the last things we're to do. Verse 18 says that we're to pray always in the Spirit. Romans 8:26 and 27 tell us the Spirit helps us know what we should pray for, so we can pray according to the will of God. If we pray according to God's will, Satan can be exposed.

Spiritual gifts (I Corinthians 12:8 and 9). The gifts of the Holy Spirit, particularly a word of knowledge, a word of wisdom, and the gift of faith, can help us detect Satan and his devices and know what other weapons to use.

The Name of Jesus (Acts 5:40 and 41; Mark 16:17 and 18; Philippians 2:9-11; John 16:24; Matthew 18:20). The authority in the name above all names—Jesus—has been delegated to the Church to carry out the will of God. Because every knee will bow at this name, it becomes a powerful weapon against the enemy.

Fasting (Isaiah 58:6). Fasting is also a Scriptural weapon for spiritual warfare. It was used many times in Scripture. (We will go into this more in a future lesson.) Isaiah 58:6 tells us that a chosen fast will *"loose the bands of wickedness, undo the heavy burdens, let the oppressed go free, and break every yoke."* Though we humans may not understand how fasting works, God somehow uses it for His purposes to overcome Satan.

Binding and Loosing (Matthew 16:18 and 19 Amplified) Jesus told Peter that upon Himself—the rock—He would build His church. He gave Peter the keys to the kingdom (the authority that would unlock its power). Then Jesus said to Peter, *"I will give you the keys of the kingdom of heaven, and whatever you bind…that is, declare to be improper and unlawful…on earth must be already bound in heaven; and whatever you loose on earth…declare lawful… must be what is already loosed in heaven"*. In other words, as we (the Church) take the authority which has been given to us, we can remind Satan of what's already bound in heaven and what's already loosed there. He and his work have been bound; the Holy Spirit and his work have been loosed.

Resist by faith (I Peter 5:8 and 9). Here we're told that when harassed by Satan we should actively resist him. We need to watch for him and take action against him.

Draw Near to God (James 4:7 and 8). Not only do we resist Satan, but we draw nigh to God so we may be in right relationship with Him. Otherwise, resisting will be in our own strength and won't work.

Abide in Christ and Pray (John 15:7; Romans 8:26 and 27). As we abide in Christ (have a continuing relationship with Him), and are open to the Holy Spirit who helps us to know how to pray, we can better wage spiritual warfare against Satan.

SUMMARY

Though it's improbable that either Delilah or Abigail saw themselves involved in spiritual warfare, we see, in their stories, principals that can help us in our battle against our enemy, Satan and his hosts. We not only learn of the tactics of Satan, but of weapons God has put at our disposal to have victory over the enemy as we wage spiritual warfare.

MODERN EXAMPLE

At 4:43 p.m., May 2, 1983, a devastating 6.7 earthquake hit the small town of Coalinga, California. As it flattened the downtown business section, the ground rippled for miles around. The residents, as well as people in nearby towns, were struck with fear when they realized what was happening. Most tried to get to their homes, but found streets blocked with debris. Anxiety mounted as they wondered about other members of their families. Yet, when everyone was finally accounted for, the news broadcasts reported a "miracle"—*not a single life had been lost,* even though stores and other businesses had been functioning as usual that weekday afternoon.

As reports began to emerge concerning the catastrophe, one could begin to see the hand of God in protection as a result of spiritual warfare waged by His children.

For about a year, all who entered Coalinga had seen, at the city limits, a large billboard proclaiming in bold letters "Jesus is Lord of Coalinga." However, few probably knew that the idea for this sign originated with a Christian in nearby Fresno who passed the idea on to Christians in Coalinga. Several church groups raised money to rent the billboard so that the declaration of Jesus as Lord could be seen by all—including Satan!

In addition, at least two women felt so burdened for their hometown that they walked the city streets at night, praying for each home they passed.

When the earthquake struck, most of the homes were spared the heaviest damage. One church building escaped with only minor damage, even though the shopping center surrounding it was completely destroyed.

Jesus was Lord over Coalinga during the terrible earthquake which hadn't been predicted. God's people, prompted by the Holy Spirit, had already taken their stand against Satan and declared that Jesus was Victor.

WHAT DO YOU THINK?

1. Do you know who your real enemy is and some of how he operates? _____

_____

_____

2. Do you wage spiritual warfare, or do you succumb to fleshly battle? _____

_____

_____

3. Do you know what spiritual weapons are? Do you know how to use them? _____

_____

_____

4. Is there a new weapon that you need to learn how to use?

_____

_____

5. What results have you seen as an outcome of spiritual warfare? _____

_____

_____

EVALUATE YOURSELF

1. In what ways are you implementing the principles learned from Delilah and Abigail? _____

_____

_____

2. In what ways are you failing to implement the principles learned from them? _____

_____

_____

3. What do you need to do to change? _____

_____

_____

4. How will you do it? _____

_____

_____

Lesson 13
Naomi & Ruth

An Example of Israel and the Church

"This mystery is that through the gospel the Gentiles are heirs together with Israel, members together in the promise in Christ Jesus."

Ephesians 3:6 (NIV)

SETTING THE STAGE

The story of Naomi and Ruth is an analogy of Israel and the Church. As we note the restoration of Naomi, following her loss and sojourn in a foreign country, we see that she depicts the condition of Israel, God's chosen people. As Ruth makes the decision to leave her natural family and follow Naomi's people and their God, we see that she represents the grafted-in Gentile, the Church, and Bride of her Kinsman-Redeemer.

When Naomi lost her husband and sons, she decided to return to her own land and people. The Lord had dealt bitterly with her, and though she returned empty, she was restored. Through the offspring of Ruth and Boaz, Naomi became part of the lineage of the Messiah.

Naomi should have been the one to marry Boaz, but because she could no longer bear children, she allowed Ruth to take her place and marry the Kinsman-Redeemer as provided by law. In like manner, Israel gave way to the Church (Jew or Gentile who accepted the redemption provided by Jesus). It now became the people of the New Covenant, the Bride of Jesus Christ.

We can be restored as individuals, as well as a nation. No decision we make is as important as the one to follow God and accept the offer of Jesus, who paid the price for our salvation.

THE INITIAL FAILURE AND FINAL SUCCESS OF NAOMI
(Based on the Book of Ruth)

During the rule of the Judges, Israel suffered a severe famine. Elimelech, a resident of Bethlehem, decided to leave Judah with his wife Naomi, and two sons. They moved to Moab, where the food seemed more plentiful. For Naomi the uprooting must have been a real sacrifice. She loved her people and was strongly attached to the traditions of her race. God wanted to care for His people even in the time of famine (Psalm 33:18 and 19), but Elimelech chose to move to another country.

Naomi probably regretted the decision more than once, for they had much misfortune in the heathen land. Her two sons married Moabite girls, which was against Jewish law. Then

Elimelech died. His death was followed by those of their two sons. Thus, Naomi was left alone with two pagan daughters-in-law in a land of idolatry.

She decided to leave Moab and return to her native country. She intended to leave alone, but both daughters-in-law left with her. Naomi, who had no way to support the three of them, pleaded with them to return to their own families. One, Orpah, decided to do just that. The other, Ruth, made a commitment to follow Naomi and her God. Thus it was that Naomi and Ruth arrived in Bethlehem together.

Naomi must have had flashbacks of her childhood, youth, and early years of her marriage. Her arrival created quite a stir. People questioned her to see if she were really Naomi, for the years had taken their toll. She returned to her homeland "empty" and in poverty.

Ruth knew that Naomi was too old to work and it was up to her to find something for them to eat, so she went out to look for work as a gleaner. In the fields, Ruth met Boaz, a relative of Naomi's. Before long, she had a job working for him. Eventually they were married. When Ruth and Boaz became parents, Naomi was happy once again. She became a nursemaid to Obed, her grandson. The family that had perished was now restored.

THE SUCCESS OF RUTH

(Based on the Book of Ruth and Matthew 1:5)

The first glimpse we have of Ruth is as a young widow whose husband, Mahlon, had died. She didn't seem to have self-pity; neither did she manifest the bitterness that gripped the heart of her mother-in-law Naomi.

A mother and two daughters-in-law were now bound together in common grief, for all their husbands had died. They found consolation in each other's company, though Naomi was one of God's covenant people, while Orpah and Ruth were pagans. When Naomi decided to return to her country and people, she begged the girls to stay in their homeland. Orpah did so, but Ruth told Naomi, *"Entreat me not to leave thee, or to return from following after thee; for whither thou goest, I will go; and where thou lodgest, I will lodge: thy people shall be my people, and thy God my God."* Thus, she accompanied Naomi back to Bethlehem.

Under Jewish law, Ruth could glean in any harvest field (follow the reapers and gather what they left behind). God designed that she meet Boaz, a godly landowner who was Naomi's relative.

Boaz was kind and was friendly with his reapers. When he discovered Ruth working in his field, he told the reapers to drop extra sheaves for her benefit. He also arranged for her to eat at his table.

Ruth was grateful for his kindnesses and reported them to Naomi. When Naomi heard of Boaz, she recalled that he was a kinsman of her deceased husband. She knew the Levirate law which said that when a husband died without an heir, the widow's brother-in-law was obligated to marry her so that their child might carry on the family name. Since Ruth had no brother-in-law left, the nearest kinsman could be called upon to act as her "redeemer."

Naomi therefore encouraged Ruth to find where Boaz slept one night and go lie at his feet. Ruth did as Naomi suggested. Boaz found Ruth when he awoke and listened to her tell of her predicament. Since there was a closer relative than him, Boaz first went to consult him. But, the relative was unable to fulfill his duty. The elders gave Boaz permission to buy Ruth's inheritance and marry her.

God blessed their union with a son named Obed. Obed became the father of Jesse, and Jesse, the father of David. Thus, in the lineage of Jesus, we find Ruth, the Gentile idolater who gave up her country and gods to join Naomi.

God's Purpose in Israel

When God chose Abraham it was because He wanted to form a people through whom His light would shine. They would be His vessel to take the salvation of God to all nations of the earth.

The temptation of the Jewish people has been to make this divine calling an end in itself. They didn't recognize and receive the Messiah when He came. Salvation came to only a small minority of Jewish people. Yet their rejection of Jesus made it possible for salvation to come to the Gentiles.

Romans 4:11 and 12 and Galatians 3:7 and 29 tell us that Abraham is the father of all who believe, Jew or Gentile. We can see this further spelled out in Ephesians 2:11-18 where we learned that, through the blood of Jesus, both Jew and Gentile have access by one Spirit to the Father. Jesus broke down the wall between the "uncircumcised" and the "circumcised." Ephesians 3:6 says, *"The Gentiles should be fellow heirs, and of the same body, and partakers of his promise in Christ by the gospel."* Galatians 3:28 reminds us that, *"There is neither Jew nor Greek, there is neither bond nor free, there is neither male or female; for ye are all one in Christ Jesus."*

In Romans 11, Paul speaks of how the Gentiles became God's people by being grafted in, much as branches are grafted into a tree. He also says that, if the Jews leave their unbelief and come back to God, God will graft them back into the tree again. The Jew becomes part of the Church the same way the Gentile does—through believing in Jesus as the Messiah.

In New Testament times, when a Jew became a follower of Jesus, he maintained his "Jewishness" and Jewish culture. Today, however, a Jew who becomes Jesus' disciple is often identified as a Christian. Actually, he has fulfilled God's original calling and can be known simply as a Jew who has accepted his Messiah.

The Church doesn't replace Israel in God's plan. The Jews, whether or not they accept Jesus as their Messiah, are still an elect people. Romans 11:29 (NIV) says, *"God's gifts and his call are irrevocable."* The Jews remain a chosen people. God's gifts and call upon them continue for Abraham's sake.

When the purpose of God to draw in the Gentiles has been accomplished, the veil on the Jew's heart will be removed with glorious consequences. Then the suffering and sorrow of the last 2,000 years will give way to radiant glory and blessing. The end result will be the Bride of the Messiah, the New Jerusalem, in the light of which the nations will walk. The fullness of the Gentiles and the fullness of the Jews will be brought into the Body of Christ, the Messiah.

Deuteronomy 28:64-66 God said He would _____

_____

_____

Deuteronomy 29:24-28 God said He would scatter His people because _____

_____

_____

II Kings 17:20-23 What happened to the northern kingdom of Israel? Did they ever return to their own land? _____

_____

_____

II Kings 25:21 What happened to the southern kingdom of Judah? _____

_____

_____

Ezra 1:1-11 Under what circumstances did Judah return from captivity? _____

_____

_____

Romans 11:7-10 Except for the remnant which believed in Jesus, what happened to the Jews? _____

_____

_____

Romans 11:11 Through the failure of the Jews to believe in Jesus, the _____

_____

_____

Romans 11:25 and 26 What will happen when the time of the Gentiles is fulfilled? (See also Luke 21:24) _____

_____

_____

LESSONS FROM NAOMI AND RUTH
Naomi—The Restoration of God's People

Naomi can symbolically represent Israel, the covenant people of God. She left her homeland and endured suffering. Because of a daughter-in-law who chose to accept her God, a Gentile was grafted into the family. By being thus joined, they received the same promise of inheritance. It's interesting to note that it should have been Naomi who married Boaz, but, because she was no longer able to bear children, she allowed Ruth to take her place. So also must Israel allow the Church to be the people of the New Covenant, the Bride of Christ.

As Naomi returned to her own country, she was restored into fellowship with her people and into the blessing of God. When her former countrymen questioned who she was, she told them not to call her Naomi, but Mara, because God had dealt very bitterly with her.

After Ruth married Boaz and bore a son, it was said of Naomi, *"Blessed be the Lord, which hath not left thee this day without a kinsman, that his name may be famous in Israel. And he shall be unto thee a restorer of thy life."* (Ruth 4:14 and 15). Naomi's life was restored; she had a new family. Naomi belonged to God, just as the Jews belong to Him. He completed the work in her by bringing her back to Himself, just as He will eventually restore His own people, the Jews.

Ruth 1:20 and 21 Naomi went out full, but now was _____

_____

_____

Ruth 4:14 and 15 Naomi was not left without a _____

_____

_____

Jeremiah 32:37-44 God has promised His people that ____

_____

_____

Zephaniah 3:20 When God gathers up His people, He will

_____

_____

Hosea 2:14-23 To restore Israel, God will _____

_____

_____

Joel 2:23-32 In restoring Israel, God will _____

_____

_____

Jeremiah 30:17 A promise of restoration is _____

_____

_____

Ezekiel 28: 25 and 26 When Israel is restored, she will ___

_____

_____

Ezekiel 16:59-62 God will remember His promises to Israel by

_____

_____

_____

Isaiah 54: 5 and 6 Israel is here described as _____

_____

_____

Isaiah 59:21 God's covenant with Israel is _____

_____

_____

Isaiah 45:17 The eventual condition for Israel is _____

_____

_____

Ruth—A Type of the Church

At the feast of Pentecost, Jews read the story of Ruth. This is very appropriate. Ruth can be a picture of the Church, which was born at Pentecost!

Ruth was a Gentile, grafted into the Jewish nation. She was a foreigner, but chose to accept Naomi's God and, thus, become part of her inheritance. Ruth made a clean break with her natural family, and never went back to them. The Church is composed of regenerated Jews, as well as Gentiles who have been "grafted in."

By the grace and provision of God, Ruth became the bride of Boaz, a type of Christ. He found her in the field which was "white unto harvest" and bestowed his love and mercy upon her. She then came into a special relationship with him, not because she deserved it, but because he was willing to pay the price of kinsman-redeemer for her.

Ruth 1:16 Ruth's decision was to _____

_____

_____

Ruth 3:8 and 9 Ruth claimed Boaz as her _____

_____

_____

Ruth 4:13 Boaz and Ruth _____

_____

_____

Romans 11:13-24 Gentiles become part of God's people by

_____

_____

122

Matthew 10:37 We are not worthy of Christ if _____

_____

_____

Matthew 12:46-50 Jesus' true family is _____

_____

_____

Acts 11:1-18 Peter was shown that Gentiles _____

_____

_____

Acts 13:46-48 When the Jews rejected Paul and Barnabas, they _____

_____

_____

Acts 15:1-19 The result of the council at Jerusalem was _____

_____

_____

Our Attitude Toward Israel

Genesis 12:2 and 3 God will bless _____

_____

_____

and curse _____

_____

_____

Psalm 122:6 We are to pray for _____

_____

_____

with the promise that _____

_____

_____

Genesis 17:7 God made a _____

_____

_____

Romans 11:13-26 We are not to be ignorant of _____

_____

_____

WOMEN IN THE BIBLE

SUMMARY

Naomi depicts Israel, God's covenant people who experienced loss and were dealt with severely by God before they were later restored. Ruth is the grafted-in Gentile, the Bride of her Kinsman-Redeemer (Boaz). We, as individuals, can also experience the loss and pain of Naomi, as well as restoration. Like Ruth, we can find our place in the family of God, as we decide to accept the God of Israel through our Kinsman-Redeemer, Jesus Christ.

In blessing Israel, we are blessed.

MODERN EXAMPLE

"We'll let you know as soon as we can!" With those words, my husband put the telephone receiver down, just as I came into the room. "Who was that?...And what will we let them know?" I asked, imagining everything from accepting a invitation to dinner with friends to being responsible for some job in the PTA.

"That was Ljuba. She wants some money. She's about to lose her house for back taxes."

"Ljuba?" I questioned. "It's been a long time since we've heard from her! How is she?"

"Quite depressed. She really needs the money. She has no other place to go."

We had been newlyweds when we met our German-Jewish friend 17 years earlier. My husband was in seminary, and the front door of her apartment faced the back door of our student housing. She often sat on her porch, resting in the sunshine, and we would exchange casual greetings as we came and went to school and work.

As time went by, we talked of other things. Ljuba was crippled from polio, but also suffered poor health due to several years of internment in a German concentration camp during World War II. She was utterly dependent upon friends and neighbors. We soon found ourselves going over to shake her rugs, carry in groceries, or just to take her for a ride.

All too soon, the three years of neighborliness came to an end. We moved to another state, and Ljuba moved to a different city. We continued to correspond, and even had the opportunity for an occasional visit. Eventually, however, our communication dwindled to annual Christmas greetings. We had been out of touch for several years when the telephone call came with her urgent request.

My husband and I wondered what to do. We had three growing children and a rather limited income—certainly not enough to give her what she asked. We knew, too, that because she was on a meager pension from the German government, she would most likely never be able to repay a loan.

For several days, we discussed the matter. She *did* need money. And she *was* a friend. We wanted to help, but the only way that we knew we could, was to cash in some insurance we had put aside for savings.

We finally came to the conclusion that we must send her the money and just forget about getting it back, though she had said she would secure it with a note.

At this time, we were completely unaware of the principle of

124

Genesis 12:3, which tells us that those who bless God's people will be blessed.

Years went by. In fact, it was eight Christmases later. Our usual greeting to Ljuba was returned, the envelope stamped with the simple word "Deceased." Our hearts were saddened. We hadn't known that she had passed away the previous Easter. Our only consolation was that we knew that she had accepted Jesus as her Messiah—that it would no longer make any difference that we were Gentiles who had salvation so freely given, while her people had had to suffer.

We were doubly saddened, however, when we realized she would not be rejoicing with us in the news our Christmas letter contained. We were planning to go to Israel, the Lord willing, the following April with a group from our church. We didn't really have enough money for the trip. We were just trusting the Lord to provide since He had put such a strong desire in our hearts.

January and February came and went—still no money. We considered taking out a loan, but didn't feel comfortable about doing that. Full payment for the tickets was due in March, just three weeks before we were to leave. The departure date itself, on the day following Easter, would now be like an anniversary celebration of Ljuba's homegoing. We would be visiting the land of her heritage just a year from the day she had entered into her full inheritance. We decided to plant some trees in Israel in her name.

But those were discouraging days. We had felt so right about signing up for the trip. Now our hopes were being dashed; our faith was ever so small.

Then, one beautiful spring day, the mail arrived.

"This is strange," my husband said as he brought it into the house. "There's an official-looking letter from the county where Ljuba lived."

Curious, we tore open the envelope. Before we could read the letter itself, a check fell into our laps. We could hardly believe our eyes. It was made out to us, for the exact amount that we needed for our trip.

"I can't believe it!" "I can't believe it!" "I can't believe it!" These seemed to be the only words we could utter. Our hands were trembling so much that we could hardly read the letter. It's message was simple. "The estate of Ljuba _____ has been settled. Enclosed, please find a check for the payment of your loan, plus eight years' interest."

We jumped for joy, danced around the room, and ran outside to tell our neighbors. Then, after many excited phone calls, we drove to the travel agency and paid for our tickets. All the way across the city, the only words we could say were, "Thank you, Lord. Thank you, Lord." Our finite minds couldn't comprehend God's unfathomable ways. He had worked every circumstance in our lives so that we would receive, on the very day that we needed it, the exact amount of money necessary for a trip to Israel—all because eight years earlier we had blessed a Jewish friend and neighbor whom we had known from the beginning of our married life. We could never even imagine such perfect timing, on this our 25th wedding anniversary, let alone His abundant grace, mercy, and love.

WOMEN IN THE BIBLE

So it was, with new eyes of belief and renewed faith in our Heavenly Father, we visited His land and His people, reassured that God, indeed, blesses those who bless His own.

WHAT DO YOU THINK?

1. What is your attitude toward the Jewish people? Is it Scriptural? _____

_____

_____

2. If Jewish, do you fully appreciate your spiritual heritage?

_____

_____

3. If Gentile, do you fully appreciate the provision of being "grafted-in?" _____

_____

_____

4. Is there any way you can bless Israel or even one Jewish person? _____

_____

_____

EVALUATE YOURSELF

1. In what ways are you implementing the principles learned from Naomi and Ruth? _____

_____

_____

2. In what ways are you failing to implement the principles learned from them? _____

_____

_____

3. What do you need to do to change? _____

_____

_____

4. How will you do it? _____

_____

_____

Lesson 14
Hannah, Rizpah & Ichabod's Mother

An Example of Prayer

"And all things, whatsoever ye shall ask in prayer, believing, ye shall receive."

Matthew 21:22

SETTING THE STAGE

Prayer is man's means of communication with God. It's the way God brings His will into being on earth.

Prayer involves the Trinity. The Holy Spirit helps us know the Word of God (Jesus), which is in agreement with the will of the Heavenly Father. I John 5:14 and 15 tell us that, when we pray according to His will, God hears us, and if He hears us, then He will grant our petitions. The secret of effective praying, then, is to determine the will of God, pray according to His Word, and claim the answer by faith.

Too often, our prayers are simply those of petition—much like making out a grocery list of what we want. But, prayer also involves intercession—travailing on behalf of the needs of others. Prayer is one of the weapons of spiritual warfare.

THE SUCCESS OF HANNAH
(Based on I Samuel 1; 2:1-21)

Hannah was the favorite wife of Elkanah, a man who followed the common custom of polygamy.

Since it was the desire of every Hebrew parent to have a son, it was a reproach to Hannah that she was barren. Though provoked by Elkanah's other wife, Peninnah, Hannah maintained a constant observance of the religious ordinances of her nation. Her husband loved her dearly, but she was unhappy and cried out to God day and night for a child. She wasn't guilty of bitterness or revenge. She knew that God was her only hope.

On one particular occasion, Hannah's supplication was made without speech; her lips moved, but no sound came forth. When Eli the priest saw her praying and thought she was drunk, he upbraided her for coming into God's house in such a condition. Hannah protested her innocence and poured out her soul to Eli. He replied, "Go in peace, and the God of Israel grant thee thy petition, that thou hast asked of him." She went home believing, and her burden was lifted.

God granted her desire. The yearned-for child, Samuel, was born.

Hannah had made a vow unto God. If God would give her a son, she would give him back to the Lord all the days of his life. So when God gave her Samuel and she weaned him, she took him to the house of the Lord, "there to abide forever." She visited him once a year.

Samuel grew up to reflect his mother's godliness, even though he was raised by Eli who had been a poor father to his own two sons. Hannah and Elkanah were blessed with other children, but none were the object of as many prayers as Samuel.

LESSONS FROM HANNAH
Prayer—Petition to God

The child Samuel was born as a result of Hannah's petition to God. Unlike other barren women in Scripture (such as Sarah, Rebekah, Elizabeth), God hadn't told Hannah beforehand that she would have a child. She had no idea God would send her Samuel—the judge, prophet, and priest that He would use to anoint the first and second kings of Israel. All she knew was that she desperately wanted a child. So she petitioned God for one.

No one knows whether or not God would have given Samuel to Hannah if she hadn't prayed for him. But it does make us wonder if we're missing some of the desires of our hearts because we don't ask for them in prayer. Prayers for our family, prayers for our financial needs, prayers for healing for our bodies, prayers for guidance in our work, prayers for deliverance from temptation, prayers for protection—the list could go on and on. God delights in hearing from us. He's waiting for us to come to Him with our heart's desires.

An interesting phrase occurs twice in the story of Hannah and Elkanah. I Samuel 1:3 says that Elkanah went up yearly to worship and to sacrifice *unto the Lord of Hosts* in Shiloh. I Samuel 1:11 says, "And she (Hannah) vowed a vow, and said, '*O Lord of Hosts...*'" This is the first place God is mentioned in this way, though He's referred to as the Lord of hosts over 200 times from that point through the end of the Old Testament.

The Hebrew word for hosts is *tsbaah,* which means "an army poised and ready for battle." As we leave the Book of Judges and move into I Samuel, we find Israel in the time of the kings. We see God recognized as the One who is mighty and powerful, with an unseen army assembled, ready to battle on behalf of the kingdom.

We have the perspective of time that Hannah didn't have. We know the power of the Almighty God through His Son Jesus and the Holy Spirit. We have history, through which we can see the supernatural acts of a mighty Lord of hosts. And, we have the Word, which tells us of the spiritual warfare we're in and of the weapons available to us.

Like Hannah, we need to see God as the *Lord of Hosts,* as One who has an army assembled, mustered, and waiting for instructions. In fact, if we accept Psalm 68:17, it's quite an army. The chariots of God are 20,000 and there are even thousands of angels.

Scripture gives us some ways and reasons to pray:

Philippians 4:6 and 7 _____

_____

_____

I Timothy 2:1-4 _____

_____

_____

James 4:2 and 3 _____

_____

_____

I Peter 4:7 _____

_____

_____

Psalms 55:22 _____

_____

_____

Luke 11:13 _____

_____

_____

Romans 10:13 _____

_____

_____

    How did God show that He answers prayer in the following situations?

I Kings 18:15-45 _____

_____

_____

Exodus 33:12-23 _____

_____

_____

Daniel 9:20-23 _____

_____

_____

Acts 12:5-12 _____

_____

_____

Persistence in Prayer

There are times when we know that we're praying in the will of God because what we ask is according to the Word of God. Yet, the answers don't seem to come quickly. There may be reasons for hindrances to the answers.

We'll consider these later in this lesson. For now, let's look at examples in Scripture when it seemed that God simply wanted *persistence* in prayer.

Genesis 32:24-29 tells how Jacob wrestled with God and prevailed until he got a new name and a new blessing.

I Kings 18:41-45 After years of severe famine, Elijah prayed seven times before the rains came.

Daniel 9:3 Daniel set his face to seek the Lord through prayer, supplication and fasting until the angel Gabriel came and told him of the future of the sinful nation of Israel.

Daniel 10:12-14 We find that another delay to Daniel's prayer was due to a spiritual battle in the heavenlies which detained the answer from getting through.

Nehemiah 1:4 Nehemiah wept certain days until the heart of the king was touched and God's people were given favor to return to Jerusalem and rebuild the walls.

Ezra 8:21-23 God was entreated for the protection of the people on the way back from exile. They afflicted themselves, fasted, and prayed.

Esther 4:16 Esther called for three days of prayer and fasting by the Jews to seek God's deliverance from the edict in Persia which was to annihilate them.

Mark 7:24-30 A Syrophoenician woman persisted in asking Jesus to heal her daughter until He did so.

Luke 18:1-8 In this parable, we see how a widow was avenged by the judge because she troubled him continually concerning her case. Persistent prayer takes faith. This pleases God.

Matthew 26:44 If Jesus Himself, petitioned God, praying the same words *three* times, can we be satisfied in doing less?

Prayer is Asking and Receiving

Matthew 7:7 and 8 Ask and it shall _____

_____

_____

Matthew 6:9-13 In the "Lord's Prayer," we are told to ask for

_____

_____

John 14:13 and 14 Whatever we ask in Jesus' name, _____

_____

_____

John 16:23 and 24 We are commanded to _____

_____

_____

Matthew 21:21 and 22 If we, by faith, ask all things in prayer,

_____

_____

THE SUCCESS OF RIZPAH
(Based on II Samuel 3:7; 21:8-14)

Like thousands of women thoughout the ages, Rizpah was a victim of national strife and war. She found herself bereft of her husband and two sons and left alone to fight the battle of poverty.

King Saul had broken an oath that had been made by Joshua with the Gibeonites. Even though Joshua had been deceived into making it, the oath stated that the Israelites wouldn't destroy the Gibeonites by the sword (Joshua 9:17-20). But when Saul came into power, he tried to annihilate the Gibeonites, along with Israel's other enemies. Then Saul met his death on Mt. Gilboa.

A severe famine overtook the land for three years. David, now King, was divinely informed that the famine was due to Saul's slaughter of the Gibeonites (breaking the oath that had been made). Thus, the Israelites had to give into the Gibeonites' demands for compensation. The Gibeonites wanted the seven sons of Saul hanged.

Five of the young men were actually Saul's grandsons, who had been raised by Michal after her sister died. The other two were sons of Saul's concubine, Rizpah. Seven innocent men were slaughtered as restitution for sin in their family; the children paid for the sins of their father.

What a ghastly scene it must have been during barley harvest, to see seven bodies hanging from the trees. And then to find Rizpah, mother of two of these, standing by, protecting the corpses from vultures. Through the days and weeks that followed, she watched the bodies gradually blacken and decay and she cared for them the best she could. (Leaving bodies unburied testified to the vengeance of man, for God's law demanded that anyone hung must be buried by sunset the same day.)

Rizpah continued her watch through anxious days and nights; her nostrils were filled with the stench of death. She spread sackcloth on the rock indicating not only her mourning for the dead, but her public display of humiliation. Thus, she defended her dead. When the rains came, a token that God had withdrawn His judgment, Rizpah's long vigil was over. She was now at liberty to bury the corpses.

David heard of Rizpah's motherly devotion and long vigil. Remembering that the uncared-for bones of Saul and Jonathan were still exposed in the streets of Beth-shan, he commanded that they should be recovered and mingled with the precious bones which Rizpah had guarded and buried in the family grave at Zelah. "God was entreated for the land," and Rizpah's desire for proper respect for her dead was fulfilled.

LESSONS FROM RIZPAH
The Ministry of Intercession

"I have set watchmen upon thy walls, O Jerusalem, which shall never hold their peace day and night; ye that are the Lord's remembrance, keep not silence, and give Him no rest." (Isaiah 62:6 and 7)

Prayer is petitioning God, asking and receiving things from Him. These are usually to benefit ourselves in some way. Another form of prayer is that of lifting up the needs of others; this is the ministry of intercession.

Rizpah is a type of intercessor. Though she could no longer petition God on behalf of her sons who were now dead, she maintained a vigil, doing what she could to ward off the enemy. She humbled herself before God until His judgment came to an end and He was entreated for the land.

The prophet Ezekiel had a vision (Ezekiel 9) in which the glory of the Lord departed from the temple. A linen-clothed man with a writing kit in his hand was told to go throughout Jerusalem and put a mark upon the foreheads of those who would grieve and lament over all the abominations that would occur as the city was destroyed. These would be ones who would see the young, old, women, and children slain. Marking these persons was to begin at the sanctuary.

Though we do not know why these persons were marked for this unpleasant task, we observe that God seems to raise up people to identify with those in real need. Perhaps in their crying and sighing, they will be repenting of sin, caring for physical needs, or standing in the gap as intercessors in prayer before God. Intercessors take up the burden of those who do not know to pray for themselves, or do not want to pray, or do not have the strength to lift their own voices to the Lord. An intercessor is so grateful for the mercy and love of God in his own life, that he is willing to deny himself, whatever the cost, to see another saved or ministered to by the Lord.

Let's look at those in Scripture who interceded on behalf of others, and see what we can learn from their experiences.

Moses (Exodus 32:11-13) _____

_____

_____

Joshua (Joshua 7:6-9) _____

_____

_____

Jehoshaphat (II Chronicles 20:5-13) _____

_____

_____

Isaiah (II Chronicles 32:20-22) _____

_____

Daniel (Daniel 9:3-19) _____

_____

_____

Paul (Colossians 1:9-12) _____

_____

Jesus as Our Intercessor

In John 17, we find Jesus' prayer of intercession on behalf of the disciples He would soon be leaving behind. He prayed for the Church which would come into being, when He said (in verses 20 and 21), *"Neither pray I for these alone, but for them also which shall believe on me through their word...that they all may be one; as thou, Father, art in me, and I in thee, that they also may be one in us; that the world may believe that thou hast sent me."*

His work was finished. It was necessary for him to return to heaven so the Holy Spirit could be poured out on all flesh.

Where did Jesus go? According to Romans 8:34, He ascended into heaven where He is now at the right hand of God making intercession for us. Hebrews 5:7 recalls the intercession Jesus made for us while He was on earth. *"Who in the days of his flesh, when he had offered up prayers and supplications with strong crying and tears unto him that was able to save him from death, and was heard in that he feared."* Now that Jesus is at God's right hand, He ever liveth to make intercession for those whom He saves (Hebrews 7:25).

God Calls Us to Be Intercessors

In a world with millions perishing, intercessors are desperately needed. God is able to save and meet the needs of people, but He depends upon prayer to act. He gave the following instructions in His Word:

"Ye have not chosen me, but I have chosen you, and ordained you, that ye should go and bring forth fruit, and that your fruit should remain: that whatsoever ye shall ask of the Father in My name, He may give it you." (John 15:16)

"And I sought for a man among them, that should make up the hedge, and stand in the gap before me for the land, that I should not destroy it; but I found none." (Ezekiel 22:30)

"And He saw that there was no man, and wondered that there was no intercessor." (Isaiah 59:16)

"Praying always with all prayer and supplication in the Spirit, and watching thereunto with all perseverance and supplication for all saints." (Ephesians 6:18)

THE FAILURE OF ICHABOD'S MOTHER

(Based on I Samuel 4)

The Bible doesn't give us the name of this woman. She was the wife of Phinehas, one of Eli's sons. Phinehas and his brother died during the battle in which the ark of the covenant was taken. When Eli was given the news, he died, thus leaving Phinehas' wife alone and expecting to give birth soon.

All we know of her is her anguish in childbirth and the name she gave her son, whom his father never saw. Labor pains seized her after she heard that the ark of the Lord had been lost.

The death of her husband, Phinehas, and her father-in-law, Eli, didn't seem to affect her as intensely as the loss of the ark of the covenant. When her child was born, she named him Ichabod, lamenting, *"The glory is departed from Israel, for the ark of God is taken."* Disappointed though she was (because God's honor was her honor), she didn't speak against her worthless husband (See I Samuel 3:13-14) or complain to God about his death. But prayers had not been answered. To her, the glory of the Lord was in the ark. When the ark was taken away, so was the presence of God.

LESSONS FROM ICHABOD'S MOTHER
Unanswered Prayer

Ichabod's mother gave up all hope when she heard that the ark had been captured. She knew that the glory of the Lord had departed. There are times when we, too, feel that God's presence has departed—that our prayers are going no farther than the ceiling. What does Scripture give as reasons prayers go unanswered?

I Peter 3:7 In order that prayers not be hindered, husbands must _____

_____

_____

Psalm 66:18 God doesn't hear those who _____

_____

Isaiah 59:2 Our _____

_____

so that _____

_____

Proverb 28:9 The prayer of one who _____

_____

is _____

_____

I John 5:14 For God to hear us, we must _____

_____

_____

Matthew 21:22 When we ask in prayer, we must _____

_____

Matthew 18:19 and 20 God will answer prayer when _____

_____

_____

Mark 11:24 When we pray, we must _____

_____

_____

I Thessalonians 5:17 We are to pray _____

_____

_____

Hebrews 11:6 He that comes to God must _____

_____

_____

James 1:5-8 If we _____, we won't _____

_____

_____

Deuteronomy 1:43-45 God won't hear those who _____

_____

_____

Proverbs 1:28-30 God won't answer when _____

_____

_____

Proverb 21:13 Whoever _____ won't be heard. _____

_____

_____

Isaiah 1:15 God doesn't hear the prayers of _____

_____

_____

Zechariah 7:9-13 Sometimes, man doesn't hear from God

because _____

_____

_____

James 4:2 and 3 We don't have the things of God because

_____

_____

SUMMARY

Three women—Hannah, Rizpah, and Ichabod's mother—show us three aspects of prayer. We see Hannah petitioning God for a son and receiving an answer to her prayer. Rizpah is a type of intercessor—fasting, praying, and standing guard in the midst of what seems to be a futile situation. With Ichabod's mother, we learn why some prayers seem to go unanswered.

MODERN EXAMPLE

Among those who persist in prayer while they observe many suffering for the lack of God's Word, are the Wycliffe Bible translators. These dedicated Christians live among various hard-to-reach tribes of the world. They not only translate the Bible into native tongues, but, often, must first put the languages themselves into written form! It's an arduous task, away from family and friends, for which they forfeit much physical comfort and earthly gain.

Two of these patient, persistent translators are Jim and Marj of Jigalong, Australia. They've been at work translating the Bible for many years while living among the Aborigines in the outback of Australia. In early December of 1982, when they returned to their work in Jigalong, after a four-month stay at the Linguistic Centre in Darwin, a visiting group of Aboriginal Christians shared what God was doing in their lives and gave the Jigalong people the opportunity to make a public commitment to Jesus Christ.

What Jim and Marj had waited for so long finally happened. People responded and received the living Lord into their hearts.

Soon new Believers started coming to them to ask about the Scriptures. They wanted to find out what God had to say about living the Christian life. Some had dreams and visions for which they needed interpretations. Others walked about declaring, "I'm a new man!"

Drawn together by a new bond of love, they began to meet every evening under a white gum tree. Here they worshiped God, praised Him in song, prayed, and shared their needs and victories. Needless to say, Jim and Marj were thrilled to see their 15-year-old dream finally come true. They watched God move by His Holy Spirit among the people. The Lord added daily to those being saved, and supplied enough water in the frequently dry creek to baptize new Christians. New songs came forth as the people became hungry for the Word of God.

Who knows why it took the Lord 15 years to answer their prayers or what may have hindered the answers along the way. But, persistence in prayer—as well as continual interces-

136

sion by their supporters—found fulfillment in the birth of the church in Jigalong, for which many important Scriptures had already been translated!

WHAT DO YOU THINK?

1. How would you describe your prayer life? What can you do to improve it? _____

_____

_____

2. Are your prayers mostly of petition, or do you intercede on behalf of others? _____

_____

_____

3. Do you have prayers that seemingly haven't been answered? What is your attitude toward God in this dilemma? _____

_____

_____

EVALUATE YOURSELF

1. In what ways are you implementing the principles learned from these three women? _____

_____

_____

2. In what ways are you failing to implement the principles learned from them? _____

_____

_____

3. What do you need to do to change? _____ _____

_____

_____

4. How will you do it? _____

_____

_____

Lesson 15
Michal & Bathsheba

An Example of Marital Relationships

"For we are members of his body, of his flesh, and of his bones. For this cause shall a man leave his father and mother, and shall be joined unto his wife, and they two shall be one flesh."
Ephesians 5:30 and 31

SETTING THE STAGE

David, like other Old Testament kings, had more than one wife. Although the Bible names several of them, we'll look at only two. These are Michal, David's first wife, and Bathsheba, his last wife named in the Bible. We're told several things concerning their marriage relationships.

Michal, who was also King Saul's daughter, was infatuated with the young hero who slew the giant Goliath. She was, no doubt, very happy when her father arranged for her to become David's wife. But they had several strikes against a happy relationship. We'll look at these and discover how David and Michal were unequally yoked.

David and Bathsheba's relationship is a different story. Their marriage began with adultery, murder, and deceit. (David later repented of these and received God's forgiveness.) Bathsheba's sin was of a more subtle nature. She "stumbled her brother."

God dealt with each of these relationships. He didn't allow Michal to bear David any children, and He took the child of David and Bathsheba's adulterous union.

We can learn truths from these two husband-wife relationships which will help us in our own marriages. We'll consider the problem of being unequally yoked as we look at David and Michal's relationship.

We'll also see how forgiveness is necessary if marriage is to succeed, when we look at the relationship of David and Bathsheba.

THE FAILURE OF MICHAL
(Based on I Samuel 14:49; 18:20-28; 19:11-17; 25:44; II Samuel 3:13 and 14; 6:12-23; I Chronicles 15:29)

Michal was the younger daughter of King Saul and his wife Ahinoam. Although she was a princess, Michal didn't seem to have a very commendable character. She sought prestige at the expense of others, was easily infatuated with David, and seemed to be indifferent toward God.

When Michal saw David, the young shepherd boy who killed the giant which had terrified her father and his nation, she made no effort to conceal her "love" for this handsome young hero.

King Saul had vowed that the man who killed Goliath would become his son-in-law. Merab, his eldest daughter, should have been the one given to David. She was the promised bride. But Saul regretted his promise, postponed the marriage and eventually gave Merab to another man.

Then, because of his jealousy over the fact that David had become a hero, he devised a plan whereby David would be killed by the Philistines. Knowing that Michal loved David, Saul asked David for a dowry for Michal in the form of the foreskins of 100 Philistines. David slew 200, forcing Saul to give Michal to him.

Still bent on destroying David, Saul had David's house surrounded. His messengers were ready to slay David at daybreak, but Michal became suspicious and let David down through a window so he could escape.

She tricked her father's men by putting a hair-covered image in David's bed. Saul accused Michal of deception. In response, Michal pretended that David had threatened to kill her if she didn't help him escape.

After this incident, Michal's love for David evidently waned. No doubt she was tired of his being a fugitive, always on the run from her father. Once, while David was gone, she allowed her father to give her to another man.

After Saul's death, his cousin Abner made arrangements to assist David in taking over the kingship of the nation. In the process, David asked that Michal be returned to him. She was willing—probably not because she loved him, but because she saw it as a way to the throne.

The final picture we have of David and Michal is very sad. After making Jerusalem his capital, David wanted to bring the sacred ark of the covenant into the city. On of the day of the ark's return from the hands of the Philistines David was so joyful that he sang and danced through the streets as he led the procession. Michal watched him from a window and, when she saw him so jubilant, despised him in her heart. Although she had once loved him and even risked her own life for his safety, she now hated him for his unabashed enthusiasm for the Lord.

Nursing her contempt, she waited until David came home. When they met, she sneeringly remarked, *"How glorious was the King of Israel today, who uncovered himself today in the eyes of the handmaids of his servants, as one of the vain fellows shamelessly uncovereth himself."* David was curt in his reply. He made it clear he was not ashamed of what he had done "before the Lord," who had chosen him rather than any of Saul's children, to reign as King.

We assume this was the end of their relationship. *"Michal, the daughter of Saul, had no child unto the days of her death."* She ended her days without the love and companionship of a husband, raising her dead sister's five children, all of whom were ultimately beheaded (as we learned in the story of Rizpah).

140

LESSONS FOR MICHAL
Being Unequally-Yoked

David and Michal's relationship began as a fairy tale—she, the lovely young princess, he, the handsome hero with a very promising future as King. Michal, however, is always referred to as the "daughter of Saul," not the "wife of David." She never truly submitted to the new King. She was not "transferred" from the old kingdom to the new.

When couples don't find their expectations fulfilled, they often become disappointed in one another, angry at God and bitter within themselves. This is especially true if they aren't of the same kingdom. They're unequally yoked. II Corinthians 6:14 and 15 (Amplified) says, *"Do not be unequally yoked up with unbelievers...do not make mismated alliances with them, or come under a different yoke with them (inconsistent with your faith). For what partnership have right living and right standing with God with iniquity and lawlessness? Or how can light fellowship with darkness? What harmony can there be between Christ and Belial (the devil)? Or what has a believer in common with an unbeliever?"* In light of this Scripture, let us consider the following questions:

(1) Why should you, as a Christian, not date or marry an unbeliever?

Every marriage begins with a single date. Because it becomes difficult to break a relationship once it is begun, one should ask for the Lord's wisdom *before* dating. In an unequal relationship there is always competition and compromise. It becomes increasingly difficult to stay true to one's commitment to God because there are continual conflicts in loyalties. If the unbeliever isn't willing to make a commitment to God before marriage, it's very unlikely he will after marriage.

(2) What should you, as a Christian, do if you're already married to an unbeliever?

Such a wife will spend much time in prayer, asking the Lord for wisdom, guidance, and strength. She won't enjoy the intimate oneness with her husband that's possible with couples who both know the Lord, nor is she free to leave and begin a new relationship with someone else—even a Christian. God will use her situation to work His nature in her, if she will allow it. And she'll find that He will be her true husband, caring for all her needs, as she submits to the one she married.

I Corinthians 7:10-17 In summary, the instructions given here for the one married to an unbeliever: _____

_____

_____

John 8:42-44 If one doesn't belong to Jesus, his father is __

_____

_____

Matthew 6:24 When one tries to serve two masters, _____

_____

_____

Colossians 1:13 When one accepts Jesus and His work of atonement, he's _____

_____

_____

Romans 6:8-13 If we are in Christ, _____

_____

_____

Making Choices

How do we make life choices? If we want the Lord's wisdom and guidance, we'll make our decisions according to specific guidelines. All three guidelines must agree before we can have a clear "go ahead" with our decision.

(1) Does the decision agree with the Word of God?

This doesn't mean just one verse out of context, rather, agreement with the *whole* counsel of God. God's Word is always confirmed, even in His own Word. II Corinthians 13:1 and Deuteronomy 19:15 both tell us that in the mouth of two or three witnesses, every word is established. We can see an illustration of this, also, in the advice concerning those unequally yoked. II Corinthians 6:14 and 15 tell us that we aren't to be unequally yoked with unbelievers. I Corinthians 7:13-15 confirm that when one is yoked with unbelievers, it becomes a very difficult situation. We need to always pray that God will show us direction *from His Word.*

(2) What are the circumstances saying?

Both God and Satan can arrange circumstances in our lives. If we have prayed to God about specific direction, we must believe that He is the One arranging the details of our lives. We're told in Psalm 37:5 to *"Commit thy way unto the Lord; trust also in him, and he shall bring it to pass."* Proverb 16:9 says, *"A man's heart deviseth his way; but the Lord directeth his steps."*

(3) Do you have peace in your heart?

God's ways aren't our ways, and our thoughts aren't His thoughts (Isaiah 55:8 and 9). But His Holy Spirit can give us a peace that passes understanding when we're in God's will. Therefore, if we have anxiety or are "uptight" after making a decision, we should take another look at it and seek the Lord some more.

Thus, we see how the Trinity is involved in helping us make life choices. Jesus is the Word of God; our Heavenly Father arranges our circumstances as we seek His will; the Holy Spirit confirms our decisions with the fruit of peace.

If we sincerely submit to all three guidelines, and still think we've made a wrong decision, we can be assured that God will (if we allow Him) work all things together for good. Romans 8:28 assures us of this. God wants to lead us. He wants us to choose Him and His ways. He has a plan for our lives. He's pleased when we seek His will.

THE FAILURE, AND THEN SUCCESS, OF BATHSHEBA

(Based on II Samuel 11:1-12 and 24; I Kings 1:11-31; 2:13-19; I Chronicles 3:5)

Bathsheba was the wife of Uriah, the most loyal of David's men. After the murder of Uriah, she became the wife of David and the mother of five of his sons.

Her relationship with David begins with the sentence, *"But David tarried still in Jerusalem."* The Israelites were at war with the Ammonites. The King should have been with his army. But David had become either self-indulgent or weary of war, so he decided to stay home and not fight the battle of the Lord. In so doing, he put himself in the position of being open to temptation, and soon found himself in trouble.

While out on the rooftop one evening, he looked over at a nearby house and happened to see Bathsheba preparing for a bath. He sent a messenger to her door, asking that she come see him.

It wasn't long before they committed adultery in the king's bedchamber while Bathsheba's husband, Uriah, was in the forefront of battle.

In time, Bathsheba discovered that she was pregnant. Learning of her condition, David immediately ordered Uriah home, hoping that he would spend the night with his wife. But Uriah was a very proper soldier and refused any physical contact with his wife while he was still on duty.

David's clever plan failed. He sent Uriah back into battle, this time with the order that he be sent to the front line. Thus, as David had hoped, Uriah was killed. Now murder was added to David's sins of lust, adultery and deceit.

After the accustomed period of mourning, Bathsheba became David's wife. The child of their adulterous union was born, only to die within a week of his birth. David was deeply grieved over the sickness and death of the child. Both he and Bathsheba must have experienced much agony, knowing the death of their son was a divine judgment against their sin.

When the prophet Nathan confronted David with his sin, the King openly admitted he had sinned against God.

We aren't told of Bathsheba's repentance. She must have seen her sin as well, and confessed it, for God blessed her and David with another son, Solomon, who succeeded David as King. Bathsheba must have raised her son in the fear of the Lord. He came to the throne a God-fearing man.

After the birth of Solomon, we don't hear of Bathsheba again until, at the time of David's death, she reminded him of the promise to make Solomon king. Bathsheba's success was that, although she committed adultery, she was forgiven and restored by God.

LESSONS FROM BATHSHEBA
Forgiveness

When we hear the story of David and Bathsheba, we usually think of David's sins of adultery and murder. But what about Bathsheba? What was her sin? What about her forgiveness?

To keep these questions, let us look at Romans 14. Paul instructs us to keep from putting a stumbling block in our brother's way. In other words, we shouldn't do anything which will make another person sin or keep him from a right relationship with God.

We're usually aware of our witness before unbelievers.

We're anxious to set a good example so we might win them for the Lord. It's interesting to note, however, that Paul reminds us not to cause our *fellow believers* to stumble.

How do we do this? Bathsheba simply didn't "pull the shades." Her immodesty invoked lust in David and, when he called her to his palace, she evidently didn't have the courage to remind him that she was married. She caused her own king to stumble by her actions.

Sin, whether it's obvious or subtle, separates us from God and from each other. The only means of true reconciliation is through forgiveness.

We've previously seen how God provided for our forgiveness through the atoning blood of Jesus Christ. He promises us in His Word that, *"If we confess our sins, he is faithful and just to forgive us our sins, and to cleanse us from all unrighteousness"* (I John 1:9). Not only that, but God forgets them as well. According to Jeremiah 31:34, *"I will forgive their iniquity, and I will remember their sins no more."* David's *repentance* (in Psalm 51) for his sin of adultery and murder is what made him a man after God's own heart (Acts 13:22).

Because of God's forgiveness toward us, we should forgive others. Yet asking for and receiving forgiveness from God is often easier than asking for and receiving forgiveness from each other—especially those with whom we're closely associated, such as husbands and wives. But asking for and receiving forgiveness is absolutely essential in the marriage relationship.

In order for forgiveness to be fully realized, it must be *both* asked for and received. If we wait until we *feel* like forgiving or asking for forgiveness we'll never do it. Instead, forgiveness must be *an act of the will*, asked for or received with the expectation that God will provide the *feeling* later.

What is to be the meaure of our forgiveness of one another?

Luke 6:37 and 38 _____

_____

_____

Matthew 18:21 and 22 _____

_____

_____

Luke 17:3 and 4 _____

_____

_____

Ephesians 4:32 _____

_____

_____

Some of the benefits of forgiving others are:

Mark 11:25 and 26 _____

144

II Corinthians 2:7-11 _____

_____

_____

James 5:15 and 16 _____

_____

_____

WOMEN
IN THE BIBLE

SUMMARY

Two of David's several wives give us insight into marital relationships. Michal was *unequally yoked* with David. She remained her father's daughter, uncommitted to David's God. Bathsheba became David's wife through an adulterous relationship which God judged. The lesson we learn from their relationship is that of the need for forgiveness—both from God and each other. Despite these imperfect relationships, God still called David a man after His own heart, because David acknowledged his sins and repented of them.

MODERN EXAMPLE

Debbie was born to an unwed mother who eventually gave her up for adoption at age six. Having been knocked around from one bad situation to another, she finally found security in the home of a Christian family. They taught her well. They also gave her the love she so desperately needed. Through their example and sharing, Debbie accepted Jesus and grew in His Word.

As she entered adolescence, she began to wonder about her "real" mother—what kind of person she was and if she had ever found the Lord. Though she never made contact with her mother, Debbie's concern and compassion motivated her to reach out to the lost and lonely.

So, it wasn't surprising when, in her late teens, she met a young man who seemed to need the help and care she had to offer. Also of illegitimate birth, he'd practically raised himself while his mother worked hard to make ends meet. Curt wasn't a Christian. In fact, he was resentful towards God for the lack of homelife he'd seen other children enjoy.

Debbie was aware of his unbelief, but she thought that, through her love and attention, she could help him find the Lord as well as the companionship he'd always wanted. Against her adopted parent's counsel, she pursued the relationship. Within a few months she and Curt were married.

In an attempt to please Debbie, Curt began attending church with her. But the more she wanted to get involved, the less interested he seemed. To keep peace, she stayed home with him. The result? By the time their baby was born, she was almost entirely out of fellowship with other Christians.

As Debbie began to feel the responsibility of raising her child, she began to feel the increased need of spiritual food herself. But when she thought of the disappointment she was to her parents, and of her back-slidden condition with the Lord, she felt guilty. Feeling bad about herself, she blamed Curt. It wasn't long before their relationship disintegrated so much she was hardly aware of the verbal and even physical abuse she was receiving from him. Whatever he did only seemed to justify the guilt she felt within and confirmed the low self-esteem she now had.

On several different occasions, Debbie took her daughter and left Curt, only to return when she became lonely. They would then renew their commitment to each other and things would go along fine for a while. Then she would become discouraged again as he refused to get counsel and spiritual help. He would become angry, and the abuse would begin all over again—and Debbie would allow it, to salve her guilty conscience. Then she would leave, become lonely, return to Curt, and the cycle would begin again.

There are times when it seems as though things will be better, and then the cycle begins again. Debbie and Curt continually reap the consequences of being unequally-yoked.

WHAT DO YOU THINK?

1. What problems of the past have your husband and/or you brought into your marriage? How have you dealt with them? _____

_____

_____

2. What can you do when problems arise in your marriage which you know to be your fault? _____

_____

_____

3. Are you unequally yoked? How do you deal with this?

_____

_____

4. Have you and your husband learned how to give and receive forgiveness? _____

_____

_____

EVALUATE YOURSELF

1. In what ways are you implementing the principles learned from Michal and Bathsheba? _____

_____

_____

2. In what ways are you failing to implement the principles learned from them? _____

_____

_____

3. What do you need to do to change? _____

_____

_____

4. How will you do it? _____

_____

_____

Lesson 16
Witch of Endor and Jezebel

An Example of the Occult

"Let no one be found among you who sacrifices his son or daughter in the fire, who practices divination or sorcery, interprets omens, engages in witchcraft, or casts spells, or who is a medium or spiritist or who consults the dead. Anyone who does these things is detestable to the Lord..."

Deuteronomy 18:10-12

SETTING THE STAGE

From the moment Satan fell and became god of this world (II Corinthians 4:4), there has been an ongoing spiritual battle between the forces of evil and those of God. Jesus came to earth to destroy the works of the devil, as well as to pay the price of man's sin (I John 3:8). Those who become children of God, by accepting the atoning work of Jesus' shed blood, are given the authority over Satan as well as weapons to wage war against him.

However, man can still open himself up to the power of Satan and his host by submitting to the devices Satan continues to offer. We call these means the *occult*. They include psychics, fortunetellers, horoscopes, palm readers, Ouija boards and certain other games, levitation, fetishes, idols, and anything that symbolizes or recognizes a power other than God. Even though they appear to be supernatural in effect, they are opposed to God's power and the truth of His Word. They seem to be harmless but are, in truth, counterfeit.

In both the Witch of Endor and Queen Jezebel, we have stories of women who were involved with the occult. They tapped into a power other than God. We'll not only see what we can learn from them, we'll also look at other things the Word has to say concerning the subjects of the occult and witchcraft.

THE COUNTERFEIT SUCCESS OF THE WITCH OF ENDOR
(Based on I Samuel 28)

When anointed by Samuel to be king, Saul was "head and shoulders" above his fellowmen. But rebellion and disobedience reduced him to a physical and spiritual wreck. When faced with an approaching confrontation with the Philistines, Saul became frightened and cried out to God, but God didn't answer. He'd rejected Saul because of Saul's previous disobedience. Driven by despair, Saul sought to consult the prophet

Samuel, the prophet who had helped him earlier in his reign. Samuel was now dead, but Saul hoped to find a "medium" who could bring back Samuel's spirit. (Actually, there shouldn't have been any of these around. Saul, himself, had earlier banned them from the land because they were an abomination to God!)

The witch of Endor was introduced to Saul by his servants. She had a *familiar spirit* which was supposed to help her compel a departed spirit (actually a demon in disguise) to revisit the earth and submit to questioning. The witch of Endor knew the practice of her art was forbidden. She asked her visitor if he were trying to "lay a snare" for her. Saul assured her she wouldn't be punished.

When she asked Saul who he wanted her to bring up for him, he told her he wanted Samuel. When Samuel appeared, the witch became frightened. She now recognized Saul and realized that another power had brought the real Samuel forth.

God allowed Samuel to speak to Saul, for He wanted Samuel to tell Saul, *"Because you did not obey the Lord or carry out his fierce wrath against the Amalekites, the Lord has done this to you today. The Lord will hand over both Israel and you to the Philistines, and tomorrow you and your sons will be with me. The Lord will also hand over the army of Israel to the Philistines."* (I Samuel 28:18 and 19 NIV).

This proved too true the next day when Saul committed suicide by falling on his own sword after the battle went against him.

The witch of Endor seemed to have come out looking good. It appeared that she brought Samuel back for Saul. She was compassionate when he heard the bad news, and insisted on fixing him a nice meal. True to the characteristics of Satan, she appeared as *an angel of light.*

LESSONS FROM THE WITCH OF ENDOR
The Occult

All forms of fortunetelling, magical practice, and spiritism are an abomination to God. The seriousness of this offense is seen in the case of King Saul. He fell under God's curse, was rejected as ruler of Israel, and was put to death by divine decree because he attended a seance and sought help from a medium! I Chronicles 10:13 and 14 says, *"Saul died for his transgression which he committed against the Lord, even against the word of the Lord, which he kept not, and also for asking counsel of one that had a familiar spirit, to inquire of it; And inquired not of the Lord: therefore he slew him, and turned the kingdom unto David the son of Jesse."*

What Saul did was against God's Word. In Deuteronomy 18:9 God warns not to practice the abominations of heathen nations. Scriptures say there should be no person who uses divination (fortune-teller), no observers of times (astrologers), interpreters of dreams (soothsayers), magicians, witches, charmers (hypnotists), mediums, psychics, or necromancers (mediums who consult the dead). Scripture says *all* who do these things *are an abomination unto the Lord.*

Here we see methods by which some seek to unveil hidden

150

knowledge, predict future events, uncover secret wisdom, and exercise supernatural powers. In contrast to the methods pagans use to uncover secrets of the spiritual realm, God's people learn the things they need to know concerning the future and His will for them, not by discovery through methods of divination and occult practices, but by revelation. This comes by His Word through His spokesmen, the prophets. Thus, we are forbidden, in Scripture, to seek information or guidance from unauthorized, unscriptural sources. The believer is admonished to ask of *God* (James 1:5), because the secret things belong to Him, (Deuteronomy 29:29).

Modern-day occultists had their ancient heathen counterparts in necromancers, consulters of spirits, wizards, soothsayers, diviners, and sorcerers, among other things. Man has always been intrigued with the idea of uncovering hidden knowledge which belongs only to God. Satan has always accommodated such seekers with substitutes for truth and counterfeits for genuine revelation, thus deceiving the gullible who think that the supernatural belongs only to God.

God's Word clearly condemns all forms of occultism, *"They which do such things shall not inherit the kingdom of God "* (Galatians 5:19-21), nor enter into God's presence (Revelation 22:14 and 15), but *"...shall have their part in the lake of fire which burneth with fire and brimstone" (Revelation 21:8)*. God not ony forbade participation in all forms of occultism, calling it spiritually defiling (Leviticus 19:31), but made such disobedience punishable by death (Exodus 22:18) and sufficient grounds for rejection of that soul by God (Leviticus 20:6). Those who defile themselves in this manner are an abomination to the Lord (Deuteronomy 18:9-12).

Let's now consider other scriptures in light of the above.

Exodus 20:3 and 5 Occult involvement breaks which commandment? _____

_____

_____

Deuteronomy 6:13-15 What happens when God's people seek after other gods? _____

_____

_____

Deuteronomy 17:1-5 What acts demanded death by stoning?

_____

_____

Leviticus 19:26 and 31 What did God command? _____

_____

_____

Leviticus 20:6 and 27 What deserved punishment by death?

_____

II Kings 21:5 and 6 How did Manasseh provoke the Lord's anger? _____

_____

Isaiah 8:19 To whom should man look for wisdom and guidance? _____

_____

Jeremiah 27:9 and 10; 29:8 and 9 What do false prophets, diviners, etc., do? _____

_____

Malachi 3:5 Whom will God judge? _____

_____

I Timothy 4:1-5 What can we expect in the last days? _____

_____

Galatians 1:6-9 Of what are we warned to beware? _____

_____

II Corinthians 11:4 and 13-15 Of what are we warned here?

_____

Revelation 21:8 What is the end result of those involved in the occult? _____

_____

Occultism in New Testament Times

Those who have become involved in any form of occultism will, eventually, suffer Satanic oppression in some manner. Through we aren't specifically told in Scripture that the demon-possessed to whom Jesus ministered were that way because they'd been involved in the occult, this could have been among the reasons. When one opens himself to demonic power, demons use that person and can possess or oppress him.

Evil spirits (demons) can oppress people in various ways.

152

There are blind spirits, deaf spirits, epileptic spirits, deceiving spirits, lying spirits, spirits of pride, lust, fear, suicide, and others. Their primary intention, as disembodied spirits, is to oppress or possess a person congenial to their particular nature in order to escape detection.

Oppression resulting from occult involvement, means that one or more of these spirits are afflicting the victim with any of the many forms of mental, physical, emotional, or psychic ailments and distresses. **On the other hand, we must not conclude that these symptoms automatically presuppose demonic origin. The fact is that, through the occult, one opens himself up to the** *possibility* **of such ailments.**

Let us now look at some incidents which occurred in the early Church and see how occultism was dealt with then. Read the following stories and see what happened.

Acts 8:5-25 _____

_____

_____

Acts 13:6-11 _____

_____

_____

Acts 16:16-18 _____

_____

_____

Acts 19:11-19 _____

_____

_____

Deliverance from the Effects of the Occult

Those who have allowed themselves to become bound by these dark powers can only be freed by confession of occult sins and renunciation of Satan and his work in their lives. There must be a direct command to Satan himself to depart in the name of Jesus. This can be done with true repentance to God and a simple statement to Satan such as, "Satan, I hereby renounce you and all your works in my life. I command you, in Jesus' name, to depart and trouble me no more. I hereby refuse to participate in any of your activities any longer. I am covered by the blood of Jesus Christ, my Lord."

If you still feel the need of more ministry, consult your pastor.

Some present-day occult practices include: astrology, clairvoyance, spiritualism (communication with the dead), ESP, eastern religions, Edgar Cayce, evolution, free masonry, fortune-telling, handwriting analysis, hypnotism, horoscopes, levitation, mediums, magic charms, numerology, Ouija boards, Dungeons and Dragons game, palm reading, pagan artifacts, reincarnation, religious science, scientology, drugs, seances, tarot cards, telepathy, transcendental meditation, water witching, yoga, and the signs of the zodiac.

THE COUNTERFEIT SUCCESS OF JEZEBEL
(Based on I Kings 16:31; 18:4-19: 19:1 and 2; 21:1-25; II Kings 9)

Jezebel was the daughter of Ethbaal of the Zidonians, who was both king and priest of Baal worshippers. The gods of the Phoenicians were Baal and Ashtaroth. Ahab installed 450 of their priests in a magnificent temple which he built in Samaria. Another 450 priests were honored in a sanctuary that Jezebel built for them. Jezebel came from an idolatrous nation when she married Ahab, king of Northern Israel. In marrying her Ahab sinned. The nation Israel suffered for it.

Jezebel was no ordinary woman. Savage and relentless, she carried out her wicked schemes. She was persuasive, domineering, and talented. Not content with establishing idol worship in her own country, she tried to convert Israel to Baal worship and tried to drive out the true prophets of Jehovah.

After causing three years of famine in the land, God sent Elijah to King Ahab to confront him with his sin of forsaking the Lord and turning to Baalism. Elijah challenged God's people to choose between God and Baal. A contest was held on Mt. Carmel between Elijah and the prophets of Baal. Elijah placed a bullock upon an altar and challenged the 450 prophets of Baal to do the same. They would then pray and see whose god would send fire to consume the sacrifice. The God of Elijah responded, though the prophets of Baal prayed all day. The people of God then fell on their faces proclaiming, "The Lord, he is the God; the Lord, he is the God." The 450 prophets of Baal were slain; then rain came upon the land. But Jezebel became so incensed that Elijah had to flee for his life.

Ahab was like a puppet in Jezebel's hands. The tragedy of Naboth and his vineyard reveals what a despicable woman she was. Naboth owned a vineyard next to the palace. Ahab wanted it for a garden, but Naboth refused to sell or exchange his inheritance. When Jezebel saw Ahab pouting, she determined to get the vineyard for him.

She ordered a public fast, at which Naboth was brought into the center of attention. Jezebel arranged to have Naboth falsely accused of blasphemy. He was found guilty and stoned to death. Then Ahab took possession of the vineyard.

The Lord then told Elijah to go to Ahab and give him the message that *"in the place where dogs licked the blood of Naboth shall dogs lick thy blood"* (I Kings 21:19). This prophecy was fulfilled shortly afterwards, when war broke out between Israel and the Syrians, and Ahab received a fatal wound while riding in a chariot. The blood-soaked chariot was taken to the spring which ran through Naboth's vineyard where dogs came and licked the bloody water.

Concerning Jezebel, Elijah said, *"The dogs shall eat Jezebel by the wall of Jezreel"* (I Kings 21:23). Jehu was appointed avenger for Jehovah and set out to bring justice to the land. He slew Jezebel's son and grandson. Grandmother though she was, Jezebel took time to arrange her hair and paint her face. She then watched out a window for Jehu to pass by. When he reached the palace, Jehu looked up at the window. Jezebel taunted him and he ordered her eunuchs to throw her down.

As she fell from the window, her blood sprinkled the walls. When her body landed on the ground the horses trampled it. The triumphant Jehu entered the palace over Jezebel's dead body. Later he ordered her buried, but dogs had already eaten her flesh. The only things left of her were her skull, her feet, and the palms of her hands!

LESSONS FROM JEZEBEL
Witchcraft—Manipulation

Jezebel not only submitted herself to Baal, but used her own power to manipulate people and situations. We see this in the story of the purchase of Naboth's vineyard. She schemed to get it for her husband through trickery and lies.

Though we usually think of witchcraft as calling upon the powers of Satan and his host, we can also see that it is using any power opposed to the power of God, including that of our own flesh. In fact, Galatians 5:20 calls witchcraft a work of the flesh. We try to be as God by manipulating people and situations into doing what *we* want. In doing this, we don't allow God to be in control. In fact, we become a barrier between others and God. We put ourselves on the throne, instead of letting Jesus be Lord and allowing the Holy Spirit to do His work.

Women are especially prone to manipulate. As a result, men often become "spiritual dropouts." Thus, they can't be the authority that God ordained unless the woman relinquishes her control. This is a most difficult lesson for women, but perhaps the study of Jezebel will help us see the consequences of manipulation and determine to "let go and let God."

In seeing witchcraft as a work of the flesh, (using the power of our flesh instead of submitting to the Spirit of God) how do we see manipulation at work in the lives of the following Bible women? In each case, what was the result?

Eve (Genesis 3:1-6) _____

_____

_____

Sarah (Genesis 16:1-12) _____

_____

_____

Rebekah (Genesis 27:5-17) _____

_____

_____

Potiphar's wife (Genesis 39:6-20) _____

_____

_____

Delilah (Judges 16:4-20) _____

Zeresh (Esther 5:14) _____

_____

_____

Herodias and Salome (Mark 6:17-28) _____

_____

_____

Sapphira (and Ananias) (Acts 5:1-10) _____

_____

_____

Revelation 2:18-29 warns us about Jezebel, as one who seduces the saints. We are to beware of this trait in others, as well as ourselves, lest we find that we're participating in Satan's kingdom of darkness instead of God's kingdom of light.

SUMMARY

Though Jesus destroyed all the works of the devil at the cross and we can claim protection through His shed blood, we can still open ourselves up to Satan by submitting to the devices he offers. We call these the *occult*. It includes horoscopes, levitation, psychics, fortune-telling, magical practices, spiritism—anything which symbolizes or recognizes a power other than God. Both the witch of Endor and Jezebel tapped into sources of power other than the one true God. We learn of God's judgement from their experiences of occult involvement.

MODERN EXAMPLE

Don was pastoring a small church in a large city during the late sixties. With the hippie movement at its height, he felt unprepared in meeting the needs of the young people within the congregation. Part of this was due to his liberal seminary education. It had diluted his faith in God and included no teaching on Satan at all.

When the church custodian told Don of a healing he had received due to the supernatural powers of a certain woman, Don was intrigued. Soon he, too, visited the woman. She seemed to be a Christian. She talked of God and of the need for young people to get their lives straightened out. In fact, she had many answers, as well as miracles, to share. Before long, Don was taking some of the church young people to meet with her. And they seemed to benefit from her counsel. Though there were times when he detected a bitterness toward God, the help the woman gave overshadowed the doubts Don began to have.

Because he was searching for answers himself, Don met

156

with other people, including pastors. Some thought this woman was legitimate. Others obviously didn't.

Things came to a head one Sunday afternoon when Don needed some information and decided to call her. An elderly woman in the congregation was extremely burdened by the disappearance of her granddaughter.

Don called his friend and asked if she could tell him anything of the girl's whereabouts. After a lengthy silence, she said that she could—that the girl was with a hippie commune in another state, but that she was alright (all of which later proved to be true).

Thanking her for the information, Don closed the telephone conversation by mentioning the fact that, since there was nothing going on at his church that evening, he would be visiting a certain other church. Immediately, her voice flared and she nearly shouted, "You won't find what you're looking for there!" Stunned, Don hung up the receiver and wondered at her outburst of anger, especially when she'd apparently been so pleased that he had called concerning the girl.

After a call to the grandmother with the news, he went to the church he had mentioned. There, his eyes were opened. At the close of the service, a loving group of people ministered the truth of God's word to him. They shared concerning the reality and tactics of Satan, as well as the need for discernment. Through the Spirit of Truth, Don was shown that this woman was a "medium," one who appeared as "an angel of light." By the time he finished late that night, he knew exactly why she had become so upset when she discovered where he was going that evening.

Of course, Don had to acknowledge his ignorance of God's Word, as well as repent for leading the young people astray. When Don later called the medium to tell her he wanted nothing more to do with her, she was furious. The mild-mannered woman who had enticed him by her supernatural powers, had been exposed for the tool of Satan which she truly was. Don was free. Since that time, Don has been very careful to test the spirits while claiming the victory Jesus has already won through His shed blood.

WHAT DO YOU THINK?

1. Have you ever been involved in any occult activity? If so, have you repented of this and been set free? _____

_____

_____

2. What do you do to prevent occult influence over your life, your home, your family? _____

_____

_____

3. Do you try to manipulate people and situations? How can you remedy this? _____

_____

_____

WOMEN IN THE BIBLE

EVALUATE YOURSELF

1. In what ways are you implementing the principles learned from the witch of Endor and Jezebel? _____

   _____

   _____

2. In what ways are you failing to implement the principles learned from them? _____

   _____

   _____

3. What do you need to do to change? _____

   _____

   _____

4. How will you do it? _____

   _____

   _____

Widow of Zarephath, Widow with Pot of Oil, Shunammite Woman

An Example of Responding to God's Word

"But he that received seed into the good ground is he that heareth the word, and understandeth it; which also beareth fruit...."

Matthew 13:23

SETTING THE STAGE

God gave us His written Word (the *logos*) through men moved by the Holy Spirit. His Word is for all who will believe it. However, as we find in the parable in Matthew 13:1-23, not everyone's heart is prepared to receive the Word. Some of the Word falls by the wayside. Some falls into hearts that are too hard or full of the cares of this life. But some is received by faith into prepared hearts and accomplishes what God desires.

As the Holy Spirit anoints a particular Word, we can receive it as God's utterance to us. This is the *rhema* word of God. As we are obedient to it, we can be assured of its promise, and as we are assured of the promise, we must not only obey the Word, but continue to claim it until it's fulfilled.

The widow of Zarephath did, in faith, what Elijah asked her to do, and God met her every need. The widow with the pot of oil obeyed the Word of God through Elisha, even though it seemed foolish. Again, God was faithful and abundantly supplied more than she asked. The woman of Shunem provided lodging for the prophet Elisha and came to trust in the word he brought from the Lord. She was then able to receive it by faith. When it came to pass, she worshipped God.

The Shunammite woman obeyed Elisha and as a result, her family prospered.

We each have a choice as to how we'll respond to the Word of God. The choice we make determines whether or not it comes true for us.

The *Word* of God

There are two terms for the *word* of God. One is *logos*. The other is *rhema*.

The *logos* is something said (or thought)—past tense. This is essentially God's *written* Word, applicable to everyone as His truth. God said it; it's an established fact "which lives and abides forever." (I Peter 1:23). It's this Word of God which we can choose to hear or not to hear (Acts 4:4).

The *logos* is the Word described in the parable of the sower in Matthew 13. A sower went out to sow. Some of his seeds fell by the wayside, and birds came and ate them up. Some fell in stony places and, because there was no depth of soil, the plants which came forth soon withered and died. Some fell among thorns, which eventually choked them. Others fell into good ground, and brought forth much fruit.

Jesus explained the seeds were like the Word of God—the *logos*, God inspired to be written so that we might believe. This Word of God can fall into unprepared hearts and the devil will snatch it away. It can fall into shallow lives and, because it doesn't take root, withers and dies. Or, it can be received into hearts and then choked by the cares of this world. The final possibility is that the Word can be received with open heart, take root, and bear much fruit.

The *rhema* Word of God has a different meaning. It is an *utterance*—present tense. It's the Word of God (logos) which has been quickened by the Holy Spirit. In the rhema Word, we find God's personal word to us for a specific situation. As we receive it by faith and act upon it, we are assured it will come to pass.

This is the word which Paul speaks of in II Corinthians 13:1 when he says that the Word will be established in the mouth of two or three witnesses. It's the Word of Ephesians 6:17, described as the sword of the Spirit. It's the word of Matthew 4:4, which proceeds out of the mouth of God and gives us His Bread (Jesus), by which we live.

John 8:47 says, *"He that is of God heareth God's words (rhema); ye therefore hear them not, because ye are not of God."* We must believe in Jesus as we allow God, by His Holy Spirit, to give us the *rhema* word. It is available to only those who are of God and are open to His voice.

THE SUCCESS OF THE WIDOW OF ZAREPHATH

(Based on I Kings 17:8-24; Luke 4:25 and 26)

This widow, whose name is never given, lived in Sarepta, which belonged to King Zidon, Jezebel's father. When Israel was unsafe, Elijah found a welcome refuse in this heathen country. Ironically, it was the home of Jezebel, from whom he was fleeing.

Here, Elijah was directed by God, to stay with a widow.

160

Though she lived in a pagan land, it seems she knew something of the faith of the Hebrews before Elijah came to stay. No doubt, she knew even more about God as Elijah sojourned with her in her poor home.

The widow had a child to care for. With a few olive trees and a small barley field, she was able to eke out a frugal living.

When famine struck, she didn't know where the next meal would come from to keep the two of them alive.

Little did the distressed widow realize that deliverance was at hand in the form of a rough-looking stranger who appeared at her door.

When Elijah met the widow, she was gathering sticks to make a final scanty meal. Once this meal was eaten, there would be nothing to do but await death by starvation.

Although she came to speak of Elijah as "the man of God," there's no evidence that she recognized him as such when he came asking for water. But when Elijah told her to go on with the preparation of what she thought would be her last meal, she obeyed him. She even served him first, as he asked. How hope must have filled her heart when she saw fresh meal, and the empty oil cruse refilled. For nearly two years, the widow experienced a continuing miracle.

As time passed, she must have come to feel secure with Elijah. But one day when her son was suddenly seized with an illness and died, she once again knew despair. In her grief, she wondered if the boy's death was a form of divine judgment because of sin.

When she asked Elijah about it he said nothing except, "Give me thy son." The prophet took the lifeless body up to his chamber and asked God why He had allowed such a grief to overtake the widow who had been so kind to him. Three times he stretched himself upon the child and prayed most earnestly for the child to live again. For the mother downstairs it must have been an agonizing wait. But she was to witness another miracle when her son returned to life. This truly convinced her that Elijah was, indeed, a man of God.

It must have been a sad day when God called Elijah to leave the shelter and love of the widow's home and go to Ahab and pronounce an end to the three-year drought. The Bible doesn't tell us any more about the widow and her son. Yet Jesus mentioned her while in the synagogue in Nazareth. He said that, though He was sent to the Jewish people, He would be more easily accepted by the Gentiles, just as Elijah was accepted by the widow.

Let us now look at another widow who also was asked to obey by faith. As she obeyed a seemingly foolish command, God blessed her abundantly.

THE SUCCESS OF THE WIDOW WITH THE POT OF OIL

(Based on II Kings 4:1-7)

This bereaved woman was the widow of one of the prophet Elisha's pupils. As one of the "sons of the prophets," her husband hadn't been able to leave adequate provision for his family, and she was afraid that her two sons would be taken as payment for the debts she owed.

Elisha was deeply concerned about their welfare, so he asked her, "What do you have in your house?" When she replied that she had nothing but a pot of oil, he gave her a strange order. He instructed her to borrow pots and pans from her friends and neighbors.

Then, she and her two sons were to go back home and close the door. There, they were to pour olive oil from the jars into the pots and pans, setting them aside as they were filled.

She did what he instructed. Her sons brought the pots and pans to her, and she filled one after another, until every container was full to the brim. When she ran out of pots and pans, the oil stopped flowing.

Elisha then told her to go sell the oil and pay her debts. He assured her that not only would she now be out of debt, but she would even have enough money to live on.

THE SUCCESS OF THE SHUNAMMITE WOMAN
(Based on II Kings 4:8-37; 8:1-6)

A prominent woman in the city of Shunem once invited Elisha into her home to eat. After that, he stopped in whenever he passed that way, so the woman and her husband prepared a room just for the prophet.

Once when he was staying there, he told his servant to express his appreciation for the room and ask what he could do in return. Though the woman said she couldn't think of anything, the servant noted that she really wanted a son. So he reported this to Elisha. Elisha, himself, then talked to the woman and told her she would have a son in about a year. Though she couldn't believe it would happen, she did become pregnant and have a son, just as Elisha predicted.

One day several years later, the child went to the field to see his father. While there, he complained of a terrible headache, so the father had a servant take the boy home—where he soon died. The woman of Shunem carried her son up to Elisha's bed and shut the door, then sent word to her husband that she wanted to find Elisha.

She saddled a donkey and went to find the prophet. As she approached Mt. Carmel, Elisha saw her coming and told his servant to go meet her. When she finally reached Elisha, she fell to the ground and told him what had happened. She also told him that she wouldn't return home without him. So Elisha and his servant went with her.

The servant reached the child first and laid his staff upon the boy's face, but nothing happened. He told Elisha that the boy was, indeed, dead.

However, when Elisha arrived he went to the room and closed the door. There he prostrated himself upon the boy's body, with his mouth over the boy's mouth. The child began to grow warm again! Elisha did it again. This time the boy sneezed and opened his eyes.

Elisha sent for the woman and gave her back her son. She fell to the floor at his feet, then picked up her son and went out.

Later, Elisha told the woman to take her family and move to another country because there would be a famine in Israel for

162

seven years. They moved to the land of the Philistines. After the famine was over, they returned to Israel. She went to the King to see about getting her house and land back. As she entered, she found the king asking Elisha's servant about some of the great things the prophet had done. The servant told him about bringing a boy back to life. Needless to say, the servant was surprised to find the boy's mother standing there, just as she was surprised to hear him telling the story. When the king asked if the story was true, she told him that it was. He then directed that everything be restored to her, plus the value of any crops harvested in her absence.

Faith

The widow of Zarephath is an example of one who had faith to believe that, if she obeyed what she was asked to do, the word given would come to pass. She acted before she saw any result. This is the faith of Hebrews 11:1, which says, *"Now faith is the substance of things hoped for, the evidence of things not seen."* The widow heard the word the Lord spoke through Elijah, and was given faith to believe for a miracle.

Romans 10:17 says that *"faith cometh by hearing, and hearing by the word of God."* Hearing the Word is what gives us faith, for faith is a gift of God, not something we can muster up ourselves.

John Wesley once said that the devil has given the church a substitute for faith, and that it is called "mental assent." Many people read God's Word and agree that it's true, but they're agreeing only with their minds. That isn't what gets the job done. It's heart faith, given of God, that is necessary.

"For verily I say unto you, That whosoever shall say unto this mountain, Be thou removed, and be thou cast into the sea; and shall not doubt in his heart, but shall believe that those things which he saith shall come to pass, he shall have whatsoever he saith" (Mark 11:23). Heart faith sees the answer as having already happened.

I Corinthians 2:14 tells us that the natural mind doesn't receive the things of the Spirit of God. Hebrews 4:2 says that the preaching of the Gospel doesn't profit those who don't hear it "mixed with faith." So faith must, in a sense, be mixed with the Word to receive faith.

This is why we *must* depend upon the Spirit of God to open and unveil the Word of God to us. We must allow Him to give us the gift of faith, which is mixed with the Word (logos) and then becomes rhema to us. As we act upon this word in faith, we have fulfillment. The Word gives us faith, and faith brings the Word to pass!

The importance of faith can't be minimized. Here's why:

*We can't be saved without faith. John 3:36; Luke 7:50
*We can't live victoriously over the world without faith.
  I John 5:4
*We can't please God without faith. Hebrews 11:6
*We can't pray without faith. James 1:6
*We can't have peace with God without faith. Romans 5:1
*We're justified by faith, not by works. Galatians 2:16
*We're to live by faith. Galatians 2:20
*We're made righteous by faith. Romans 10:1-4
*Christ dwells in our hearts by faith. Ephesians 3:17

*The Holy Spirit is received by faith. Galatians 3:2
*Whatever isn't of faith is sin! Romans 14:23

Obedience

Along with faith, comes obedience; obedience is an expression of one's faith. The widow of Zarephath could have said, "Yes, I have faith that the oil will increase as I pour it." But her faith would never have become reality until she actually *did* what she believed. Obedience is the works of James 2:17-26 which makes faith live.

Let's review the widow of Zarephath in light of her obedience by faith. When Elijah arrived at her home, he made some unusual requests:

(1) He asked for water in a land undergoing a drought.

(2) He asked for bread when there was only enough oil and meal to make one last meal for the widow and her son.

(3) He didn't seem to be suffering from malnutrition, he'd just come from the brook Cherith, where he was fed by ravens.

But as the widow obeyed, Elijah was not only fed, but she and her son were provided for for many days. Look up the following Scriptures and answer these questions. What seemingly foolish command was given? What happened when it was obeyed, by faith?

Genesis 6:1-22 _____

_____

_____

Genesis 12:1-4 _____

_____

_____

I Kings 17:2-6 _____

_____

_____

II Kings 5:1-14 _____

_____

_____

Matthew 17:24-27 _____

_____

_____

Acts 9:10-19 _____

_____

_____

Acts 10:9-48 and 11:2 _____

164

The Shunammite woman not only accepted the Word of God by faith and obeyed it, but she claimed it until it was fulfilled. She didn't let the promises made to her slip away. Let's see how she did this, using her story as an analogy of our own relationship with the Word of God in our lives. We will be the woman of Shunem; Elisha represents God's written Word.

(1) Just as this woman prepared a place for a continuing relationship with Elisha, we can prepare our hearts for continuing communion with God in His Word.

(2) Just as she didn't give in to negative confession when her son died, we can confess God's words of promise when problems arise.

(3) Just as she went directly to Elisha and reminded him of the promise he gave, we can claim God's Word to us until it comes to pass.

(4) Just as she accepted no substitute for Elisha, we must go straight to God's Word and accept no shortcuts devised by man.

(5) Just as she bowed to the ground in gratefulness when her son was restored to life, we can give God the glory when His promises to us are fulfilled.

SUMMARY

We each have a choice as to how we respond to God's Word. If our heart is hard, the Word won't take root and grow. If we're open to God, His Word can accomplish much in us. However, like the woman of Zarephath, we must take the Word by faith and act upon it. In the widow with the pot of oil, we find one who obeyed the Word even when it seemed foolish to her. Finally, in the Shunammite woman, we find the Word having power and result as she claimed its promises for her own. God speaks to us through His Word; we can accept it or not.

MODERN EXAMPLE

Through a rhema word, my husband and I were able to release a blessing upon the marriage of our oldest daughter and son-in-law.

As Christian parents, we had, over the years, prayed for the future mates of our children. But we were unprepared for the ways of God in the life of Donna, our oldest daughter.

While working on her Master's Degree at a secular university, Donna met an Iranian student whose company she particularly enjoyed. But because we were already concerned about her disappointment in losing another relationship as well as failing to get the job she had applied for following graduation, we cautioned her about getting too involved. We knew she was in a vulnerable position and, since another job didn't open up right away, we advised her to go somewhere to get some space. To please us, she decided to return to a city where we had formerly lived. After about six months there, she joined Youth With a Mission and went to Hawaii for training.

Meanwhile, with the relationship called off, the young man finished his schooling and began working in agriculture, his field. Nearly a year later however, Donna and he met at the wedding of mutual friends. They resumed their relationship, even though Donna was now living in Hawaii and Farshad lived not far from us, in California.

My husband and I knew there was nothing more we could say, but we were once again overwhelmed with fears and questions. Was he really a Christian? What would an inter-cultural marriage involve? Did he want to marry her just so he could gain citizenship—like others, whose stories we seemed to hear everywhere? What would our family and friends think with the Iranian hostage situation so fresh on everyone's minds?

Yes, we admitted, we could see the hand of God in bringing them together; but our hearts were in turmoil. We cried out to God for His wisdom and peace. He gave them in a most unusual way.

One day, my husband went apart to fast and pray while I worked on a writing assignment. I was reading the story of Samson in the 14th chapter of Judges. I thought it interesting that Samson and his parents were having a discussion concerning his desire to marry a woman of a different background and country. My eyes became glued to verse 4. *"But his father and mother knew not that it was of the Lord."* I could read no farther as God spoke to my heart. Before long I was in tears, confessing my fears to God and recommitting my daughter and her future to Him. When my husband returned, he told me that he felt we were to release her and give them our blessing.

Soon we sent a very special letter to Donna, and invited Farshad over to become acquainted. Thus it was, that we spent more time with Farshad during the first four months of their engagement than Donna did.

Since their wedding, we have seen some of what God wanted to do. They are now both on the staff of Youth With a Mission and take college students on short-term mission projects. Not only are they well-suited to working with students of all countries, but God has given them a special relationship with each other. And, their parents rejoice—all because of a rhema word which God gave through His logos.

WHAT DO YOU THINK?

1. What is your attitude toward God's Word, the Bible? Do you believe it to be entirely true? _____

_____

_____

2. How do you claim God's Word by faith for yourself? Have you seen its promises come true in your life? _____

_____

_____

3. Can you think of a time when you did what the Word said to do, even when it seemed foolish to you? What happened? _____

_____

_____

EVALUATE YOURSELF

1. In what ways are you implementing the principles learned from these three women? _____

_____

_____

2. In what ways are you failing to implement the principles learned from them? _____

_____

_____

3. What do you need to do to change? _____

_____

_____

4. How will you do it? _____

_____

_____

WOMEN IN THE BIBLE

Lesson 18

Naaman's Wife's Maid, Huldah, & the Queen of Sheba

An Example of Confessing the Word—Wisdom

"For verily I say unto you, that whosoever shall say unto this mountain, Be thou removed and be thou cast into the sea; and shall not doubt in his heart, but shall believe that those things which he saith shall come to pass; he shall have whatsoever he saith."

Mark 11:23

SETTING THE STAGE

In the last lesson we looked at how God wants us to respond to His Word in faith and obedience, claiming its reality in our own lives. We'll continue, in this lesson to look at our response to the Word of God. This time, we'll consider the ways we proclaim it, confessing and sharing it with others.

God's Word is powerful. Psalm 33:6 says that the Lord simply spoke, and the heavens and all the starry host were made His Word accomplishes what He pleases. (Isaiah 55:11).

Our words, which also come to pass, can deny the promises God has for us because we speak negative, idle, or cruel words—all of which issue from our deceitful hearts.

As we look at the maid of Naaman's wife, we find a young girl who shared her belief—and others greatly benefited. She passed good news to others, even Gentiles.

Huldah was a true prophetess of God. With courage and discipline, she said only what He told her say. His Word is truth. It's an expression of His wisdom. We not only have the priviledge of sharing the Word of God, but also the responsibility to speak the truth.

The Queen of Sheba couldn't believe reports of the great wisdom of Solomon, so she went to see for herself if what she'd heard was true. When she saw that it was, she recognized the God of Israel as the one who had given Solomon his wisdom and knowledge.

THE SUCCESS OF NAAMAN'S WIFE'S MAID
(Based on II Kings 5:1-9)

Some 20 words cover all we know of this Jewish slave girl. Her record consists of one remark, *"Would God my Lord were with the prophet that is in Samaria! For he would recover him of his leprosy"* (II Kings 5:3).

This nameless maid had been taken from a Hebrew home in which God was honored. She had been brought from the land of Israel as part of the spoils of war. During one of the Syrian attacks, she was stolen and taken across the border as to the slave market where Namaan, captain of the king's host, secured her as a servant for his wife.

Reading between the lines, we can see that Namaan's wife was kind to the young girl and even shared personal concerns with her. As the girl dutifully waited upon her mistress, she came to know of Namaan's dread disease. Evidently the maiden saw how much it distressed her mistress, so she told her that there was a man in Samaria who could help him.

The mistress shared the news with her husband, who was willing to try anything. When the kings of the two nations finally agreed to allow it, Namaan went to see the prophet Elisha. But his pride met a blow. He was met by Elisha's servant who told him to bathe himself seven times in the muddy waters of the Jordan River. Enraged and humiliated, he determined to go home without obeying.

His officers tried to reason with him and reminded him that if Elisha had told him some great thing to do, he would have done it; so he should do even the simple thing. Namaan did and, on the seventh dip, came up completely healed. A very surprised, but happy, man returned to Syria not only healed, but a worshipper of Jehovah.

Imagine the joy of the little maid when she heard the good news! How glad she must have been that she hadn't kept the truth from her mistress.

LESSONS FROM NAAMAN'S WIFE'S MAID
Sharing the Good News

Naaman's wife's maid was a young girl who took the risk of sharing her faith and the Word which she knew to be of God. She was a stranger in a strange land, yet she was willing to tell others what she knew concerning God as she had heard it from the prophet Elisha.

Among the last words Jesus gave His disciples, was the command to go into all the world and make disciples of all nations. This *great commission* is for us as well. It is often called *evangelism* when the Word is preached and spoken to many people. On a one-to-one basis, we usually call it witnessing.

To be an effective witness, our *walk* must coincide with our *talk*. We can't share the good news of Jesus Christ and live the bad news of the world if we want to be heard correctly.

In order to share our faith, or be a witness, we must not only first experience God's love within ourselves, but we must be willing to open our hearts so that God's love can flow through us. To be an effective witness, we must not just know *about* Jesus, but we must know *Him*, otherwise, our sharing will be empty words. It will be like trying to describe chocolate ice-cream to a friend when you've never tasted it yourself.

Before Jesus left this earth, He told His disciples to both go into all the world and "wait in Jerusalem." He knew they needed the empowering of the Holy Spirit (which would be poured out at Pentecost) to be able to evangelize effectively.

John 1:40-42 Witnessing involves _____

_____

_____

I Peter 3:15, and 16 We're told to always be ready _____

_____

_____

Acts 2:41 and 42 When the Word is shared in the power of the

Holy Spirit, _____

_____

_____

Matthew 28:19 and 20 Jesus' last words to His disciples were

_____

_____

as well as *Acts 1:8* _____

_____

_____

THE SUCCESS OF HULDAH
(Based on II Kings 22:14-20; II Chronicles 34:22-33; II Kings 23:28-30)

All we know of Huldah, apart from her ministry, is that she was the wife of Shallum, the keeper of the royal wardrobe. As a prophetess during the reign of King Josiah, she could be found sitting in the central part of the city, ready to receive and counsel any who wished to inquire of the Lord.

Ranking with Deborah, Huldah's standing and reputation are attested to in that *she* was consulted, rather than Jeremiah, when the lost book of the law was found. Her word was accepted as divinely revealed.

When Hilkiah the priest found the book in the Temple, Josiah sent immediately for Huldah. Verifying the genuineness of the scroll, she prophesized national ruin because of the disobedience to the commands of God. Her prophetic message and the public reading of the law brought about a revival resulting in the reforms carried out by Josiah. With renewed dedication, both king and people vowed to follow the God of their fathers more faithfully. Huldah heard correctly from God. She wasn't afraid to pass on His Word to others.

LESSONS FROM HULDAH
Speaking the Word of God

Huldah was recognized as a woman who spoke God's Word

in truth, even though it wasn't necessarily what people wanted to hear. As a true prophetess, her words came to pass because they were God's words.

Jesus exalted the mystery of the power of the confession of God's Word when He said, *"I say unto you, that whosoever shall say, and shall not doubt in his heart, but shall believe that those things that he saith shall come to pass, he shall have whatsoever he saith"* (Mark 11:23). Paul attested to this truth in Romans 10:8 when he said that *"the word of faith is in our mouth."*

God's Word is powerful (Hebrews 4:12); it always comes to pass (Isaiah 55:11); it accomplishes what He pleases (Isaiah 55:11); and it endures forever (I Peter 1:23). Jesus is God's Word made flesh (John 1:14). He is the truth (John 14:6).

The problem is, we often fail to speak God's Word. Instead, we speak our own negative, idle, false words (usually inspired by Satan, who wants to rob us of all that God has for us). Matthew 12:36 and 37 says that eventually we'll have to give account for every idle word we speak.

If we *believe* God's Word, then we must *confess* the truth of it. Thus, we must *know* it. To do that, we must *study* the Bible.

James 3 contains much instruction concerning our tongues, which verse 8 says "no man can tame." We can bless God, or curse man through the use of our tongue.

Actually, our tongues speak what is in our hearts (Matthew 12:34). Since our hearts are deceitful and desperately wicked (Jeremiah 17:9), it's only when we open our hearts to God for His cleansing (which comes through His Word) (Ephesians 5:26), that we can speak His love, His healing, His encouragement, and His forgiveness. As a man thinks in his heart, so he is (Proverb 23:7).

Look up other Scriptures to help discover the condition of our tongue and the importance of our speech.

James 3:3-12 Our tongue is _____

_____

_____

and can be used for _____

_____

_____

Psalm 141:3 We must pray that _____

_____

_____

Proverb 18:21 In the power of the tongue are _____

_____

_____

Ephesians 4:29 We're to let no _____

_____

_____

Ephesians 5:4 Unappropriate are _____

_____

_____

Proverb 6:2 We can be snared by _____

_____

_____

Matthew 12:36 and 37 We'll be held accountable for _____

_____

_____

Isaiah 55:11 God's Word _____

_____

_____

Matthew 10:19 and 20 We can be given words by _____

_____

_____

Psalm 35:28 All day long, our tongues should speak of ___

_____

_____

Psalm 119:172 Our tongues should speak _____

_____

_____

Ephesians 4:25 We should speak _____

_____

_____

Titus 2:1 and 8 We're to speak _____

_____

_____

Deuteronomy 6:7 To our children, we're to _____

_____

_____

Psalm 71:15-17 Our mouths are to _____

_____

_____

Psalm 71:24 Our tongues should _____

Psalm 77:12 We're to _____

THE SUCCESS OF THE QUEEN OF SHEBA
(Based on I Kings 10:1-13; II Chronicles 9:1-12; Matthew 12:42)

When the Queen of Sheba heard how wonderfully the Lord had blessed Solomon with wisdom, she decided to go see him. She loaded her camels with spices, gold and jewels, and set out for Jerusalem.

When she finally met with Solomon, she asked him many questions and decided that he did, indeed, have great wisdom. She was also greatly impressed with the splendor of his palace, gardens, food, servants, etc. In fact, she told him that his wisdom and prosperity were much more magnificent than she'd imagined. She even blessed the God of Israel for choosing him to set upon the throne.

Then she gave him a gift of $3,500,000 in gold, along with huge quantities of spices and precious gems. In exchange, Solomon gave her everything she asked for including the presents he had already planned. Then she and her entourage returned to her country.

We don't know how she acted upon the knowledge of God that she received from Solomon. We hear no more about her until Jesus speaks of her during His ministry.

LESSONS FROM THE QUEEN OF SHEBA
Wisdom

On at least one occasion, Jesus spoke of the Queen of Sheba as a woman who went to great lengths to hear the wisdom of Solomon. He told those listening that one "greater than Solomon" was in their midst, referring of course, to Himself. Yet they didn't listen to Him.

We have the same choice today. We can find our wisdom in the world and human resources, or we can find our wisdom in Jesus and God's Word.

According to Webster's New World Dictionary, wisdom is the power of judging rightly, following the soundest course of action based on experience, knowledge, and understanding.

Proverb 9:10 tells us that _"the fear of the Lord is the beginning of wisdom."_

After Solomon succeeded his father David as King, the Lord appeared to him in a dream one night and asked Solomon what he would like from Him. Solomon replied that he would like an understanding heart. His request pleased God, who replied, _"Because thou hast asked this thing, and hast not asked for thyself long life; neither hast asked riches for thyself, nor hast asked the life of thine enemies; but hast asked for thyself understanding to discern judgment; Behold, I have done according to thy words: lo, I have given thee a wise and understanding heart; so that there was_

174

none like thee before thee, neither after thee shall any arise like unto thee." (I Kings 3:11 and 12).

But in the chapter which follows the story of the Queen's visit, we have some very sad news. Solomon married many strange women during his life. Women who turned his heart to worshipping their gods. The wisest man who ever lived, the king who had built the most beautiful temple for the worship of the one true God, lost his fear of the Lord *and* His wisdom. He did evil in the sight of the Lord, and God stirred up adversaries against him. His two sons divided the kingdom. It was never again reunited.

During the period of his life when Solomon listened to God's wisdom, he wrote some of the literature which we now have in the Bible. These include Proverbs, the Song of Solomon, and possibly, Ecclesiastes. The Book of Proverbs has been called the book of *wisdom*. It's crammed with witty, humorous, and profound truths which can help us in our everyday lives. Included are proverbs on the subjects of sex, money, family relationships, anger, pride, fear and more. Let's take one of these catagories and see what wisdom we can gain from Proverbs on this subject.

Women and Wives

Proverbs:

11:22 ___discretion: religion, grace_____

___beauty or comeliness of body is a jewel of___

___gold, a thing very valuable_____

12:4 _____

_____

_____

14:1 _____

_____

_____

18:22 _____

_____

_____

19:13 and 14 _____

_____

_____

21:9 _____

_____

_____

25:24 _____

_____

21:19 _____

_____

_____

27:15 and 16 _____

_____

_____

What kind of wisdom do you want? How do you obtain it?

James 3:13-17 Describe the two kinds of wisdom. _____

_____

_____

James 1:5-8 How do we receive God's wisdom? _____

_____

_____

I Corinthians 1:19-2:16; 3:19 What other kind of wisdom is there? In spite of all that wisdom, ignorance still prevailed, iniquity still abounded. Puffed up & alienated from God

Exodus 36:1 and 2 Wisdom is given by _____

_____

_____

Luke 21:15 Wisdom is given by _____

_____

_____

I Corinthians 12:8 Wisdom is given through _____

_____

_____

Proverb 9:10 Wisdom comes from _____

_____

_____

Colossians 2:3 In Jesus are _____

_____

_____

176

I Corinthians 1:30 God made Jesus Christ our _____

_____

WOMEN
IN THE BIBLE

SUMMARY

Our response to God's Word should involve the confession of our lips, for we have what we *say*. In witnessing to this truth, Naaman's wife's maid helped bring about the healing of the Syrian commander, Naaman. Because Huldah always spoke what God had said, she became a true prophetess. And, after visiting King Solomon, the Queen of Sheba recognized the wisdom of God and proclaimed it. Whether we witness to others about what God has said; whether we confess Scriptural promises for ourselves; or whether we proclaim the wisdom of God, we need to speak God's truths with our mouth. We receive what we "speak into being."

MODERN EXAMPLE

We first met Tammy in the county jail. She sat opposite us, behind the glass panel which separated inmates from visitors. She was the roommate of Keri, a young woman whom we had just visited. Keri was a backslidden Christian who had become involved in drugs. She seemed repentant and we were trying to give her counsel. It appeared that she was sincere in wanting to get right with the Lord. She'd shared the gospel with Tammy, and now Tammy wanted to talk to us.

Our hearts went out to this 19-year-old, who was now seven months pregnant. She would soon be released and had no where to go. The home she'd left was not a good one for any kind of rehabilitation.

We began to share Jesus with her—to reinforce the gospel message and assure her that He was the only One who could truly help her now. Meanwhile, we checked into the possibility of finding a place for her through a Christian crisis pregnancy center. But because of her background, some of the sheltering homes were reluctant to take her in. Finally, one of the staff members felt that the Lord was leading her family to provide for Tammy. So, when she was released from jail, Tammy had a place in a loving Christian home.

The family took Tammy to church with them, and shared their lives with her day by day. One evening, they went to hear a speaker who had found new life in Christ after several years in prison. He invited those present to come forward to accept Jesus, so that they, too, could experience deliverance and salvation. Tammy responded to his invitation and received Jesus into her heart. Expressing her transformation, she said, "I've never felt so clean inside!"

"Clean" and "teachable," Tammy began to grow in the Lord as her family shared the Word and Scriptural principals daily. By the time her little girl was born, she was becoming well-grounded in her faith.

WHAT DO YOU THINK?

1. With whom have you shared the gospel of Jesus Christ?

_____

_____

2. Have you ever given testimony to others of how God's Word has come true for you? _____

_____

_____

3. Why is it so important that we speak positively and not negatively? _____

_____

_____

4. Can you see any result of having what you have confessed with your lips? _____

_____

_____

EVALUATE YOURSELF

1. In what ways are you implementing the principles learned from these three women? _____

_____

_____

2. In what ways are you failing to implement the principles learned from them? _____

_____

_____

3. What do you need to do to change? _____

_____

_____

4. How will you do it? _____

_____

_____

178

Lesson 19
Manoah's Wife & Job's Wife

An Example of Response to the Ways of God

"For my thoughts are not your thoughts, neither are your ways my ways, saith the Lord."

Isaiah 55:8

SETTING THE STAGE

God's thoughts are not our thoughts, nor our ways His ways. In fact, they're usually in opposition to one another unless our flesh is reckoned dead and we're submitted to the Holy Spirit. We're reminded in I Corinthians 1:27, that God has chosen the foolish things of the world to confound the wise, and the weak things of the world to confound those who are mighty.

The two women in this lesson were victims of God's surprising ways. Manoah's wife was barren, so she wasn't expecting to have a child of her own to raise when an angel appeared to her to tell her that she would bear a special son. She responded to the news by seeking advice from her husband, the one God ordains to be a woman's head.

The Lord blessed her by giving her Samson, who grew up to be one of the Judges of Israel.

Job and his wife were prosperous and blessed by God when the Lord allowed Satan to suddenly take away their children, servants, livestock, home and belongings, and then cover Job with boils as trial for this perfect and upright man. As calamity befell them, Job fell to the ground in worship of God; however, his wife became bitter and urged him to curse God.

We have choices as to how we'll respond to the surprising ways of the Lord. We can accept His ways and benefit from them, or we can become bitter and make life miserable for ourselves and others.

THE SUCCESS OF MANOAH'S WIFE
(Based on Judges 13; 14:1-5)

One day the Angel of the Lord appeared to the wife of Manoah, of the tribe of Dan, who lived in the city of Zorah.

"Mrs. Manoah?"

"Why, yes. Who are you? What do you want?

"I've just come to tell you that, though you've been childless, you'll now conceive and bear a son.

"Me?"

"Yes, the Heavenly Father has chosen you. I have some further instructions for you."

"What are they?"

"You aren't to drink any wine or other fermented drink, and you aren't to eat any unclean thing. You're not to let the child's hair be cut, as this child is to be a Nazarite, one set apart to God from birth."

Before Manoahs wife could respond, the Angel of the Lord disappeared as quickly as it had come. Somewhat frightened, she got up and ran outside to find her husband. When she saw him, she ran towards him, blurting, "Manoah, my husband a man of God came to me. He looked like an angel. I don't know where he came from, and he didn't tell me his name. But he told me that I would have a son, and then gave me other instructions on how to raise him. What do you think, Manoah?"

Manoah, still reeling from the description of the angel's visit and announcement, said, "Well, I guess we should pray." Putting his arm about his wife, he whispered, "O Lord, I beg you, let the man of God you sent to us come again to teach us how to bring up the boy that is to be born." Manoah felt his wife's body relax a bit, and he realized she would be willing to submit herself to God's will for their lives.

A few days later, while she was alone in the field, the angel appeared a second time. Not wanting to be in the same predicament, she ran to the house before he could say a word. She found Manoah, took him by the arm, and said excitedly, "Manoah, come with me! He's here! The man of God is here again!" Together, they ran back to the field where the angel was still standing. Since the angel looked to be just an ordinary man, Manoah asked, "Are you the one who talked to my wife?"

"Yes, I am," replied the Angel of the Lord.

"So," Manoah continued, "when your words are fulfilled, what is to be the rule for the boy's life and work?"

The angel of the Lord answered, "Your wife must do all that I have told her. She mustn't eat anything that comes from the grapevine, or drink any wine or other fermented drink, eat anything unclean. She must do everything I have commanded her."

Manoah then offered to prepare some food for the man to eat, but the man refused. He told them that, if they wanted to prepare a burnt offering, they could offer it to the Lord.

Still not realizing that he was speaking to an angel of the Lord, Manoah questioned the man further. "What's your name, so that we may honor you when your word comes true?"

The angel replied, "Why do you ask my name? It's beyond understanding."

Then Manoah took a young goat, together with the grain offering, and sacrificed it upon a rock to the Lord. As he did, the flame blazed up from the altar toward heaven, and the angel of the Lord ascended in the flame.

Manoah finally realized that is was indeed, an angel of the Lord, and exclaimed, "We're doomed to die! We've seen God!" But, Manoah's wife replied, "If the Lord had meant to kill us, he wouldn't have accepted a burnt offering and grain

180

offering from our hands, or shown us all those things, or told us what he did."

In due time, the wife of Manoah bore a son and called his named Samson. And the child grew, and the Lord blessed him.

LESSONS FROM MANOAH'S WIFE
The Ways of God

Bible characters didn't always understand the ways of God in their lives. Only as we read what later transpired, do we begin to see why God might have done what He did.

Nor do we, today, always understand the ways of God while things are happening to us. Sometimes we later see the answers to our "whys." Some answers will be revealed only in eternity.

Isaiah 55:8 and 9 God's thoughts _____

_____

_____

nor are _____

_____

_____

I Corinthians 2:12 We have received the Spirit of God that

_____

_____

Deuteronomy 29:29 The secret things _____

_____

_____

Romans 9:14-21 God will have mercy on _____

_____

_____

Romans 11:33-36 God's judgments and ways are _____

_____

_____

Deuteronomy 32:4 God's work is _____

_____

_____

and his ways are _____

_____

_____

Hosea 14:9 God's ways are _____

_____

_____

Revelation 15:3 God's works and ways are _____

_____

_____

Proverb 16:29 A violent man's way _____

_____

Proverb 16:2 The ways of man _____
but_____

_____

Proverb 14:12 There is a way that _____

_____

_____

Judges 21:25 When no one respects authority, everyone __

_____

_____

THE FAILURE OF JOB'S WIFE
(Based on the book of Job, particularly Job 2:9 and 10; 19:17; 31:10)

It's strange that we have the names of Job's three daughters but not the name of the wife who was with Job through all his trials and tribulation! She's identified by only ten words, which she uttered to her husband when she saw him suffering from much bodily pain. She urged him to curse God and die, and thus relieve himself of further anguish.

The story of Job and his wife actually took place during the time of the Book of Genesis. We read in Genesis 46:13 that Job was a son of Issachar, one of the twelve sons of Jacob.

The story begins with God and Satan having a conversation concerning the perfect and upright Job, a man who feared God and avoided evil. Satan had noticed Job in his travels over the earth and suggested to God that Job was only a righteous man because all was going well with him. To disprove that, God allowed Satan to do whatever he wanted with Job, except touch him. With God's permission, Satan caused all of Job's children to be killed, most of his servants to be slain, some of the animals to be consumed by fire while others were slain, and his home to be destroyed. Job's response to this great catastrophe, all of which occured on the same day, was to fall to the ground and worship God.

This only irritated Satan more. He talked God into allowing him to touch Job's physical body with disease. Even at this point, it wasn't until Job's wife encouraged him to curse God and his friends sat silently with him for seven days, that Job,

182

unable to take it any longer, cried out, cursing the day that he was born.

Because he believed that all that happened to him was in God's hands, Job could say, *"The Lord gave: the Lord hath taken away: blessed be the name of the Lord"* (Job 1:21).

Mrs. Job, meanwhile, suffered along with her husband. Though she wasn't stricken with illness, she, too, lost her children, her livelihood, and her wealth. What's more, she probably also lost respect from her friends and neighbors, because her husband no longer held a prestigious position. She, who had probably encouraged her husband in his priestly function with their children, now became so overwhelmingly frustrated that she told him to curse God and die! She'd had it! Job's response? He neither blamed his wife, nor cursed God.

The story continues with the suffering of Job and tells how his friends tried to minister to him. Though Job mentions his wife a time or two, we don't actually hear from her again. We assume, however, that she was a part of Job's restoration since he had more sons and daughters.

LESSONS FROM JOB'S WIFE
Bitterness

In the story of Job and his wife, we see two contrasting responses to the ways of God. Job recognized God's hand in all that happened, even though he didn't understand any of the reasons. His wife, on the other hand, responded bitterly, encouraging Job to curse God.

Bitterness often results from being hurt. It's unavoidable to be hurt, but the way we deal with our hurt makes a big difference in our lives. Bitterness can take root and defile others. It also greatly harms the one who allows it to take place.

One of the tragic results of bitterness is that it increases with time. That's why Hebrews 12:15 describes bitterness as a *root*. It not only takes hold of us, but it causes all we come in contact with to suffer as well. Many people can be hurt by one person's bitterness. We can see why when we note the characteristics of a bitter person.

A bitter person:

*lacks concern for others.

*is sensitive and touchy.

*has few close friends, and is possessive with the ones he does have.

*tends to avoid meeting new people.

*shows little or no gratitude.

*usually speaks words of criticism.

*holds grudges and finds it difficult to forgive.

*usually experiences extreme changes in moods.

How can we get out of the bitterness trap? Take some time alone to do the following:

(1) Make a list of the people who have hurt you.
(2) Make another list of the things you've done to hurt others. (This is more difficult; one tends to forget these.)

(3) Take a good look at how you've hurt the Lord. Genesis 6:6 remind us that, *"The Lord was grieved that He had made man on the earth, and His heart was filled with pain."* Man can hurt God by his responses to Him.

(4) Pray, and ask forgiveness from God and others. This may take a few phone calls, letters, or trips.

(5) Destroy the lists—as well as the "files" in your memory.

   Matthew 6:14 and 15 says, *"For if you forgive men for their transgressions, your heavenly Father will also forgive you. But if you do not forgive men, then your Father will not forgive your transgressions."* We must forgive if we want to be forgiven. If we choose not to forgive, bitterness will take root in our lives and many will be defiled.

Ephesians 4:31 We're to put away from us all _____

_____

_____

James 3:14-18 The result of bitter envying and strife is _____

_____

_____

but God's wisdom is _____

_____

_____

Hebrews 3:7-15 We can miss having the promises of God because _____

_____

_____

Acts 8:21-23 Peter perceived Simon the sorcerer _____

_____

_____

Therefore, _____

_____

_____

Proverb 14:10 Our hearts know _____

_____

_____

   We can prevent bitterness from taking root, to begin with, by:

I John 1:9 _____

_____

_____

184

I Thessalonains 5:18 _____

_____

_____

The Benefits of Accepting God's Ways

As Job trusted in God throughout the unusual trials God allowed him to suffer, God began to reveal Himself and show Job his own self-righteousness. Job received insight as to the need of a Redeemer. In the pit of despair, he had an amazing revelation. Job proclaimed, *"I know that my Redeemer liveth, and that he shall stand at the latter day upon the earth; and though after my skin worms destroy this body, yet in my flesh shall I see God!"* (Job 19:25 and 26) Job learned to trust in God, not in man. As Job endured his trials, he learned patience. The Heavenly Father, who saw it all happen, blessed Job and his wife doubly in the end.

It's interesting to note how God trains the leaders He will use. Most often He allows them to go through suffering and trials which they don't understand. He allows them, like the children of Israel whom He brought out of Egypt, to go through a wilderness to prove themselves, to see what's in their hearts. Then, He calls them from unusual circumstances to use them in ways they hadn't dreamed. Look up the following scriptures. See where these leaders were when God called them. What was their response to His call?

Genesis 37:20, 27 and 36; 39:20, 40:15, and 23, 41:38-43; 47:11 and 12 Joseph _____

_____

_____

Exodus 3 and 4 Moses _____

_____

_____

Judges 6:11-40 Gideon _____

_____

_____

I Samuel 9 and 10 King Saul _____

_____

_____

I Samuel 16 David _____

_____

_____

Matthew 4:18-22 Peter, Andrew, James and John _____

_____

_____

WOMEN IN THE BIBLE

We see that *"all things work together for good to them that love God, to them who are called according to his purpose"* (Romans 8:28). God can take circumstances in life, whether He has caused them, whether Satan has been allowed to bring them about, or whether they happened because of our own doings, and work each thing together for our good and His. Our response is to accept His ways and not let bitterness take root in our lives because we don't understand what happens to us.

SUMMARY

The wives of Manoah and of Job were victims of God's surprising ways. Manoah's wife was barren when an angel appeared to her and told her that she would have a special child. Job's wife was with him when sudden calamity took away their children, servants, livestock, home and covered Job with boils from head to foot. The first of these women responded in a good way; the second did not. Likewise, we each have a choice as to how we will respond to the unusual ways of God. We can accept His ways and benefit from them, or we can become bitter and make life miserable for ourselves and others.

MODERN EXAMPLE

Fanny Crosby was born in 1820 in rural New York. Because of an eye infection at 6 weeks of age, she lost her sight. Before she was one year old, her father died. So, her grandmother became her babysitter and her mother went to work.

Thus, her grandmother became her closest companion, describing the wonderous world which only the sighted can observe. Fanny was an adventurous child, but also spent long hours learning poetry and memorizing Scripture. She could repeat the entire book of Ruth, as well as lengthy portions from the Psalms, Proverbs, and the New Testament.

At age 14 Fanny was sent to the New York Institute for the Blind where she learned Braille. Her creativeness motivated her to spend many hours reading and composing poetry.

Fanny experienced more heartache when, after marrying a blind musician, their only child died in infancy.

When Fanny Crosby died of a cerebral hemorrhage at age 94, she had written between 5,500 and 9,000 poems and hymns. Some of these were set to music. We know them as "Blessed Assurance," "Near the Cross," and "Saved by Grace." Perhaps it's this latter hymn that best typifies her faith in a God who never allowed her to see the beauty of His earthly realm. After each verse which describes passing from this life into the next, she gives the refrain: "And I shall see Him face to face, And tell the story—Saved by grace." Unable to see during her lifetime, she knew and longed for the joy of *seeing* her Lord *face to face.*

Though she couldn't understand the tragedies she experienced, Fanny Crosby accepted God's ways, and He used her to inspire millions of His people to sing praises in worship of Him.

WHAT DO YOU THINK?

1. Have you ever been the victim of God's surprising ways?

186

How did you respond? _____

_____

_____

2. Can you recall an example of a time when God's ways definitely differed from yours? What happened? _____

_____

_____

3. Have you ever experienced bitterness? How did it affect you and those with whom you had contact? _____

_____

_____

4. Have you ever been the object of another's bitterness? How did it affect you? _____

_____

_____

EVALUATE YOURSELF

1. In what ways are you implementing the principles learned from these two wives? _____

_____

_____

2. In what ways are you failing to implement the principles learned from them? _____

_____

_____

3. What do you need to do to change? _____

_____

_____

4. How will you do it? _____

_____

_____

Lesson 20
Esther

An Example of Feasting and Fasting

"Whether therefore ye eat, or drink, or whatsoever ye do, do all to the glory of God."

I Corinthians 10:31

"Is not this the fast that I have chosen? to loose the bands of wickedness, to undo the heavy burdens, and to let the oppressed go free, and that ye break every yoke?"

Isaiah 58:6

SETTING THE STAGE

The Book of Esther is usually associated with a special *Fast* of the Hebrew people which proved to be significant in their history. Through this particular Fast, they were miraculously delivered out of the hands of their captors.

Feasts also played an important role in Hebrew life. These were a means for God's people to recall His will and work in their lives. If we count the number of feasts or banquets in the Book of Esther, we'll find that the story revolves around seven such meals.

In this lesson, we'll survey the Feasts the Jewish people were commanded to keep. We'll also consider what partaking meals together should mean to us as families.

We'll then look at the subject of Fasting, a discipline often neglected among Christians today.

Fasting, denying one's body food, seems to have been an expected discipline throughout Scripture. We find that fasting was done by many persons, as well as by groups of people. We know that Jesus fasted for 40 days and nights while being tempted by Satan in the wilderness. In fact, the only ones who evidently didn't fast, were the disciples of Jesus while He was alive (see Matthew 9:14 and 15). Even then, Jesus said that, when He (the bridegroom) was taken away, the disciples would return to fasting.

Let's look at Esther as we consider feasts and fasts.

THE SUCCESS OF ESTHER
(Based on the Book of Esther)

In order to understand the success of the woman Esther, we need to know the story in the Book of Esther.

The book opens with the announcement of a feast to be given by King Ahasuerus. He was ruler of Persia, an empire that stretched from India to Ethiopia. Though it was the greatest kingdom of its day, this king wasn't satisfied. He wanted to conquer Greece.

Probably as a military strategy, he invited all his princes and military advisors to his palace in Shushan for an immense feast to last a full six months. As if that weren't enough, at the end of the first feast he proclaimed another seven-day feast for all the people of the land, both great and small. This celebration, no less elaborate, was held in the palace gardens.

On the last day of the second feast Ahasuerus, a bit drunk from his own good wine, asked that his wife, Queen Vashti, be brought in so that he could show her off to his friends. She refused to be made a spectacle, and as a result the king was enraged. Subsequently, he issued a decree that she could no longer come before him, saying that he would instead, give her position to another.

A beauty contest was held among all the young maidens in the land, and Esther won the king's favor. He made her his queen and, again, called for a feast to celebrate the occasion. The King's first feast brought him honor; his second feast brought Queen Vashti dishonor; the third feast exhibited the king's favor toward Esther, the new Queen.

Ahasuerus didn't know that Esther was a Jewess. Neither did he know that Mordecai was her uncle, nor that, in days gone by, this same Mordecai had risked his own life to prevent an assassination attempt on the king.

Since Mordecai was a Jew he refused to bow down to Haman, the King's chief advisor. This infuriated Haman, who decided to get even by asking the King to annihilate all Jews. When Esther heard of this, she called all Jews to fast for three-days. She believed God had brought her into her position in the kingdom for this purpose. Through the Fast, she believed, God would deliver His people.

In order to ask Ahasuerus to recind his order against the Jews, Esther prepared a banquet and asked both the King and Haman to attend. At this time, the King told her, in front of Haman, that he would give her whatever she desired. She chose not to tell him what she wanted at that time, but rather, invited both him and Haman to a second banquet, saying she would then let him know what she wanted.

In the time between these two meals, events took place that caused both Ahasuerus and Haman to have a change of heart. Haman went home and told his wife about Mordecai's unsubservience. She encouraged him to ask the King to require Mordecai's death. With eager anticipation, Haman ordered gallows made and looked forward to making his request when he saw the king at the banquet the next day.

The king, in the meantime, had gone to bed but couldn't sleep. He ordered some of the palace record books be brought to him. In reading these, he discovered that Mordecai had once prevented him from being killed, but had never been honored for doing so. He immediately called Haman and asked him what he should do to honor a person worthy of some recognition. Haman jumped to the conclusion that the king was talking about him, so he told the king to dress this person in royal garments and let him ride down the streets of the city for all to see. When Ahasuerus then suggested that this be done for Mordecai, Haman was more than humiliated. He was doubly angry—not only for Mordecai's not having bowed down to him, but now, because the king wanted to honor the man whom he wanted to hang. Besides, he would receive no glory for himself.

With these new motives and feelings, Ahasuerus and Haman went to Esther's second banquet, where the king again asked her what she wanted. She told him that she would like deliverance for her people. When the king learned that Haman was the one who requested that all the Jews be killed, he demanded Haman's death and made possible Esther's request.

Haman was hanged on the very gallows he had prepared for Mordecai. The Jews were spared destruction; Mordecai was honored, Haman was hanged, and Esther was used by God to save His people.

LESSONS FROM ESTHER
The Feasts of Israel

To celebrate their deliverance from Haman's plot, the Jews proclaimed a Feast Day of their own. In order to remember this episode in their history, they instituted the Feast of Purim. *Pur* means *lot*, and *Purim* comes from the fact that Haman had decided to find out which would be the propitious day to destroy the Jews by casting lots. The lot fell on the 13th day of Adar (our March). It's still observed by Jews today.

The other feasts of Israel were to be memorials of God's dealings with the Hebrew people. They're also a prophetic symbolism of God's dealings with His Church. We find most of them listed in Leviticus 23:

Passover commemorates the deliverance of the Jews from Egyptian slavery. Jesus instituted the Lord's Supper on Passover night.

The Feast of Unleavened Bread occurs simultaneously with Passover. During this time, the Jewish people put away all leaven from their houses. Thus they are purged of sin. (Leaven is any substance used to make dough rise, and a symbol of moral influence.)

Pentecost commemorates a harvest festival. This feast took place 50 days after the Passover sabbath. (Pentecost means 50.) During this feast, the priests offer two loaves of bread made with newly harvested grain and baked with leaven. The Holy Spirit was poured out on Pentecost.

The Feast of Trumpets is commonly called Rosh Hashanah. This marks the beginning of the Jewish New Year. God commanded the blowing of trumpets to call the congregation of Israel together for a solemn assembly. It's the beginning of 10 days of introspection and repentance and leads into the most solemn day of the Jewish year.

Day of Atonement (Yom Kippur) is a time of fasting and prayer. It's the only time the high priest can enter the Holy of Holies. Because of Jesus, Christians now have access to God.

The Feast of Booths is the final fall harvest festival, a time of ingathering at Jerusalem. The Jewish people built booth-like structures and lived in them during this feast as a reminder of the temporary dwellings the Israelites had in the wilderness. Booths also speak of rest, as well as the final harvest.

Other Meals in Scripture

It's amazing what we discover when we search God's Word concerning meals. To begin with, Adam and Eve fell from

God's grace into sin because they didn't eat according to His instructions (Genesis 3:6-19) Jesus, in not yielding to Satan's temptation to eat, overcame the enemy and was blessed by God (Luke 4:2-4). Abraham entertained angels with a meal (Genesis 18:5-8), as did Lot (Genesis 19:1-3). Hebrews 13:2 tells us not to forget to entertain strangers, for we may unknowingly entertain angels. Esau sold his birthright for a meal (Genesis 25:34). We find Jacob offering his family a meal at the time he and Laban were reconciled (Genesis 31:49-55). Joseph gave a banquet for his brothers at their reunion (Genesis 43:16-34). Then, there are the Passover meal of Exodus 12 and the feasts previously mentioned.

We also have some important meals described in the New Testament, such as the feast prepared for the return of the prodigal son. (Luke 15:11-27). There is the meal to which Jesus was invited after Matthew decided to follow him (Matthew 9:9-13), and the meal Jesus was eating in a Pharisee's house when a woman of the city came to anoint His feet and wash them with her tears (Luke 7:36-50). Jesus told us, in Matthew 25, to feed the hungry. He said not to be anxious about what we shall eat, because God will provide if we seek Him first (Matthew 6:25-33). Paul instructs us, in Romans 14, not to cause our brothers to stumble by what we eat or don't eat. It's also significant to note that it was during a meal following the resurrection, that two of Jesus' disciples, who had already walked the Emmaus Road with Him, finally recognized Him (Luke 24:30 and 31). It was in this same glorified body that Jesus also ate a breakfast with His disciples (Luke 24:39-43).

The climax of Jesus' ministry centered around a meal. *"The Lord Jesus the same night in which he was betrayed took bread, and when he had given thanks, he broke it, and said, Take, eat; this is my body, which is broken for you; this do in remembrance of me..."* (I Corinthians 11:23 and 24). At the Jewish Passover celebration, Jesus instituted a meal which became known as the Last Supper, or Lord's Supper. Here, Jesus established a memorial to His death. As we partake of the bread, which is His body, and the wine, which is His blood, we are to remember His death (I Corinthians 11:26). Jesus is the Passover Lamb.

Upon His return, there will be another meal. This meal is the culmination of all history—the Marriage Supper of the Lamb of God and His Bride, the Church of Jesus Christ (Revelation 19:7).

The invitation is out now, to this great feast. We can say "yes" or "no" by accepting Jesus as Savior. He not only calls unbelievers to come to Him, but He also calls His own to come and sup with Him (Revelation 3:20). Even now, Jesus calls us to share a meal with Him. He wants a relationship which comes from sharing spiritual food together. We do this by partaking of His Word, so we might be edified and cleansed. We commune with Him in prayer and meditation, allowing His strength, love and power to come into our lives as He indwells us by the Holy Spirit. As we sup with Him, our lives are changed.

How Our Lives Are Affected by Sharing Meals with Others

Eating plays a greater role in our lives than we may think. A birthday celebration isn't complete without a piece of cake. To get acquainted with neighbors, we invite them over for coffee. What's the Fourth of July without a picnic; Thanksgiving without a turkey dinner; or Christmas without goodies to share? Everyday meals we share with our families are also important times in our lives.

Scripture tells us it isn't good to eat with the wrong company or for the wrong reasons. What do we learn from the following?

Philippians 3:17-19 _____

_____

_____

_____

Luke 17:26-29 _____

_____

_____

Luke 21:34 _____

_____

_____

Fasting

Fasting is a means of diligently seeking God and prevailing with Him. It should be accompanied by prayer and repentance, as one humbles himself before God by denying the flesh of its lusts and pleasures. Fasting isn't a hunger strike to force God's hand and get our own way. Rather, it's a weapon in spiritual warfare against the principalities and powers of darkness.

The subject of fasting is well described in Isaiah 58. We're told the benefits of God's chosen fast, as well as given a warning against fasting for the wrong reason or with the wrong attitudes.

No man knows how fasting works, but we do know that it's necessary for both our own benefit, as well as for victory in certain areas. Somehow, heaven is ready to bend its ear and to listen when prayer is accompanied with fasting. Perhaps it demonstrates our "wholeheartedness." When we're willing to deny our flesh and concentrate on praying, we demonstrate our earnest desire to seek God and not to let go until He answers. This can be true for individuals or for groups. God wants us to return to Him *with all our heart,* and with fasting (Joel 2:12 NIV).

In Bible times there were three types of fasting.

1. *Absolute fast*—no food or water

   Ezra 10: 6 _____

   _____

   _____

   Esther 4:16 _____

Acts 9:9 _____

_____

Exodus 34:28 _____

_____

An exceptional measure for an exceptional situation, this type of fast should be no more than three days and even then, supernaturally inspired.

2. _Normal fast_—no food, but water
This was, evidently, the kind of fasting Jesus did in the wilderness.

Matthew 4:2; Luke 4:2 _____

_____

This is also the type of fast usually assumed in other situations.

3. _Partial fast_—eliminates certain foods or meals over a period of time.

Daniel 1:12-16 _____

_____

Daniel 10:2 and 3 _____

_____

I Kings 17:4 and 9-15 _____

_____

Mark 1:6 _____

_____

Should We Fast?

Matthew 6:2, 5 and 16 In Jesus' Sermon on the Mount, He

doesn't say "if" ye give alms, pray and fast, but _____

Matthew 9:15 While Jesus (the bridegroom) is away, His discii ples are to _____

_____

Isaiah 58:3 and 4 We aren't to fast while _____

_____

Isaiah 58:5-12 God's chosen fast results in _____

_____

Romans 13:14 We're to put on the Lord Jesus Christ, and to make no _____

_____

I Corinthians 9:25-27 We're to bring our bodies under subjection that _____

_____

_____

Titus 2:12 We're to deny our flesh that _____

_____

(Note: As we can see from Scripture, _fasting_ isn't the same as _dieting_. Nor are those who suffer from eating disorders fasting for spiritual purposes.)

Look up the following verses and see who, in Scripture, fasted and why:

Deuteronomy 9:9 and 18 _____

_____

_____

I Samuel 1:7 _____

_____

_____

II Samuel 12:16 _____

WOMEN IN THE BIBLE

I Kings 19:8 _____

_____

II Chronicles 20:1-4 _____

_____

Ezra 8:21-23 _____

_____

Ezra 10:6 _____

_____

Nehemiah 1:4 _____

_____

Nehemiah 9:1 and 2 _____

_____

Esther 4:15-17 _____

_____

Psalm 35:13 _____

_____

Jeremiah 36:6 _____

_____

Daniel 9:2 and 3, 21 and 22 _____

_____

Joel 2:12-17 _____

196

Jonah 3: 5 and 10 _____

_____

_____

Luke 2:36 and 27 _____

_____

_____

Luke 4:2 _____

_____

_____

Acts 9:9 _____

_____

_____

Acts 10:30 _____

_____

_____

Acts 13:2 and 3 _____

_____

_____

Acts 14:23 _____

_____

_____

WOMEN
IN THE BIBLE

SUMMARY

Though eating is a daily activity, feasts are usually occasions of joyous celebration. The Hebrew people had several feasts that they observed throughout the year. Fasting, denying food to one's body, is a Scriptural discipline as well. In the Book of Esther we find several feasts as well as an important historic fast. After looking at these, we'll consider other instructions in God's Word about eating and not eating. Then we'll apply them to our own lives.

MODERN EXAMPLE

The following incident took place in a church summer camp where my husband and I served as counselors for a week.

It was an evening mealtime and my husband and I, as counselors, were seated around a table with eight 11, 12, and 13-year-olds. Since it was mid-week, we had, by now, eaten at least one meal with each of the campers—and we were disturbed.

Though we'd prepared ourselves for sharing meals with some picky eaters, we were surprised at how difficult it was to maintain edifying group conversations during the meals. Not only were there a variety of complaints about the food, but there was an absence of table manners as well. Some of the young people gulped their meals in silence; others didn't seem to eat at all. And sharing in caring communication during meal time seemed to be an experience lacking altogether. So, we determined at the next meal to ask each one to describe his or her family mealtimes at home. Their answers gave us much insight.

"We hardly ever eat together. Everybody has different schedules."

"We eat together, but the TV is usually on—especially if it's news time.

"Sometimes we eat together. Lot's of times we don't. Personally, I don't care, because I'd just as soon fix what I want."

"We try to eat together, but lots of times the phone rings or somebody comes by."

"We all eat together, but Dad rarely talks and Mom usually fusses with my younger brother."

"My parents and I nearly always end up arguing, because they don't think I eat enough."

Only two of the eight seemed to have regular family mealtimes, which included balanced diets and sharing in loving concern. This experience not only opened our eyes to the many benefits of family mealtimes, but renewed our own commitment to more quality mealtimes at home.

Multiple work schedules, television, fast foods, eating disorders, lack of communication, ignorance of God's Word, many factors destroy family mealtimes. And with them, many benefits which God intended are lost. We saw this in the young people at the junior-high camp. Though predominately from church families, they were losing out not only physically, mentally, and socially, but spiritually as well. What's in a mealtime? There are potentially many more blessings in these daily family occasions than most of us realize.

WHAT DO YOU THINK?

1. Have you ever participated in a Jewish feast? What occurred? _____

_____

_____

2. Have you taken part in any other feasts? _____

_____

_____

3. How would you describe your family's mealtimes? How can they be improved? _____

_____

_____

4. Do you fast? If so, what do you see as the benefit? If not, can you begin? _____

_____

_____

EVALUATE YOURSELF

1. In what ways are you implementing the principles learned from Esther? _____

_____

_____

2. In what ways are you failing to implement the principles learned from Esther? _____

_____

_____

3. What do you need to do to change? _____

_____

_____

4. How will you do it? _____

_____

_____

WOMEN IN THE BIBLE

Lesson 21
Gomer

An Example of God's Mercy and Love

WOMEN IN THE BIBLE

"Behold, what manner of love the Father hath bestowed upon us, that we should be called the sons of God."

I John 3:1

"Thou shalt not commit adultery."

Exodus 20:14

SETTING THE STAGE

God is love. Most people understand little about His kind of love. We love our husbands. We love our family. We love our friends. We love our hometown. We love our pets. We love to hike. We love chocolate cake. We use the word *love* so commonly, it's often meaningless.

Gomer was a woman who didn't truly understand or accept love. She knew infatuation, worldly love, and perhaps, even self-love. Hosea loved her in spite of who she was and what she did. Though she was unfaithful to him, he gave his all so she could be reconciled to him.

The story of Hosea and Gomer is a picture of God's love toward Israel, who committed spiritual adultery. It's also an illustration of Jesus' love for the Church, for whom He was willing to pay the supreme price—His life—for her reconciliation.

What is *love?* What is the love relationship we're to have with God, with our husbands, with others? What if we've committed physical or spiritual adultery? Can we ever know God's kind of love? These are questions which we'll consider in this lesson.

THE FAILURE OF GOMER

(Based on Hosea 1:1-3:5)

Hosea prophesied in the Northern Kingdom (Israel) during the time Isaiah prophesied in Judah. Hosea prophesied Israel's impending exile. God used Him to demonstrate His love for His people.

God commanded Hosea to take a wife who was a prostitute. Believing that Gomer was God's choice for him, Hosea married her. Soon she bore him a son who was named Jezreel in reference to God's coming punishment of the house of Jehu for the massacre at Jezreel. Not long after Jezreel was born, Gomer conceived again and bore a girl whom they called Loruhamah, in reference to the fact that God would have no more mercy on Israel, though He would show love to Judah. When Gomer weaned her daughter, she had a third child.

This child was named Loammi, for God was declaring that the Israelites weren't His people nor He their God any longer.

Gomer left Hosea to raise the three children and turned to adultery. Hosea loved her. He did much pleading to get her to return, and he determined to bring her back. He cried out to God as he thought of how his beautiful wife was playing the harlot.

One day he found her—a slave on an auction block. He paid the required price and bought her back. He took his wayward wife home and nursed her back to health, loving her with a love no other could understand.

LESSONS FROM GOMER
The Love of God

In the story of Hosea and Gomer we see the symbolic relationship of God with Israel, the people with whom He made a covenant (much like we are to make in marriage). We can also see the love relationship Jesus wants with His Bride, the Church, in that He paid the price for her reconciliation. In both cases, we find *agape* love—the benevolent, sacrificial love whose source is God.

Though in English we use only one term, there are various kinds of love. We know, for instance, that in our sex-saturated society, we find a very lustful, worldly passion called love. We also experience love for our families, love for brothers and sisters in the Lord, love for mankind, as well as love for our husbands. Occasionally, we may have even sacrificed our own rights and desires to benefit someone else because of love we're willing to give. Everyone will agree that none of these relationships are the same, none of the feelings are the same. Though we use one word, the Greek language has several words for *love*.

Since the New Testament was written in Greek, it would be a good idea to learn the various meanings of the Greek words. Let's look at some of these.

See Chart 21A

The Father Heart of God

To understand God's *agape* love, we must first recognize His love as that of a Heavenly Father who truly cares for us enough to die for us. Acceptance of this love is essential if we're to know love in our earthly relationships as well. Until we *know* that we are loved, we can't give love.

Some people think of God as a remote, impersonal being somewhere off in space. Others think of Him as an old gentleman sitting upon a throne, waiting to judge our every move. But, until one knows Him as a Heavenly Father, he really cannot relate to God as His child.

A wrong concept of God often results from a poor relationship with one's earthly father. If this relationship isn't healthy, one experiences many emotional wounds that keep him from any desire to have an intimate relationship with a Heavenly Father. Even the word "father" may connote rejection, abuse, disappointment, hurt, bitterness, neglect, or other negative feelings. Who wants to experience those feelings again?

Let's look at some of the attributes of fathers and see, from

202

LOVE

agapē

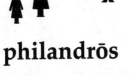

God →

affection or benevolence
sacrificial love—Godly
love
*"Behold, what manner of love the
Father hath bestowed upon us, that
we should be called the sons of
God..."*
(I John 3:1)

philadēlphia

brotherly love (kindness)
love of the brethren
*"But as touching brotherly love ye
need not that I write unto you; for
ye yourselves are taught of God to
love one another."*
(I Thessalonians 4:9)

philandrōs

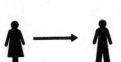

affectionate (as a wife)
love of husband
*"That they may teach the young
women to be sober, to love their
husbands, to love their children."*
(Titus 2:4)

philĕō

personal attachment (love
for family or friends)
*"He saith to him again the second
time, Simon, son of Jonah, lovest
thou me? He saith unto him, Yea,
Lord; thou knowest that I love
thee..."*
(John 21:16)

eros

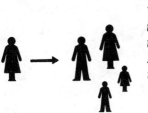

eros (not found in
scripture) ("erotic")
pleasure directed, self-
fulfilling, lustful, sexual
type love

Scripture, how God is a perfect Father:

Authority The father is intended to be the authority figure in the family. Hebrews 12:10 (LB) says, *"Our earthly fathers trained us for a few brief years, doing the best for us that they knew how, but God's correction is always right and for our best good, that we may share his holiness."*

Concern Earthly fathers shouldn't be too busy to attend to the personal needs of their children. I Peter 5:7 (LB) reminds us that God is concerned about us. *"Let him have all your worries and cares, for he is always thinking about you and watching everything that concerns you."*

Trust Though our earthly fathers may "let us down," our Heavenly Father never will. II Timothy 2:13 (LB) says, *"Even when we are too weak to have any faith left, he remains faithful to us and will help us, for he cannot disown us who are part of himself, and he will always carry out his promises to us."*

Affection Though our own fathers may have provided well for us, they might not have show us much affection. God does. I John 3:1 says, *"Behold, what manner of love the Father hath bestowed upon us, that we should be called the sons of God."*

Commitment We may think our earthly fathers deserted us at critical times, but God never will Hebrews 13:5 (NIV). *"Keep your lives free from the love of money and be content with what you have, because God has said, 'Never will I leave you: never will I forsake you.'"*

Communication Earthly fathers don't always communicate with their children, but God always wants to be in communication with us. We have the promise in Jeremiah 33:3. *"Call unto me, and I will answer thee, and show thee great and mighty things, which thou knowest not."*

Acceptance We may not have always felt accepted by our earthly father, but God loves and accepts us, unconditionally. Romans 5:8 reminds us of this. *"But God commendeth his love toward us, in that, while we were yet sinners, Christ died for us."* And in John 3:16. *"For God so loved the world that he gave his only begotten Son, that whosoever believeth in him should not perish, but have everlasting life."*

Ephesians 2:4-7 God's love is so great that _____

_____

_____

Jeremiah 31:3 God loves with an _____

_____

_____

Romans 5:5 The love of God is _____

_____

_____

I John 4:7-12 God's love is _____

_____

_____

I John 4:16 God is love and _____

_____

_____

I John 4:18-21 Concerning God's love, we learn that _____

_____

_____

I John 3:1 and 2 What manner of love has God bestowed upon us? _____

_____

_____

Luke 15:11-32 What does this parable tell us concerning a father's love? _____

_____

_____

Adultery

In the story of Hosea and Gomer, God visibly illustrates His own relationship with Israel, the chosen wife with whom He had a covenant. Through her, He demonstrated His everlasting mercy and agape love.

Thus we also have a picture of God's intended relationship with us, His people. He paid the price for our redemption even though we may have played the harlot by enjoying the company of other gods many times. We've committed spiritual adultery, just as Hosea and Gomer bore the pain of physical adultery.

Adultery is a grievous sin in the sight of God. He says so in His Word from Genesis to Revelation. Let's first see what He says concerning physical adultery:

Genesis 38:24 During pre-Mosaic times, adulterous wives were put to death.

Job 31:9-11 In this book, one of the oldest in Scripture, we find Job saying that adultery is *"an heinous crime; yes, it is an iniquity to be punished by the judges."*

Exodus 20:14 One of the ten commandments instructs man not to commit adultery.

Numbers 5:12-31 When a wife was suspected of adultery, a Jewish man could bring her to the priest, who made her drink water mixed with dust from the Tabernacle floor so the curse of God would come upon her.

Leviticus 20:10; Deuteronomy 22:22 An adulterer would surely die. It was a sin unto death among the Hebrew people.

Proverbs 7:10-27 Here we find that the house of an adulteress is the way to hell. All through the times of the Judges, Kings, and Prophets we find stories of adultery and its consequences—from the sons of Eli to King David himself. Ezekiel 16 graphically describes Israel as a harlot and an abomination to the Lord. She was a wife who committed adultery—a wife who took strangers instead of her husband (Ezekiel 16:32).

Matthew 5:27 and 28 Jesus, Himself, speaks of the consequences of adultery, as He describes how it relates to divorce and remarriage.

Romans 7:1-3 Paul gives further insight on the subject of adultery. He says death is the only accepted end to a marriage.

I Corinthians 6:9 and 10 Adultery (which is also described as a work of the flesh in Galatians 5:19) has no place in the kingdom of God.

Hebrews 13:4 God will judge the adulterers.

Revelation 21:8 The sexually immoral—and this includes adulterers—will be thrown in the lake of fire.

We find, in no uncertain terms, that adultery is unacceptable to God. It breaks the vow both to Him and to our married partner. Therefore, it's a sin punishable by death. Like any sin, there's only one way that it can be forgiven—through the mercy of God and the blood of Jesus Christ. Man's natural instinct is to overlook sin, to deny it, or to allow it to condemn him. But God wants us to recognize sin, confess it, and receive His forgiveness as we truly repent of what we have done and turn instead, to Him.

We see this dramatically portrayed in the story of David and Bathsheba, a couple who committed adultery. Their sin grieved God, and He judged them for it. Both were God-fearing persons. Yet they allowed themselves to be tempted, and succumbed to the lust of the flesh.

But because of true repentance and confession of their sin, God forgave them, and allowed His own Son, Jesus, to later be born of their seed. Yet their lives were lived out in the consequences of this one adulterous act. Their illegitimate child died soon after birth. God allowed David to be publicly exposed and shamed. Bathsheba had to bear the reproach and suffering of losing both a husband and child.

Jesus also demonstrated His mercy upon an adulteress when the scribes and Pharisees brought Him a woman taken in adultery. They wanted to trick him, in order to make further accusation against Him. They asked Jesus what His verdict should be. They were aware that He knew the commandment given by Moses, as well as His own teaching on God's love and forgiveness. He replied. *"He that is without sin among you, let him first cast a stone at her"* (John 8:7). The result was that the accusers own consciences were pricked and they left the scene. To the woman, Jesus said, *"Neither do I condemn thee; go, and sin no more."* In this act, Jesus forgave her. He expected her to truly repent, and sin no more.

As with most sin, adultery takes place first in the heart. Jesus said that whosoever *looks* upon a woman to lust after her has already committed adultery with her in his heart. He also said, in Matthew 15:19, *"For out of the heart proceed evil thoughts, murders, **adulteries,** fornications, thefts, false witnesses, blasphemies."* The things which come out of our hearts are the things which defile us.

The story of Hosea and Gomer shows God's unending grace and mercy toward us as sinners. God will always be as Hosea, willing to forgive and take us back into the relationship He desires. Gomer represents Israel and those of us who are His children, but are tempted by other lovers. We don't know the end of the story of Hosea and Gomer; we do know that only a

206

remnant of God's people chose to remain faithful to Him.

Spiritual Adultery

Though we may never actually commit physical adultery, we're always being tempted to commit spiritual adultery. This is known by other terms—half-heartedness, double-mindedness, idolatry, or being a *carnal* Christian. We're all guilty. Without the grace of God, we would be unable to have a restored relationship with Him.

What are some Biblical examples of spiritual adultery?

Judges 2:11-14 Here we have a description of Israel's apostasy. They followed other gods, the gods of the people who were round about them even though they had a covenant with the one true God. This occurred over and over again. Throughout their history. God has had to deal with them.

Ezekiel 16 The prophet describes Jerusalem's unfaithfulness as she played the harlot by committing fornication with her neighboring nations, according to verse 32, *"as a wife that committeth adultery, which taketh strangers instead of her husband!"* Verse 35 says: *"Wherefore, O harlot, hear the word of the Lord."*

James 4:4 Lest we think God's warning is only to Israel, let's see what James says to believers in James 4:4. *"Ye adulterers and adulteresses, know ye not that the friendship of the world is enmity with God? Whosoever therefore will be a friend of the world is the enemy of God."* We commit spiritual adultery when we love the world more than God.

Revelation 2:14 and 15 To one of the churches of Revelation 2, Jesus says that He is against them because of their idolatry and fornication, their lack of whole-hearted commitment to Him.

In verses 20-22 of the same chapter (but to a different church), He says that He will deal with those who succumb to false teaching and thus commit fornication. Upon those who seduce, as well as those who submit to their doctrines, He will inflict much tribulation unless they repent.

God is a jealous God. He will have no other gods before Him. (Exodus 20:3)

SUMMARY

Gomer was a woman who didn't truly understand love or accept it, even when Hosea gave her his unconditional love. The story of their relationship is a picture of God's agape love toward Israel, His "wife" who committed spiritual adultery with other nations. It can also be an illustration of Jesus' love for His Bride, the Church.

MODERN EXAMPLE

Doug and Sheryl met while working at a fast-food restaurant. Having attended the same high school, they had friends in common though they, themselves had never taken any classes together. In fact, they came from quite different backgrounds. Doug and his family were Christians and had lived in the same house most of his life. Sheryl, on the other hand, lived with her divorced mother and had moved around a lot. They struck up a friendship and began dating while working at the same place.

Because Doug was a Christian, he tried to get Sheryl to go to church with him. She did, and one day, she accepted Jesus as her Savior. In time, they were married and lived together nearly a year before Doug joined the army due to lack of steady employment. After boot camp he was sent overseas, where he wanted Sheryl to join him. But because she was pregnant, she wanted to stay with her mother and have her baby in familiar surroundings.

Doug wasn't happy about it, but agreed and told her to come as soon as she could after the baby arrived. Sheryl moved in with her mother who had various "boyfriends" over from time to time. It wasn't long before Sheryl stopped going to church, but she didn't tell Doug.

Finally, the baby was born, Sheryl spent her time caring for her little one—still postponing joining Doug until the baby was "old enough to travel." Meanwhile, she enjoyed the company of her mother's friends and even went to a movie with one of them. Because she was lonely for male companionship, she took him up on other offers, and before long, their relationship had gone too far. It was only when she discovered that she was pregnant that Sheryl panicked.

What would she tell Doug? If that weren't enough to worry her, the father of this baby left town when he learned of her situation. Not only did he not want to give up his free and easy life-style, but he also didn't want to ever meet Doug.

As Sheryl packed to go overseas, her heart was heavy. Taking their little girl to meet her father wasn't the joy she had dreamed it would be. She wondered if she should write him before she left or wait until she saw him to tell him the truth. She decided to wait.

Doug was overjoyed to meet his daughter for the first time, and delighted to see Sheryl after so many months of loneliness. However, he couldn't understand why Sheryl wasn't as happy. He decided the trip must have been too much for her.

As they began to get reacquainted, Sheryl continued to debate with herself about whether to confess her sin or just not say anything and let him think he was the father of a baby born prematurely.

Finally she could stand it no longer. When Doug asked her about how things had gone at home, she told him of her condition. At first Doug couldn't believe it. Then he became angry. In fact, he told her to pack up and go home. But he thought of how he would miss his little girl, and changed his mind. The next few weeks were almost unbearable for both of them. After much counsel from the base chaplain, Doug realized his only recourse was to forgive Sheryl and care for the baby she was carrying. He told her he loved her enough to forgive her, and he wanted to raise the baby as his own. She couldn't believe it. It made her wonder if God could forgive her, too. Broken at last, they asked for, and received, forgiveness from each other and from God. They determined to start a new life together, with God at the center.

Ironically, when they were finally at peace once again, Sheryl had a miscarriage. She was sad, not that the reminder of her sin was gone, but that she wouldn't have the child which brought her to a realization of a love beyond imagination—a love that only God could give.

WHAT DO YOU THINK?

1. Do you know the unconditional love of your heavenly Father? How? _____

_____

_____

2. What other kinds of love have you experienced? _____

_____

_____

3. Have you had any personal experience with adultery? (In your own life or its effect on someone else's life) What was the effect on all involved? Was forgiveness given and received? _____

_____

_____

4. Have you committed spiritual adultery? How can this change? _____

_____

_____

EVALUATE YOURSELF

1. In what ways are you implementing the principles learned from Gomer? _____

_____

_____

2. In what ways are you failing to implement the principles learned from Gomer? _____

_____

_____

3. What do you need to do to change? _____

_____

_____

4. How will you do it? _____

_____

_____

Lesson 22
Elizabeth & Anna

An Example of Jesus as Lord and King

"And he hath on his vesture and on his thigh a name written, King of Kings, and Lord of Lords."

Revelation 19:16

SETTING THE STAGE

As we begin our study of New Testament women, we'll look at two who were associated with the birth of Jesus. Elizabeth, mother of John the Baptist, was the first Biblical woman to acknowledge Jesus as her *Lord*, the One to whom she would commit her son's very life. We need to know this kind of commitment to the lordship of Jesus in our lives.

Anna, the elderly woman who fasted and prayed in anticipation of Jesus' birth, recognized Him as the Redemption of Israel at His circumcision ceremony when He was eight days old. Like Anna, we have the privilege, in these last days, of praying and fasting in preparation for the second advent of Jesus. This time, He will come not as Savior, but as *King of kings* and *Lord of lords*. Every knee will bow and ever tongue confess that Jesus Christ is Lord, either regretfully or joyfully, depending upon whether or not one acknowledged Him as Lord in this life.

Just as Scripture gives many names and adjectives to describe Jesus, He can be known in different ways. He is *Messiah, Immanuel, Alpha and Omega, Good Shepherd, Bread of Life.*

We'll look at some of these descriptive titles, as well as consider the power invested in the name of Jesus. We'll also try to differentiate between knowing Jesus as Savior and as Lord.

Jesus is known by many names, but it's only when the Holy Spirit allows us to confess Him as *Lord* that we truly begin to appreciate the various other aspects of His character and nature and see Him as *our* Lord.

THE SUCCESS OF ELIZABETH

(Based on Luke 1:5-80)

Elizabeth, of the priestly line of Aaron, married a priest named Zacharias. Luke describes this couple as *"righteous before God, walking in all the commandments of the Lord, blameless"* (Luke 1:6). But their sorrow was great because they had no child.

One day, when Zacharias entered the temple to burn incense, an angel appeared beside the altar. Zacharias was startled, but the angel Gabriel calmed his fears and told Zacharias that God had heard his prayers.

He and Elizabeth were going to have a son whom they were to name John. Gabriel told Zacharias this special child would be filled with the Holy Spirit from his mother's womb, and would be anointed to prepare the hearts of the people for the coming of the Lord.

When Zacharias, concerned because of Elizabeth's age, questioned the angel Gabriel about her ability to conceive, he became a mute—unable to talk until after the birth of the child.

As foretold, Elizabeth became pregnant. In her sixth month, Gabriel made another visit—this time, to Elizabeth's cousin Mary. He informed her that she, too, would have a special child. In fact, she would conceive by the Holy Spirit and bear the Son of God!

Soon after the angel's visit, Mary went to visit Elizabeth. The two women spent three months marveling at God's supernatural intervention in their lives and pondering the births of the sons they were to have.

It was in their inital greeting, however, that insight is given as to how each would view Jesus. When Elizabeth saw Mary, she was filled with the Holy Spirit and acknowledged Mary as the mother of her *Lord*. In response, Mary magnified the Lord, as *Savior*.

After Mary returned to Nazareth, Elizabeth had her baby. Friends and neighbors rejoiced as they gathered for the circumcision ceremony.

They fully expected the child would be named after his father. But Elizabeth announced that his name would be John. When Zacharias confirmed it, his tongue was loosed and he began to prophesy, telling of the purpose of his son's life. Elizabeth and Zacharias raised John until he was ready for the public ministry God had for him—calling people to repentance in preparation for the coming of the Lord Jesus Christ.

LESSONS FROM ELIZABETH
What's in a Name?

Dictionaries define *name* as a word constituting the distinctive designation of a person or thing. We identify people by their names. And though it isn't as true in our day or society, in the past a person's name often denoted something of their character or the family to which the belonged.

God Himself is known by different names which describe His character.
A few of these are:

ELOHIM—The Strong One (Genesis 1:1)

EL SHADDAI—Almighty God (Genesis 17:1)

JEHOVAH RAPHA—The Lord that heals (Exodus 15:26)

JEHOVAH SABAOTH—The Lord of Hosts (I Samuel 17:45)

JEHOVAH JIREH—The Lord will provide (Genesis 22:8)

Just as the name of God varies in Scripture, so we find many names for Jesus. Every one of the more than 220 names of

212

Jesus are given in scripture to give us new revelation of His person, character, personality, offices and qualities so that we can *know Him*.

Hebrews 1:4 says, *"Being made so much better than the angels, as he hath by inheritance obtained a more excellent name than they."* Jesus was given His name by God, a name which has within it the fullness of the Godhead. There is power in the name of Jesus because of the authority behind it. It's interesting to note that Joseph and Mary were informed separately that the baby born to them would be called Jesus. (Matthew 1:21; Luke 1:31) Let's look at a partial list of other names by which He is known.

The Names of Jesus

SON OF MAN Luke 19:10

SON OF GOD John 1:34

ALPHA AND OMEGA Revelation 22:13

HIGH PRIEST Hebrews 9:11 and 12

ROCK I Corinthians 10:4

SHEPHERD John 10:11

LIGHT John 8:12

BREAD OF LIFE John 6:35 and 48

WORD John 1:1-3 and 14

REDEEMER Job 19:25

LAMB OF GOD John 1:29

PRINCE OF PEACE Isaiah 9:6

TEACHER John 3:2

BRIDEGROOM John 3:29

DESIRE OF ALL NATIONS Haggai 2:7

IMMANUEL Isaiah 7:14

DOOR John 10:7-9

WAY, TRUTH, LIFE John 14:6

TRUE VINE John 15:1-4

DELIVERER Romans 11:26

LAST ADAM, SECOND MAN I Corinthians 15:45-47

THE HEAD OF THE BODY Ephesians 4:15 and 16

FIRSTFRUITS I Corinthians 15:20-23

MESSIAH John 4:25

CHRIST Acts 9:20 and 22

OUR RIGHTEOUSNESS Jeremiah 23:5 and 6

MEDIATOR I Timothy 2:5

KING OF KINGS AND LORD OF LORDS
Revelation 19:11-16

Look up the following Scriptures and see what the Word says about the name of Jesus:

Matthew 10:22 _____

_____

_____

Matthew 12:21 _____

_____

_____

Matthew 18:5 _____

_____

_____

Matthew 18:20 _____

_____

_____

Matthew 24:5 _____

_____

_____

Matthew 28:19 _____

_____

_____

Mark 9:38 and 39 _____

_____

_____

Mark 16:17 and 18 _____

_____

_____

John 1:12 _____

_____

_____

John 3:18 _____

_____

_____

John 14:13-15 _____

_____

_____

John 15:16 _____

_____

_____

John 16:24 _____

Acts 2:38 and 39 _____

_____

Acts 3:1-6 and 16 _____

_____

Acts 4:12 _____

_____

Acts 4:29 and 30 _____

_____

Acts 5:28 _____

_____

Acts 16:18 _____

_____

I Corinthians 5:4 _____

_____

I Corinthians 6:11 _____

_____

Ephesians 5:20 _____

_____

Philippians 2:9-11 _____

_____

Colossians 3:17 _____

_____

WOMEN
IN THE BIBLE

II Thessalonians 1:11 and 12 _____

_____

_____

Jesus As Savior and Lord

Jesus' main purpose in coming into this world was to give His life as the supreme sacrifice for sin. He came to save us from eternal damnation. Thus, He is known as our Savior.

He paid the price for sin with His own blood. He not only desires that we accept the salvation He offers, He expects us to follow Him in every way—submitting to His Word, doing His commands, and obeying Him in love.

We can see this in the relationship a master has with a servant. A master purchases a servant and expects the servant do his bidding. He feels especially honored if the servant obeys out of love rather than duty.

I Corinthians 12:3 says no one can say "Jesus is Lord" except by the Holy Spirit. When we accept Jesus as our Savior, the Holy Spirit exalts Him so that we begin to see Him as our Lord. The more we submit to Jesus as our master and yield to the leading of the Holy Spirit, the more we understand the ways to express His Lordship in our lives.

Elizabeth, by the power of the Holy Spirit, acknowledged Jesus as her lord even before His birth. We who live after His life, death, and resurrection, have the opportunity and responsibility to proclaim Jesus as Lord of our lives. For we know that, by His death and resurrection, He demonstrated victory over Satan and all his works, and He gave us the means to reckon our own flesh crucified with Him. Because the Holy Spirit was subsequently poured out in fullness, we have available to us the ability to see Jesus as *our Lord*.

Jesus As Savior

Hebrews 2:14 and 15 To save us, Jesus _____

_____

_____

Hebrews 5:8 and 9 Jesus became the author of eternal salvation by _____

_____

_____

Romans 5:19 By one man's disobedience, _____ but, by the obedience of Jesus _____

_____

_____

I Timothy 1:15 Jesus came into the world to _____

216

Luke 19:10 Jesus told Zaccheus that _____

_____

_____

Acts 16:30 and 31 Paul told the Philippian jailer _____

_____

_____

I Peter 1:18-21 We are saved by _____

_____

_____

Romans 5:9-11 We are saved _____

_____

_____

John 3:36 He that believes in Jesus _____

_____

_____

Romans 6:23 Without salvation _____

_____

_____

Romans 10:9 To be *saved*, one must _____

_____

_____

Romans 10:13 One is saved by _____

_____

_____

Ephesians 2:8 and 9 Salvation comes through _____

_____

_____

Jesus As Lord

I Corinthians 12:3 No one can say that Jesus is Lord except

_____

_____

Romans 10:9 At the time of salvation, _____

_____

Luke 24:34 The Lord is _____

_____

_____

Ephesians 4:4-6 There is one _____

_____

_____

Acts 2:36 God has made _____

_____

_____

Romans 14:9 Jesus died and lives again that _____

_____

_____

Philippians 2:6-11 Jesus became obedient unto death that

_____

_____

I Timothy 6:13-15 We are to keep God's commandments until _____

_____

_____

Revelation 1:7 Those who do not recognize Jesus' lordship will _____

_____

_____

Revelation 11:15 The kingdoms of this world will _____

_____

_____

Matthew 7:21-23 Some will call Jesus Lord, but _____

_____

_____

THE SUCCESS OF ANNA
(Based on Luke 2:36-38)

Luke describes Anna as an elderly woman who served the Lord in the temple through continual prayer and fasting. This may not seem too unusual, but when we read the three verses that tell of her, we discover that she was a prophetess—yet God hadn't spoken through prophets for four hundred years. She was of the tribe of Asher, but the tribe usually associated with temple worship was Levi. She was also an 84-year-old widow—definitely past the prime of life.

When death took her husband, Anna joined the holy women who devoted themselves in continual service in the temple. Here, she joined the congregations and poured out her soul to the Lord. Day after day, she prayed for the coming of the Messiah, and although He seemed to tarry she waited for His appearance.

One day, the miracle happened. As she entered the temple, she heard the sounds of joy proceeding from the inner court and Simeon saying, *"Now, Lord, lettest Thou Thy servant depart in peace, for mine eyes have seen Thy salvation:* (Luke 2:29). Then, when she saw the child in the arms of his parents Anna knew that the *Redemption of Israel* had come. She, who had prayed and fasted for many years, now was able to proclaim the glad tidings to those who shared her faith and hope. She and Simeon, were rewarded with the sight of the baby Jesus, and knew that He was indeed, the Christ (the *anointed one* who would be the way of salvation). Her waiting and service prepared the way for the birth of the Savior of mankind, the coming of the Lord Jesus Christ.

LESSONS FROM ANNA
Jesus' Second Coming—As King

Today we have the privilege of being part of the generation which is looking forward to the Second Coming of Jesus—this time, as King of kings and Lord of lords, to rule and reign eternally. It's also a time of anticipation for the Marriage Supper of the Lamb, when the Church (the Body of Christ) will join the Bridegroom Jesus Christ. From I John 3:2, we know that the true Church will recognize Him, for she will be like Him. She will have His nature, for she will have known Him in many ways—Savior, Word, Redeemer, Master, Bread, Healer, Good Shepherd, and, most of all, as Lord.

In the meantime we have a work to do as we wait. Let's look at Scripture and see what this involves:

Luke 21:34-36 _____

_____

_____

Luke 12:35-40 _____

_____

_____

Matthew 24:42-44 _____

_____

_____

Matthew 25:1-13 _____

WOMEN IN THE BIBLE

Matthew 28:18-20 _____

_____

_____

Ephesians 6:10-18 _____

_____

_____

II Timothy 4:1-4 _____

_____

_____

I John 3:2 and 3 _____

_____

_____

I Timothy 6:11-16 _____

_____

_____

SUMMARY

Jesus has many names and titles. *Immanuel*, for instance, was one given to Him even before His birth. Elizabeth recognized Him as her *Lord* before He was born. Anna, a prophetess, was privileged to see the infant Jesus after many years of praying for His coming. In our day, we're awaiting Jesus' coming again, this time as King. Meanwhile, we're privileged to become acquainted with Him in the various ways God has provided—Shepherd, Redeemer, Baptizer, Master, Author and Finisher of our faith, soon-coming Bridegroom.

MODERN EXAMPLE

Only because of their individual commitments to Jesus Christ as Lord, could Corrie ten Boom and "Hansi" Hirschmann exchange the love of God in a world that should deem them enemies.

Corrie was born into a Dutch family of watchmakers in the late 1800's. It was her grandfather, in response to a plea from his pastor, who gathered people into his home above a jewelry store to read the Scriptures and pray for the Jewish people, many of whom lived nearby. In the very same house, exactly one hundred years later, Corrie's entire family was arrested for hiding Jews during the German occupation of Holland. Her brother and one sister were detained a short time. Corrie's father and sister Betsie died in separate concentration camps. After many months in concentration camps Corrie was released by mistake.

It was her commitment to Jesus as Lord that gave her the ability to share her victory over those horrible prison experiences with the world following her release. She was especially tested when, after a talk in a German church, she was greeted by a man whom she recognized as one of the cruelest guards in the camp where she'd been held. When he asked for her forgiveness, she was overwhelmed with nightmarish memories.

Submitting her emotions to the will of her Lord, she stretched out her hand to her former enemy with the love and forgiveness that only God can give.

During these same war years, a young Czeckoslovakian girl named "Hansi" served in the Nazi Youth movement giving all her allegiance to her new German "god," Adolph Hitler. Though she had been raised in a Christian home, she was attracted by Hitler's philosophy, and before long she was thoroughly brainwashed. It was only after Germany was defeated and she was in a Communist labor camp that she learned of the holocost involving six million Jews and of the concentration camps such as the one where Corrie was interned.

Though her mother's persistent prayers, the hand of God brought Hansi back to the Church, and then to the cross of Jesus Christ. After finally giving Him her pride, her despair, her crippled emotions, and her confusion, she acknowledged Jesus both as Savior and Lord. Then she came to America to give her testimony to those she had been taught to hate.

It was after the release of her book, "Hansi, the Girl Who Loved the Swastika," that she met Corrie at a Christian Bookseller's Convention in Dallas. At a luncheon there, she allowed herself to hear for the first time, of the terrible suffering experienced by many at the hand of Hitler to whom she had given her idealistic youth.

Overwhelmed with "collective guilt," yet enveloped by God's mercy and grace, she took one of her autographed books to Corrie who received it with compassion and understanding love. Forgiveness was given and healing was received. The two women from opposing sides of a terrible war were made "one" in the Body of Christ because each was willing to allow Jesus to be Lord of her life.

WHAT DO YOU THINK?

1. Do you know Jesus as Lord, as well as Savior? What difference does this make? _____

_____

_____

2. In what other ways do you know Him? (such as Shepherd, the Way, Healer) _____

_____

_____

3. Are you looking forward to His coming as King? How can you prepare for this? _____

WOMEN IN THE BIBLE

_____

_____

EVALUATE YOURSELF

1. In what ways are you implementing the principles learned from Elizabeth and Anna? _____

_____

_____

2. In what ways are you failing to implement the principles learned from Elizabeth and Anna? _____

_____

_____

3. What do you need to do to change? _____

_____

_____

4. How will you do it? _____

_____

_____

Lesson 23
Mary, Mother of Jesus

An Example of Meditating on God's Word

"Let the words of my mouth, and the meditations of my heart, be acceptable in thy sight, O Lord, my strength and my redeemer."

Psalm 19:14

SETTING THE STAGE

Mary, the mother of our Lord Jesus, is one of the most special women of all time. God chose her as the one through whom the Word would be made flesh. This must have been beyond Mary's comprehension. It was only the first of many mysteries Mary had to ponder in her heart. There were also the circumstances surrounding Jesus' birth, the sudden flight into Egypt, finding her son in the temple discussing his "Father's" business, being ignored by Him while He was ministering, His calling her "woman" at the wedding in Cana, and hardest of all, having to watch Jesus die a cruel death by crucifixion.

Perhaps it was only after she received the fullness of the Holy Spirit at Pentecost, following Jesus' death and resurrection, that Mary had some of her "whys" answered. Yet she submitted to God's will for her life. She suffered much pain while living through the many things she didn't understand.

We have Jesus, God's written Word, and the gift of the Holy Spirit to help us understand God's Word to us. But to receive revelation we must, like Mary, *meditate* upon what He has said, and ponder His teachings in our hearts. This takes time, discipline, quietness, expectation, and sensitivity to the Holy Spirit. The results may be conviction of sin, need for intercession, desire to sing praise, or a deepening commitment to the Lord. True meditation creates within us a response toward God which we must obey in light of what we have received.

THE SUCCESS OF MARY
(Based on Matthew 1; 2; 12:46-50; Luke 1; 2; John 2:1-11; 19:25; Acts 1:14)

Mary the mother of Jesus, is probably the most recognized woman of the Bible; yet she is probably the least known as a person. Many things happened in her life, but we aren't told how she felt or what she thought. We only know that she had much to ponder as she accepted what came her way.

For instance, in events surrounding Jesus' birth, we can

imagine her having such questions as: "What does it mean that I will conceive by the Holy Ghost and bear God's only Son?" "How will I raise him, especially since I am not yet married?" "Why was I chosen to be this child's mother?" "Why did God announce His birth to some shepherds and not to more prominent people?" "How did the angels appear in the sky?" "What did Simeon mean when he said that Jesus would be a 'light to lighten the Gentiles, and the glory of thy people Israel'?" "What is His 'Father's business' anyway?" We could go on and on, thinking of questions we would have in our own hearts and minds if any one of these things happened to us.

When Jesus was just a baby being presented to the Lord in the temple, Simeon gave Mary a prophecy which she must have also pondered in her heart many times. He told her that the thoughts of many hearts would be revealed through her child, and that a sword would pierce her own soul.

Imagine the suffering Mary must have experienced as she saw Jesus increasingly given to His Father's business, yet being ridiculed and then tried. Imagine her agony as she watched her first-born son stripped, beaten, and nailed to a cross to hang until He died.

Mary doesn't stand apart from the rest of our sinful human race. As part of a fallen mankind, she recognized her own need for deliverance from sin and guilt when she sang, before Jesus' birth, "My spirit hath rejoiced in God my Savior." Mary was a faithful, humble, godly woman in need of a Savior.

God, in His great love and mercy, allowed her to be present for the outpouring of the Holy Spirit. As the Comforter and Spirit of Truth opened her eyes, she probably received insight and answers to the many ponderings which had been so long in her heart.

LESSONS FROM MARY
Loneliness

There's a special loneliness that accompanies "pondering things in our hearts." The kind of questions we're usually left to ponder are those which no one else understands.

No doubt Mary and Elizabeth did much talking, as they shared three common months of pregnancy. This was God's mercy to them both.

Who else could begin to understand their particular situations, let alone their feelings and questions? Mary was probably able to share some things with Joseph, though it seems likely that he died between the time Jesus was 12 and 30 years old.

Yet even with one or two who might understand, there are still intimate, personal ponderings for which no one has the answers except God. To know them, we must be alone with Him.

God knows this. He often arranges circumstances so He might be alone with His own—especially those He wants to use. He wants us to depend upon *Him* and to know *His* voice. We can't do that when there's even one other person with whom to talk. (See Micah 7:5-7).

Look at others in Scripture who were put in lonely places

and had time to ponder things in their hearts and receive God's answers:

Genesis 22:1-6 Though Abraham must have, many times, pondered whether or not he'd heard God correctly, the most poignant time must have been when God asked him to take his supernaturally-given child onto a mountain and offer him as a sacrifice. What questions do you think Abraham pondered during his lonely trek up the mountain?

Genesis 32:23-32 Jacob was returning to his homeland after marrying two wives and raising some children. He was also preparing to meet Esau after having had to flee from him many years earlier. As he sent his families on ahead, he was left behind to wrestle with a man all night. This confrontation with God left Jacob a broken man. He was even given a new name. What ponderings of the heart do you think Jacob had as he then set out to catch up with the rest of the caravan?

Genesis 43:30-33 Joseph experienced many lonely times in his life. But the zenith of his loneliness must have come when his brothers came to Egypt to get grain because of a famine. Joseph entertained his brothers while waiting for the perfect time to reveal his identity. What do you think were some of the ponderings of his heart during this time?

Exodus 32:11-20 Moses also experienced many lonely times, including 40 years on the backside of the desert prior to God's call to become the leader of His people. Later, when he came down from Mt. Sinai after receiving the ten commandments, he found the people dancing around a golden calf. What might have been some of the ponderings of Moses' heart in the lonely place of leadership?

I Kings 19:1-14 Elijah had just come from a big confrontation on Mt. Carmel with 450 prophets of Baal. Yet after all the display of God's favor and power, he found himself alone in a wilderness because of the anger of Queen Jezebel. What must have been the ponderings of Elijah's heart during this time?

Psalm 40 One look through the Psalms and we know that David experienced many lonely times, both when Saul was after him, and when he, himself, was king. This Psalm gives us some of the answers to David's experience of being alone in a pit, and to the ponderings he must have had while there. What was the result?

Nehemiah 2:11-16 Nehemiah was sent by God to return to Jerusalem and rebuild the walls of the city. What do you imagine were some of the ponderings of this man as, alone one night, he viewed the city?

Jeremiah 15:10-18 The people had forsaken God. God was angry with the people. And Jeremiah wondered why he had been born! In these verses, he laments his personal situation. What are the ponderings of his heart?

II Timothy 4:16-18 Like the prophets of old, the New Testament apostles also experienced many lonely times. They, too, weren't heard and had to suffer persecution. Paul tells of one of these times in a letter to Timothy. What are some of the things which Paul must have pondered during his lonely times?

Galatians 1:15-18 What can we assume happened to Paul during this lonely period in his life?

Meditation

We've considered the ponderings of the heart caused by things that happen, and the accompanying loneliness. Let's look at another aspect—the initiative one must take to seek solitude and meditate upon God's Word.

We recalled how Mary, and other people in the Bible, were left alone to ponder the things of God. Not included in this list was Jesus. He was one who sought to be alone and meditate upon the Father's will. In Matthew 26:36-45 we find Him going alone to pray in the Garden of Gethsemane just prior to His crucifixion. During this agonizing time, He must have pondered things He knew were to come to pass, as He submitted to the will of His Heavenly Father.

Each of us, as disciples of our Lord Jesus Christ, takes the initiative to be alone with Him so that we can meditate upon God's Word. It's during these times that our strength is renewed and our spirits are refreshed. Only then can we face the world with its emptiness, harshness, and confusion and still have the victory God intends. We're endued with His strength, and His power, and His faith.

What does the Word of God say concerning meditation the quiet contemplation of spiritual truths?

Joshua 1:8 We're to meditate _____

so that _____

_____

_____

II Chronicles 20:12 Jehoshaphat, in determining to seek the Lord, recognized that he needed to _____

_____

_____

Isaiah 40:31 Those who wait upon the Lord will _____

_____

_____

Psalm 119:18 We want our eyes open so that _____

_____

_____

Psalm 119:97 God's law is to be our meditation _____

_____

_____

Psalm 119:99 From meditation, we receive _____

_____

_____

Psalm 119:148 We look forward to the night watches that

Psalm 1:2 and 3 The godly man meditates _____
_____
_____

The result is _____
_____
_____

Psalm 49:3 Out of the meditation of our hearts will be _____
_____

Psalm 63:5 and 6 The result of meditating on God is _____
_____
_____

Psalm 19:14 We need to pray that the meditations of our heart
will _____
_____
_____

Psalm 77:11 and 12 We're to meditate upon _____
_____
_____

Psalm 104:34 Our meditation of God shall be _____
_____
_____

I Timothy 4:6-16 (KJV) Here, Timothy is told to meditate upon
_____
_____

I John 2:27 As we meditate upon God's Word, the _____
_____

Knowing Christ and meditating upon God's Word are daily necessities. The following steps are suggested to help you do this:

1. Find a quiet, private place.
2. Prepare your heart (confess sin, bind the enemy, ask the Holy Spirit for insight).

3. Focus on a few verses of Scripture.

4. Read slowly and deliberately, pondering every word.

5. Write down what God says to you through the Word.

6. Apply the verses to your own life and respond as the Lord directs.

7. If there's opportunity, share your insights with someone else.

A Warning

A study on meditation wouldn't be complete without a warning. This concept is also popularly used today for false purposes which include the following:

Transcendental Meditation   The very initiation ceremony is a purely orthodox Hindu religious ceremony. Every time a TM pupil invokes a secret word (or Mantra), he actually invokes a spirit to possess him. With its emphasis on meditation, the use of the Mantra and concentration on a single object is simply a variant of the Hindu practice of Yoga.

Yoga   From the Sanskrit root, "Yug", Yoga literally means to yoke or unite the human soul with the universal spirit. Yoga, through what is disguised as physical exercise, seeks to liberate the individual from the "cycle of rebirth," or reincarnation, which, to the Hindu, constitutes Salvation.

Drugs   Throughout history, man has sought to escape tension, elevate moods and relieve anxiety by artificial means. But in no other time has man become as drug dependent as he is today. We usually think of those who are on drugs as the ones to be concerned about. Yet millions of "normal" people are also addicted to drugs. And these do affect one's mind sometimes to the extent of making meditation upon God's Word nearly impossible. Gaining peace of mind through the use of tranquilizers and pain killers is the order of the day instead of gaining peace of mind and strength of God through His Word.

Television   Lest none of us be left out, we must consider the use of television as one of the greatest enemies to our meditation upon God's Word. Not only does it consume time we could give to meditating upon the Word, but it fills our minds and hearts with messages contrary to God's Word. We find ourselves meditating upon those things even when we aren't watching television.

SUMMARY

Mary, the mother of Jesus, is often spoken of in Scripture as "pondering this in her heart." Many things happened to her which she did not understand. She pondered these, meditating upon what they could possibly mean. We are to do this with the Word God gives to us. In doing so, God may give us additional insight. Mary was present on the Day of Pentecost when the Holy Spirit filled the Believers who were waiting for his coming. Likewise, when we received the fullness of God's Spirit, we will have new revelation, for His Spirit is the Spirit of Truth and will lead us into it.

MODERN EXAMPLE

In Christian meditation, we begin with a Word or Scriptural

principle and ponder ways to apply its truth to our everyday lives. *Or,* we can look at incidents in our daily experiences and ask the Lord to show us Scriptural truths to glean from them.

The following is an example of what the Lord showed one of his children after a day of picking Macadamia nuts in Hawaii.

Macadamia nut trees know no season. They continually bloom, bear fruit, and drop the ripe nuts onto the ground below. Harvesting these nuts is an ongoing process done by workers who must pick the nuts off the ground.

The kingdom of God also knows no season. The Father allows souls that are ripe to be gathered, while others aren't yet ready to bloom. The "harvesters" must also spend time on their knees.

The ripe "mac" nut is hard to find, especially if leaves and debris haven't been cleared by gas blowers. The workers must be properly clothed with long sleeves, long pants and gloves in order to be protected from thorns and prickly leaves. Likewise, ripe souls are sometimes hard to find, hidden under the debris of the world unless the clutter has been removed. As workers in God's vineyard, we, too, must be fully clothed— with the whole armor of God—lest we be snared by the wiles of the devil. We also need discernment as to which souls are "ready" to pick.

Macadamia nuts can be deceiving. They may look fine laying on the ground, but, must be checked carefully when picked up. Even the slightest hole may indicate that the meat has been eaten, and it's only an empty shell. We must also be careful lest we be deceived. Many people confess the name of Jesus and appear to be religious, but lack a relationship with Him. The outward appearance may be covering up an empty heart.

Workers have different techniques in harvesting macadamia nuts. Some like to dig under rocks; others crawl under bushes in the hopes of finding the best and most nuts. Christian workers also have different ways of harvesting souls. God gives varying gifts so many can be reached. Nor will we find the fruit God intended for us if we're busy watching how others do their job!

Macadamia nuts are quite difficult to crack. They're enclosed in two protective shells. The outer husk is soft and can be removed by hand. But the second shell is so hard that the nuts must be dumped into large furnaces where the heat reduces the water content. Here, they're roasted until the meat shrinks from the shell. Then they're put between large steel drums which exert 300 pounds of pressure per nut. After cracking, the nuts fall into a moving trough of water where the shells float to the top and are skimmed off. Finally, the nut meats are sorted, salted and ready to consume as a delicious treat!

It's tempting to think that, once our outer shell is removed and we are "saved," that, somehow, this is all there is to God's design for our lives. Yet the refining process must go on until the delicious fruit makes its appearance. To obtain this final result, God allows us to be thrown into the refining furnace until those hard shells of bitterness, anger, and resentment, are cracked. The steel drums of God's pressure expose us. Then, through the washing of the Word, the old man surfaces

WOMEN IN THE BIBLE

and is removed. Finally, we're ready for use—some to be packed and sent all over the world, others to be salted and left out in a dish for those nearby to nibble on. Whether we are left plain, or hidden in a box of chocolates, the choice isn't up to us. We're His.

WHAT DO YOU THINK?

1. Do you allow time for meditation upon God's Word every day? When and how? _____

   _____

   _____

2. Can you share a recent insight on Scripture which came to you through meditation on it? _____

   _____

   _____

3. Have you ever given yourself to the wrong kind of meditation? (such as Transendental Meditation) How have you dealt with this? _____

   _____

   _____

EVALUATE YOURSELF

1. In what ways are you implementing the principles learned from Mary? _____

   _____

   _____

2. In what ways are you failing to implement the principles learned from Mary? _____

   _____

   _____

3. What do you need to do to change? _____

   _____

   _____

4. How will you do it? _____

   _____

   _____

Lesson 24
Mary & Martha

An Example of Friends—Family

"Henceforth I call you not servants; for the servant knoweth not what his lord doeth: but I have called you friends; for all things that I have heard of my Father I have made known unto you."
John 15:15

"God setteth the solitary in families."
Psalm 68:6

SETTING THE STAGE

After Jesus left His home in Nazareth to enter His public ministry, Scripture is silent as to whether he returned to His family, even for visits. We do know, however, that He often went to the home of Mary, Martha, and Lazarus. These two sisters and a brother, lived in Bethany, a town just outside of Jerusalem. Jesus went here, to rest and share pleasant fellowship with His friends. It was with them that He had a poignant meal just prior to His triumphal entry into Jerusalem.

Though the two women's names are usually linked together, they're often recognized in contrast. Martha is known as the one "cumbered about with much serving," as she performed many hospitable tasks. Mary, on the other hand, is recognized as the one who "chose the good part," sitting at Jesus' feet to learn from Him. They were bound together in their concern for their brother, Lazarus, when he became ill and died. Jesus ministered to each of these sisters in a unique way. This lesson will focus on the relationship they had with each other. We'll also consider their hospitality, as they expressed their friendship to Jesus.

Jesus has called us to be His friends (John 15:14). He also wants us to relate to one another as friends. This lesson will also consider what Scripture says concerning some of the benefits and costs of friendship. Then, since Jesus enjoyed the fellowship of this specific family, we'll look at what God intends for both natural families as well as the family we become part of when we accept Jesus as our Savior.

THE SUCCESS OF MARY
(Based on Luke 10:38-41; John 11; 12:1-8)
Developing a Relationship

Mary and Martha seem to belong together just as Cain and Abel, Jacob and Esau. They, too, were opposites in many ways. Martha busy with household tasks, was a very practical person given to hospitality. Mary, on the other hand, seemed to prefer to sit quietly and peacefully at the feet of Jesus, soaking in the truths He unfolded. She wanted to learn all she could about her Master and Friend. The two sisters had their own appropriate talents, and each served their friend, Jesus, accordingly.

Mary seemed to be a more sensitive person. For example, though both Mary and Martha loved their brother we read only of Mary's weeping when he died. Though Martha went to greet Jesus when He came to be with them, Mary is the one who threw herself at His feet and wept. And, Jesus wept with her before he brought Lazarus back to life.

The night before Jesus made His triumphal entry into Jerusalem, less than a week before He would be crucified and buried in a tomb, a banquet was held in Simeon's house. Out of gratefulness for what Jesus had done for her family, Mary took a bottle of perfume and anointed Jesus' feet, wiping them with her hair. As the fragrance permeated the house, Jesus commended her. Though Mary couldn't have known of the events which lay ahead, Jesus knew and saw it as a preparation for burial. For Mary it was an act of friendship toward one who had become like one of the family.

THE SUCCESS OF MARTHA
(Based on Luke 10:38-41; John 11; 12:1-8)

Practical Hospitality

The first glimpse we have of Martha is of her giving hospitality when she received Jesus into her house (which suggests that she may have been the owner). The provision of this home meant much to Jesus. One day He said "The son of man hath not where to lay his head." But the next day, the Bible says *He came to Bethany...and Martha made him a supper.* It was to this home, just outside Jerusalem, Jesus often came to be ministered to and refreshed physically. For Martha, home responsibilities were never a drudgery. She was ever ready to entertain those who sought refuge under her hospitable roof.

Luke, who must have accompanied Jesus to the House, noticed that Martha "was cumbered about much serving," as she probably found herself drawn hither and yon by conflicting chores. She loved Jesus and she wanted everything to be ready for Him. It especially irritated her to see Mary just sitting and listening to Jesus while she was busy getting the meal ready. She begged Jesus to ask Mary to help out so that the practical things could get done. Jesus recognized that her work was for Him, but He also reminded her that she was permitting her outward activities to hinder her spiritually.

John takes up where Luke leaves off and fills in the details of practical Martha. Following Lazarus' illness and death, many friends came to comfort the grief-stricken sisters as they eagerly awaited their beloved Friend's arrival. When Jesus finally did arrive, Martha was the first to meet Him. She rebuked Him for not coming earlier. At the same time, in faith, she declared that Jesus could perform a miracle. Then followed a conversation in which Martha confessed her belief in the resurrection. Jesus had declared that *He* was the resurrection and life. Jesus didn't explain His delay in coming, but He assured Martha that her brother would rise again.

At the grave, Martha gave vent to her feelings again, and implied that it would be impossible to bring her brother back to life because he'd been dead four days. But a miracle hap-

232

pened and Lazarus came forth, much to the joy of both Mary and Martha. This physical miracle resulted in spiritual miracles, as many others then believed.

The last mention of Martha was at the supper to celebrate the resurrection of Lazarus. As usual, she served the meal. Nor did she make any objection when Mary anointed Jesus' feet with the costly perfume. She was no longer distracted over her tasks, but calm and trustful, seemingly in full agreement with her sister's act of love and devotion to their Master and Friend.

LESSONS FROM MARY AND MARTHA
Friendship

Scripture gives no account of Jesus' returning to His natural home after He began His public ministry. However, when He was in or near Jerusalem, we find that He often went to the hospitable home of Mary and Martha in Bethany. It was here that he retired to find refreshment and fellowship with friends.

Before we consider some aspects of friendship, let's look at other friends mentioned in the Bible.

James 2:23; Isaiah 41:8 Abraham was considered a friend of

_____

_____

Ruth 1:16-18 As part of Ruth's friendship with Naomi, she committed herself to Naomi by _____

_____

_____

I Samuel 18:1 Though King Saul hated David, his son Jonathon _____

_____

_____

II Kings 2:1-4 Elijah and Elisha showed their friendship for one another by _____

_____

_____

Job 42:10 What happened when Job prayed for his friends?

_____

_____

Several Proverbs instruct us concerning friendships:

Proverb 27:6 (LB) Wounds from a friend are _____

_____

_____

Proverb 27:10 (LB) Never abandon a friend, for _____

_____

_____

Proverb 17:17 A friend _____

_____

_____

Proverb 18:24 A friend _____

_____

_____

John 15:12-15 describes the friendship Jesus wants to have
with us. What does this involve? _____

_____

_____

II Timothy 1:16-18 Paul had a friend named Onesiphorus who

_____

_____

_____

Romans 16:1 and 2 Paul encouraged the saints in Rome to

_____

because _____

_____

_____

Romans 16:3 and 4 Paul declared his friendship with Priscilla
and Aquila by saying that _____

_____

_____

Romans 16:6-16 Paul names as other friends in Rome _____

_____

_____

I Corinthians 16:15-20 Paul encouraged the Corinthian
friends to _____
for they had _____

_____

_____

Ephesians 6:21-24 Paul's final greeting to his friends at Ephesus was _____

_____

_____

Philippians 4:14-23 Paul commends his friends in Philippi because _____

_____

Colossians 4:7-15 Paul said of his friends in Colosse _____

_____

_____

II Timothy 4:19-21 Paul had the following to say to Timothy about his friends _____

_____

_____

Titus 3:12-15 Paul had the following to say to Titus about his friends _____

_____

_____

Philemon 22-24 In closing his letter to his friend Philemon, Paul said _____

_____

Hospitality

One of the acts of friendship is to be hospitable.
Romans 12:13 As Christians, we are commanded to _____

_____

_____

Hebrews 13:2 In fact, our hospitality is to go beyond friends, for we are to _____

_____

_____

I Timothy 3:2 One of the requirements of a church overseer is that he is to _____

_____

Matthew 25:35-40 One of the ways we minister as unto the Lord is by _____

_____

_____

Luke 7:44 and 45 Hospitality in Jesus' day included _____

_____

_____

In the following Scripture passages, describe the hospitality shown. By whom? To whom? What happened?

Genesis 18:1-8 _____

_____

Genesis 19:1-11 _____

_____

Genesis 24:31-33 _____

_____

Genesis 43:31-34 _____

_____

Joshua 2:1-16 _____

_____

II Samuel 9:7-13 _____

_____

Acts 16:14, 15 and 40 _____

_____

Acts 28:12-15 _____

_____

Revelation 3:20 _____

_____

236

Jesus and the Family

The 30 years Jesus spent with His earthly family were preparation for His relatively short time of ministry. The word *family* never occurs in His teachings, but His emphasis on the family is evident in His love of God the Father, in His reverence for motherhood, in His tenderness toward little children, and in His association with family life.

Look up the following Scriptures and write down what occurred as Jesus related to a family or home situation.

John 2:1-11 _____

_____

_____

Mark 1:29-34 _____

_____

_____

Matthew 9:9-13 _____

_____

_____

Luke 7:36-50 _____

_____

_____

Luke 19:1-10 _____

_____

_____

Luke 10:38-42 _____

_____

_____

John 12:1-11 _____

_____

Though Jesus taught that loyalty to Him transcends loyalty to one's family, He continued to show understanding of the human ties of father, mother, son and children. In fact, these family terms gave Him words with which to explain spiritual relationships concerning God the Father. Jesus lifted motherhood to its highest recognition in history. On the way to the cross, Jesus spoke to the daughters of Jerusalem concerning weeping for their children. During His ministry, a number of mothers brought their childern to Him for prayer and blessing. He had such concern for children that He said, *"Whoso shall offend one of these little ones which believe in me, it were better for him that a millstone were hanged about his neck, and that he were drowned in the depth of the sea"* (Matthew 18:6).

Families

Mary and Martha weren't only friends of Jesus, they were *family* as well, for they were sisters in the flesh. The family belongs to God. He created it. He determined its structure. He appointed its purposes. He uses it as a training ground on earth to prepare us for the kingdom of heaven. God thinks so much of family that, in Psalm 127:1, it is said, *"Unless the Lord builds the house, those who build it labor in vain."* Psalm 68:6 reminds us that *"God sets the solitary in families."*

We usually use the term *family* to mean father, mother and children living together as a unit. But today, we have other types of *families*—single parent families, blended families (often the result of broken families), as well as many singles who live alone or together without the benefit of marriage which God meant to bring the family into being.

The family in today's society has been greatly undermined. Public schools have taken over the education of the Church, religious instruction has been turned over to the Church, and there is a tendency to let the government provide many services which were traditionally provided by the family. Yet, in God's sight, families are intended to be:

1) A place where people are cared for from infancy to adulthood—and unto death.

2) A center for creativity, where children are not only brought into being, but are nourished to be the individuals that God intended.

3) A transmitter of values, which best come through close day-to-day interaction.

4) A place where God can be glorified. It's a training ground to prepare us for relationships within His Body and with Him as our Head.

God so respected the family that two of the Ten Commandments concern it (See Exodus 20:12 and 14).

Beyond the Family

Jesus had little to say about relationships between natural brothers. His emphasis was on a new brotherhood of all men. To achieve this, He said, men must be born again. Love of the brethren was important to the followers of Jesus Christ. They believed it was evidence of a person's love of God (See I John 4:20).

Brotherly love became an outstanding virtue in the Church. Paul wrote to the Romans, *"Be kindly affectioned one to another with brotherly love"* (Romans 12:10). And from Peter, *"Finally, all of you, have unity of spirit, sympathy, love of the brethren, a tender heart and a humble mind"* (I Peter 3:8 RSV).

There were times when Jesus preached a higher loyalty than even that of the family. He knew that truth is more important than domestic harmony and that only God's kingdom has ultimate value. How do the following Scriptures express this?

Matthew 10:34-37 _____

_____

_____

Luke 14:26 _____

238

Mark 3:32-35 _____
_____
_____
John 1:13 _____
_____
_____

SUMMARY

Jesus had some special friends, two of which were sisters, Mary and Martha. Perhaps they were more like "family." He often stayed in their home when He was in the Jerusalem area. Scripture gives us guidance on friendship, as well as instruction concerning the family—both our natural one and the "new family" we have in the Lord.

MODERN EXAMPLE

One day in January we received a call from the Evangelical Sisters of Mary asking if my husband and I would be overnight host to one of their "brothers" from Germany. We'd been acquainted with their ministry while living in the Phoenix area, but we were now living on the central coast of California. They told us Brother Rufino would be taking pictures of the California coastline for use in some television "spots." It would probably be well after dark before he would appear at our house, since he wanted to get some sunset pictures; and he would leave quite early. We marked the date on our calendar.

At that time my sister and I were caring for our elderly parents who lived in their own home in the same town. But our 93-year-old mother's health failed and we had to put her into a nursing home. For two weeks we cared for Dad who remained at home, and took turns helping feed Mother at the nursing home.

Late one afternoon we received a call from the nursing home telling us that, if we wanted to see Mother while she was yet alive, we needed to come there right away. My sister, and her husband, and I left immediately, while my husband went to stay with Dad. Then, we remembered—this was the night we were to keep Brother Rufino. We had no way of contacting him since he was "somewhere" along the beach, about 30 miles away.

A Christian neighbor offered to stay at our house and welcome our guest when he arrived. As it happened, he arrived at our home the very time Mother drew her last breath, passing from death unto Life. Of course, there was a time of family grieving at Dad's, and phone calls and arrangements to make, so it was quite late when we got home that evening. But our guest had stayed up, not only to express his sympathy, but to

239

minister to us in compassion and prayer. Then, after a few hours' sleep, he was on his way again.

God, in His perfect timing, allowed us to entertain what still seems to have been an "angel unaware." We'd never seen the gentleman before, nor have we seen him since. He was only in this country a brief time. But our Father in Heaven knew what would happen that night. He gave us an opportunity to open our home to one who is part of our greater family (the Body of our Lord Jesus Christ) so that we might receive ministry in our time of need.

WHAT DO YOU THINK?

1. What part do friends play in your life? _____

_____

_____

2. How do you show friendship to other? _____

_____

_____

3. Is family important to you? How do you show this? ___

_____

_____

4. How do you relate to and/or share with your brothers and sisters in the Lord? _____

_____

_____

EVALUATE YOURSELF

1. In what ways are you implementing the principles learned from Mary and Martha? _____

_____

_____

2. In what ways are you failing to implement the principles learned from Mary and Martha? _____

_____

_____

3. What do you need to do to change? _____

_____

_____

4. How will you do it? _____

_____

_____

Lesson 25

Woman of Samaria, Widow of Nain, & the Syro-Phoenician Woman

An Example of Recipients of Jesus' Ministry

"And Jesus went about all the cities and villages, teaching in their synagogues, and preaching the gospel of the kingdom, and healing every sickness and every disease among the people."
Matthew 9:35

SETTING THE STAGE

John 21:25 says, *"And there are also many other things which Jesus did, the which, if they should be written every one, I suppose that even the world itself could not contain the books that should be written."* One wonders why we have the stories of certain incidents in the ministry of Jesus. Why do we hear about some women to whom He ministered and not others? God must have a reason which only He knows.

We do have descriptions of His encounters with three unnamed women: (1) the woman of Samaria (2) the widow of Nain (3) and a woman from Syro-Phoenicia. These were specific women from different cities, who were touched by Jesus, each in a unique way. Perhaps they also represent needs of women in general.

The woman of Samaria was not only an alien, as far as the Jews were concerned, but she was living in adultery. She needed cleansing from sin. When Jesus met her at a well, He offered her the living water of salvation. She found Him to be the Christ, her Messiah, and ran to share the good news with others.

The widow of Nain was overcome with grief when Jesus came into her city. Her only son was being carried out for burial. Jesus reached out to her, bringing her comfort as He raised her son back to life. God was glorified as the crowd recognized Jesus as a prophet.

The Gentile woman from Syro-Phoenicia came to Jesus with a need of healing for her daughter. Though at first it seemed that Jesus wouldn't hear her, He granted her request because of her persistence. In each case, we'll see how the woman transformed a *failure* to a *success* because of Jesus' unique ministry to her.

Jesus still ministers to women in need today. He offers us salvation. He comes to comfort us. He answers our cries of intercession on behalf of our family needs.

Chart 25A

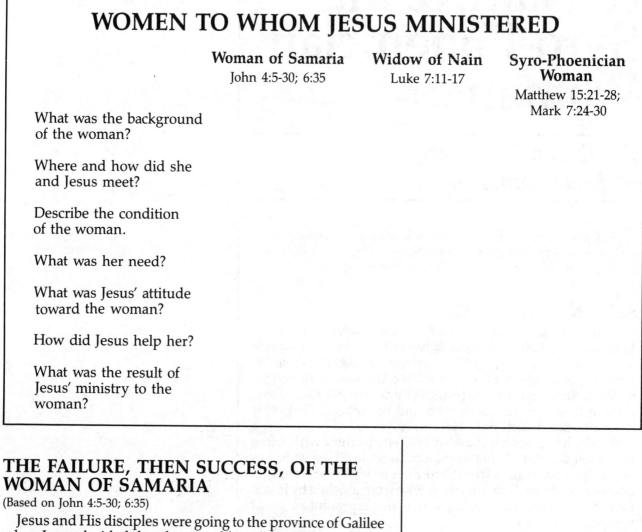

WOMEN TO WHOM JESUS MINISTERED

	Woman of Samaria John 4:5-30; 6:35	**Widow of Nain** Luke 7:11-17	**Syro-Phoenician Woman** Matthew 15:21-28; Mark 7:24-30
What was the background of the woman?			
Where and how did she and Jesus meet?			
Describe the condition of the woman.			
What was her need?			
What was Jesus' attitude toward the woman?			
How did Jesus help her?			
What was the result of Jesus' ministry to the woman?			

THE FAILURE, THEN SUCCESS, OF THE WOMAN OF SAMARIA
(Based on John 4:5-30; 6:35)

Jesus and His disciples were going to the province of Galilee when Jesus decided that they would go through Samaria. As they approached the city of Sychar, Jesus stopped to rest at Jacob's Well, while the disciples went into the city to get something to eat.

Soon a Samaritan woman came to draw water. Jesus asked her for a drink. She was surprised, but Jesus told her that, if she only knew who *He* was, she would ask for *living water.* Realizing that she was confused, Jesus went on to explain that the water which He could give would become a perpetual spring within, giving eternal life.

242

When the woman replied that she would like some of this water, Jesus gave her a strange command. He told her to go get her husband. She told him that she wasn't married, and Jesus surprised her by telling her that not only was she not married to the man she was living with, but that she'd had five previous husbands. To this, the woman declared that He must, indeed, be a prophet.

Then they had a conversation concerning true worship, which led to a discussion of the Messiah.

When Jesus revealed Himself as the Messiah the Samaritan woman left her waterpot and ran to the village to tell everyone.

The villagers came to see Jesus as the disciples returned with some food. Jesus told them that His "meat" was to do the will of God. Many of the city believed in Him because the woman told them that He knew all about her though she hadn't told Him.

The fact that Jesus even met this woman was an act of God. In those days Jews didn't travel through Samaria, even though it was the shortest route between Galilee and Jerusalem. Racial hatred kept Jews and Samaritans apart. But while the Jews had no dealings with the Samaritans, Jesus did. And He chose to go through Samaria.

The woman Jesus met was not only an enemy of the Jews, but she was also poor, evidenced in the fact that she was there drawing water. (For a Jewish teacher to speak to a woman in public was also unheard of.) The local people avoided this woman because of her reputation, which probably explains why she came at noon while other women were home fixing lunch.

The water which Jesus offered wasn't for her physical need, but was a source of quenching spiritual thirst. It was to her that He also revealed the only basis for acceptable worship, but also the truth of His Messiahship. Her response was to drop everything and run tell others the good news.

LESSONS FROM THE WOMAN OF SAMARIA

Salvation

The primary need of every person alive is for salvation. *"For all have sinned and come short of the glory of God"* (Romans 3:23). Couple this with II Peter 3:9 which says that God isn't willing for any to perish, and we can begin to understand why Jesus chose to go out of His way to confront a Samaritan woman with her need for "living water." She desperately needed the salvation and the Spirit of God to dwell within her and He earnestly desired that she have it.

In an earlier lesson we learned the need to repent so that we can confess our sins and accept the forgiveness God offers. As we do this and believe on Jesus as our Savior, we receive salvation. We're not only saved from the penalty due our sins, but we're made whole and saved for eternal life. (At this time, the Holy Spirit comes to indwell us.)

In the story of the Samaritan woman at the well, we're introduced to the term "living water." It signifies the means whereby a spiritual thirst can be quenched. The water in the

WOMEN IN THE BIBLE

well could only satisfy physical thirst. Jesus wanted the woman to "drink of Him," so that she could experience salvation and all it implies. Such water is a divine gift.

Consider these Scriptures concerning *water* and *salvation*:

Jeremiah 17:13 Jeremiah says that the Lord is _____

_____

_____

Jeremiah 2:13 God says that His people have forsaken Him, the _____.

Rather, they have _____

_____

_____

Isaiah 12:3 With joy, we can _____

_____

_____

Isaiah 55:1-3 Our spiritual thirst can be satisfied by _____

_____

_____

Ezekiel 47:8 and 9 Ezekiel tells of a river flowing from the temple of God. In these waters, there is _____

_____

_____

John 7:37-39 As we believe on Jesus and drink of Him (partake of His Life) _____

_____

Jesus was telling the people of _____

_____

who had not yet been given, because Jesus was not yet glorified. _____

_____

_____

Revelation 22:17 The final call to salvation, in Scripture, is when the Spirit and the Bride (the Church) say _____

_____

_____

Matthew 5:13 Those who have drunk of the *living water* are to be _____

so that others may become thirsty too. _____

THE FAILURE, AND THEN SUCCESS, OF THE WIDOW OF NAIN

(Based on Luke 7:11-17)

The day after Jesus healed the Centurion's servant, He and His disciples set out on a ministry tour around the Sea of Galilee. As they journeyed, the crowds followed. As they approached the steep ascent to the city of Nain, they could see burial caves lining each side of the road.

Before long, they met a funeral procession consisting of a weeping woman and a few sympathizing friends. The woman was a widow who was now about to bury her only son.

Though Elijah and Elisha had, through the power of God, raised people from the dead, Jesus had not yet done so. This was the first occasion for this type of miracle in His ministry.

The moment He saw the mother crying beside the bier, He had compassion on her. She didn't even look up to see what was happening. She only knew that she was grieving. Jesus simply said, "Weep not." Then He touched the bier—a forbidden act, for a Rabbi could not touch the dead because of ceremonial pollution. He spoke to the corpse and the young man sat up, speaking. Jesus then gave the son back to his mother. The people of Nain were overwhelmed at this resurrection miracle. Great fear came upon them all, and, they glorified God.

LESSONS FROM THE WIDOW OF NAIN
Comfort

Jesus understands the range of human emotions. He was the Word made flesh. He can identify with us because He lived on earth as man. Jesus knows us, and He has compassion on us. He wants to comfort us.

In a very comforting Scripture, Isaiah describes how God will take back His beloved Israel, though she had much sorrow. *"For the Lord hath called thee as a woman forsaken and grieved in spirit, and a wife of youth, when thou wast refused, saith thy God. For a small moment have I forsaken thee; but with great mercies will I gather thee. In a little wrath I hid my face from thee for a moment; but with everlasting kindness will I have mercy on thee, saith the Lord thy Redeemer"* (Isaiah 54:6-8).

The widow of Nain didn't cry out to Jesus. She probably wouldn't have expected Him to notice her in the crowd, even if she'd known who He was. Jesus came to her, and she let Him minister words of comfort to her aching soul. She let Him come close enough to whisper in her ear, "Weep not." As God would turn grieving Israel back to Himself, so Jesus took the initiative in ministering to the widow of Nain.

II Corinthians 1:3 and 4 God is the source of all comfort, who

Matthew 9:22 Jesus offered comfort to _____

_____

_____

Romans 15:4 Through the comfort of Scriptures, we _____

_____

_____

The Holy Spirit, as Comforter, comes to us in different ways:

John 14:16 He _____

_____

_____

John 14:26 He _____

_____

_____

John 15:26 He _____

_____

_____

John 16:7-11 He _____

_____

_____

Psalm 30:5 Weeping may endure _____

_____

but _____

_____

_____

Psalm 30:11 and 12 God turns our mourning into dancing that

_____

_____

_____

Matthew 5:4 Those who mourn will be _____

_____

_____

Revelation 7:17; 21:4 Someday, God will _____

_____

_____

Isaiah 61:1-3 The Spirit of the Lord can exchange our mourning for _____

and our spirit of heaviness for _____

_____

_____

Widows

A widow has been in need of comfort at some point in time, for she has lost her husband. Among the many widows in Israel, several crossed the pathway of Jesus. He seemed to have a special, tender care for these women.

The lot of widows, who, from earliest times wore a distinctive garment (Genesis 38:14 and 19), was generally precarious. They were, therefore, regarded as being under God's special care. (See Psalm 68:5; 146:9; and Proverb 15:25). Childless widows usually returned to their parental home (Leviticus 22:13). Those who ill-treated a widow were punished. (See Exodus 22:22-24; Deuteronomy 14:29; II Samuel 14:4-10; II Kings 4:1; Isaiah 1:17, 23 and 24; Jeremiah 7:6 and 7).

The early Church cared for its widows, especially if they had been noted for good works. (See Acts 6:1; I Timothy 5:4, 9, 10 and 16; James 1:27). Perhaps the most well-known widow in the Bible is the poor one who put her two mites into the offering plate, surrending her all.

THE FAILURE, THEN SUCCESS, OF THE SYRO-PHOENICIAN WOMAN

(Based on Matthew 15:21-28; Mark 7:24-30)

This persistent woman lived on the coast of Tyre and Sidon, a region given over to idolatry. Why Jesus made this unusual trip outside of Palestine is not known. It may have been that He wanted to get away for a while. But His fame followed Him and news of His arrival reached this distraught mother. She found Him and told Him her sad story.

At first, Jesus was silent. He seemed to turn His back on the suffering woman. Perhaps this silence was meant to try her faith. It did!

Persistent, she was determined not to take "no" for an answer. She knew Jesus was able to cure her daughter, and she would get His help.

So she pestered the disciples for another audience with Jesus. This time, Jesus told her that He hadn't been sent to Gentiles, but to the lost sheep of Israel.

Even this rebuff didn't deter her from falling at His feet and sobbing, "Lord, help me!" She begged for mercy. When He further denied her by telling her that is wasn't fitting to take the children's bread and feed the dogs, she kept on pleading.

She hadn't asked for a whole loaf of bread, she said, only for the crumbs falling to the floor. Jesus, who had been so austere, was moved by the woman's persistence, which evidenced her faith in Him. In response, He healed her daughter, from a distance. For upon her return home, the Syro-Phoenician woman found the child in her right mind, lying quietly on her bed.

LESSONS FROM THE SYRO-PHOENICIAN WOMAN
Needs

We've seen how, as women, we need salvation and the indwelling of Christ as *living water* in our lives. We also need comfort and ministry for our personal concerns. We need the ministry of Jesus as we bring our concerns for others to Him. He is, even now, seated at the right hand of the Father interceding for us (Romans 8:34; Hebrews 12:2). We have access to this throne by the blood of Jesus, to find grace in our time of need (Hebrews 4:16).

The persistence of the Syro-Phoenician woman shows us our part. We are to seek Jesus, step out in faith as we make our requests, and persist in claiming His Word until our requests are fulfilled. Let's look at some other examples of persistence.

Genesis 32:24-32 Jacob wrestled with _____

until _____

_____

_____

Deuteronomy 8:1-10 God kept the Hebrew people from entering the Promised Land immediately in order to _____

_____

_____

Luke 18:1-8 This widow came to the judge for justice and

_____

_____

Matthew 7:7-11 When we asked something of the Lord, we're to _____

_____

_____

SUMMARY

Jesus ministered to many persons, including three unnamed women of different backgrounds and situations. He knew how to meet specific needs of individuals, as well as those of large crowds. Often, we find Him ministering to women. Women today, also have many needs. Jesus, who is the same yesterday, today, and forever, can minister to us. We need only be willing to receive from Him salvation, comfort, health, truth, peace, and more.

MODERN EXAMPLE

It was because of Vera's handicap that I first met her. A victim of polymyositis, she had difficulty walking because of muscle atrophy in her legs. She used a walker to transport herself from her apartment to her church, little more than a block away.

On her way home one Sunday morning, she fell. Two of my friends were parked in a nearby car, and jumped out to see if they could help. About the same time, two young men stopped their van, got out, raised her to her feet, and left! My friends then took Vera home. While there, they invited her to a Bible Class I was teaching. Vera has been a faithful member ever since. To this day, she declares that the Lord let her "slip to the sidewalk," sent two "angels" to pick her up, and brought her together with some special women so that she could find a new and vital relationship with Jesus, through the Holy Spirit. My eyes were opened to see how our Father in Heaven does, indeed, have His ear tuned to the heart cry of the widow.

Vera had been living in our city only a short while, having moved to it to be near a daughter. Her husband had recently passed away, but she still wanted to maintain her own home, even though she was physically handicapped. The apartment near her church and town seemed to be the answer. However, she also put her name on a waiting list for a "handicapped apartment" in a low-cost housing project several blocks away.

The Lord provided for her in many miraculous ways as she continued to live in this apartment over the next several years. Week after week, at our Bible Study, she gave testimony as to how the Lord had protected her, provided for her, and healed her from the results of several falls.

Meanwhile, it became more difficult to walk distances. She began looking into getting an electric chair-cart, which could be driven on sidewalks and in bike-lanes. She also sought the Lord concerning the rather large financial investment it would be. After several months of this, she suddenly had a strong urge to get one. So she made a call and placed an order even though she really didn't have a good place to store it when it wasn't in use.

She knew that she must have it even though it would take several weeks to be delivered from across the country.

Vera had hardly placed her order when the phone rang. It was the housing project asking if she would be interested in a handicapped apartment which would soon be available. Though surprised at the sudden call, she told them that she would. Then she sat down to reflect on the chain of events! She could see the hand of the Lord in them, for to be able to move into the new apartment, she would need some form of transportation. She would now have an ideal spot to keep her new motor-chair. What she didn't know then was that, in God's perfect timing, her first trip in her new chair would be from her old apartment to the new one.

God's favor is for the widow. Jesus can minister to each one in a unique way.

WHAT DO YOU THINK?

1. Can you recall an instance when Jesus met a specific need that you had? What happened? _____

_____

_____

2. What special needs do you have now? How can you allow Jesus to minister to you in them? _____

_____

_____

3. How are you Jesus' hands and feet and (and yes, "ears"!) in ministering to others in His name? _____

_____

_____

EVALUATE YOURSELF

1. In what ways are you implementing the principles learned from these three women? _____

_____

_____

2. In what ways are you failing to implement the principles learned from them? _____

_____

_____

3. What do you need to do to change? _____

_____

_____

4. How will you do it? _____

_____

_____

Lesson 26
Woman with the Issue of Blood

An Example of Healing

"Who his own self bare our sins in his own body on the tree, that we, being dead to sins, should life unto righteousness: by whose stripes ye were healed."

I Peter 2:24

SETTING THE STAGE

In the Old Testament, we find the Lord God proclaimed as Jehovah-Raphah, *the One who heals*. The Gospels tell of many persons whom Jesus healed. Through the power of the Holy Spirit, many are healed today.

The woman with the issue of blood is but one of the persons whom Jesus healed during His earthly ministry. For 12 years, she was plagued with a disease which not only debilitated her physically, but made her a social outcast as well (see Leviticus 15:19-31). Therefore, she was probably in need of inner healing as well as physical healing.

One day, when she heard that Jesus would be in her city, she laid down her pride, her reputation, her weakness, and persevered through every obstacle which seemed to be in her way. She got close enough to Jesus to simply touch the garment He was wearing, and her mustard-seed faith was rewarded. In that instant, she was made whole.

As believers in the Lord Jesus Christ, we have the same promise of healing through His Word. But we must know this Word, believe it, and accept it in order to have it manifested in our lives. This is done by the faith which comes from hearing the Word. In this lesson, we'll study Scriptures having to do with healing. Perhaps these will build the necessary faith to realize the healing Jesus provides for each of us.

THE FAILURE OF THE WOMAN WITH THE ISSUE OF BLOOD

(Based on Luke 8:43-48)

We all feel like failures when we're ill, especially when the illness lingers. Such was the case with the woman in Luke 8. For 12 years, she hemorrhaged. Though she went to doctor after doctor, she found no relief. The continual loss of blood left her very weak and so exhausted that to leave her house was a real effort. Besides that, she was discouraged and financially drained. As if these things weren't enough, her particular illness made her an outcast. Her blood condition rendered her ceremonially unclean (Leviticus 15:25-27).

Jesus came to the Sea of Galiliee area to teach, to heal, and to minister to the crowds of people that followed Him. He delivered a man of unclean spirits and the news spread. Everyone was excited. A great crowd thronged to the shore.

They all wanted to see the One who had performed so many miracles. Even Jairus, one of the rulers of the synagogue, ran to meet Jesus before He barely got off the boat. Jairus' daughter was dying and he wanted Jesus to come lay hands on her so she would be healed.

Unnoticed by the crowd, this woman slipped in and began to inch her way toward Jesus. She believed He could heal, and so, with every ounce of strength she could muster, she crept until she could barely touch the border of His garment. (See Matthew 14:36) With further study, one can discover that the hem of Jesus' garment held great significance. For, as a Jewish teacher, He could have had four tassels connected by a blue thread to the hem of His garment. These were reminders of the law given in Numbers 15:37-41. By touching them, one could recall God's covenant and the provisions in it.

When her hand finally touched the hem of His garment, she knew that she had instantly been healed. At the same time, Jesus felt healing virtue leave His body. He turned around and asked who had touched Him.

If the woman had admitted touching Him, she would, undoubtedly, have heard the crowd shout "unclean." Everyone would have turned from her, and perhaps, Jesus. Instead, however, she fell down at Jesus' feet and confessed that she had been the one to touch His garment. She humbled herself before Him, willing to be rejected by the crowd and, perhaps, by Him.

Her courage and belief pleased Jesus. He told her that her faith in Him had made her whole. She was totally healed because she had been willing to reach out to Him, regardless of what others might think or say. Her failure in health turned to success in physical wholeness because of her faith in the ministry of Jesus.

LESSONS FROM THE WOMAN WITH THE ISSUE OF BLOOD
God's Provision for Healing

The special name which God desired to be known by His covenant people was Yahweh, or Jehovah (See Exodus 6:3 and 4) The compound names of Jehovah were those given in crisis situations, so that God could manifest Himself as the One to meet that particular need. The first time God reveals Himself is as Jehovah-Raphah (the healer), in Exodus 15:26. The children of Israel had just been delivered from 400 years of bondage in Egypt through a supernatural act of God. He parted the Red Sea for them to escape and then drowned the enemies who tried to pursue them. After a time of rejoicing, they found themselves near some other water. This time, it was bitter. Thirsty, the people began to murmur. And Moses prayed. Then God showed him what to do. He was to cut down a certain tree and cast it into the water. The water became sweet. Through a seemingly foolish act of obedience, the people were given water to quench their thirst.

Then God made His healing covenant with His people. Read Exodus 15:26 and list the four conditions of this promise:

(1) _____

(2) _____

(3) _____

(4) _____

Again, in giving the laws, in Exodus 23:25-27, God reminded the people that, He will take all sickness away from the midst of them if _____

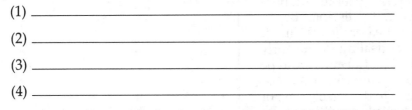

God was Israel's only physician for many years. Solomon, through his marriages to Egyptian wives, probably brought the first physicians into the land. We don't hear of any there until the time of Asa, the third King of Judah (II Chronicles 16:12).

The first healing in Scripture actually took place in Genesis 20:17. Here we find Abraham praying for the healing of Abimelech, his wife, and his maidservants, because the Lord had shut the wombs of all those in Abimelech's household. God did this to protect Sarah. He was soon to give her Isaac, whom He had promised years before.

As we are *grafted in* (Romans 11:17) and become part of God's people through Jesus Christ, we too, can claim all the covenant promises of God. God's promises are irrevocable. He is faithful to perform His Word as we do our part.

Healing Through Jesus

As God incarnate, Jesus is also the source of health and wholeness. The recreative power to bring healing to the physical body, as well as wholeness to the mind, exists in God and is channeled through Jesus in His Word, His touch, and His authority.

In prophecy, Isaiah 53:4 and 5 tells us that both healing and redemption were accomplished by the Messiah. *"Surely He has borne our griefs...sickness, weakness and distress...and carried our sorrows and pain (of punishment). Yet we ignorantly considered Him stricken, smitten and afflicted by God (as if with leprosy). But He was wounded for our transgressions, He was bruised for our guilt and iniquities; the chastisement needful to obtain peace amd well-being for us was upon Him, and with the stripes that wounded Him we are healed and made whole."* (Amplified)

Thus Jesus became our scapegoat (See Leviticus 16:22). The sins of the whole world were placed upon Him, so that He could carry them away on the cross in His suffering and death. In Hebrew, the word *griefs* actually means *sickness* or *disease*. The word *sorrows* means *pain*. Isaiah's prophecy really means that, in the substitutionary sacrifice of the Messiah, Jesus bore and carried away sickness, as well as our transgressions and iniquities.

On the cross, Jesus did battle with the debilitating powers of sickness, sin and death. Those who accept the atoning work of the cross and receive Him as Savior, receive forgiveness of sin, as well as healing of the body and wholeness of mind.

When Jesus rose from the dead, He commissioned His disciples to preach, teach, and heal (Mark 16:15-18). They were given power, through the Holy Spirit. After the fullness of the Holy Spirit was given at Pentecost, the disciples began to minister healing as they witnessed of the Lord Jesus Christ. Provision was made for the ministry of healing in the early Church. James exhorted believers to call for the elders and be anointed with oil when they were sick (James 5:16).

As time passed and the Church began to disperse, some of these commands were neglected. Coupled with lack of emphasis of spiritual healing was the growth of the practice of medicine. Claiming God's provision by faith lessened.

In the 20th century, there has been a new move of the Holy Spirit and a "rediscovery" of the healing ministry intended by God. Now many more fully see the task of the local church—to preach and teach wholeness, and to help its people claim their rightful heritage of healing through prayer.

Matthew 4:23 When Jesus walked our earth, He healed ___

_____

_____

Matthew 10:1-8 When Jesus sent out His disciples, He gave them power to _____

_____

_____

Matthew 13:58 There were occasions when Jesus could do only a few miracles because _____

_____

_____

Inner Healing

Many people want healing for the body, and we have seen that God made provision for this. But of equal or even greater importance, is the necessary healing of our souls commonly called *inner healing*.

Man is a three-fold being—body, soul, and spirit. The Fall affected each of these areas. The spirit of man was deadened by sin. The soul was burdened by sorrow, grief, despair, fear and other things. The body became subject to sickness, pain, and death.

Our spirits are made live by accepting the salvation provided by Jesus. On the cross, Jesus also bore our sickness and pain just as He conquered death. But God also made provision for healing the soul—the mind and emotions.

Isaiah 53:3 reminds us that Jesus was despised and rejected. By suffering this rejection for us, he made provision for inner healing.

It's interesting to note that the Bible tells us that, during Jesus' suffering in the Garden of Gethsemene He sweat drops of blood. We are told only of His physical pain on the cross, however. Through these two experiences, He paid the price for both kinds of healing. He bore our emotional agony and by the stripes laid upon Him, He bore our physical pain.

In Exodus 15, we see the story of Moses and the Israelites at the bitter water of Marah, where Moses threw a tree into the water. This tree represents the cross. Therefore, whenever we find ourselves in bitter circumstances (which can cause wounds that later need inner healing), we should throw the cross into the midst of them. As we submit to the work of that cross, and all it has accomplished for us, we'll know the inner healing that God has provided and the covenant we have with Him.

People Jesus Healed

Look up the following Scriptures and answer the questions concerning the various incidents in the healing ministry of Jesus.

John 5:1-5 The paralyzed man at the pool of Bethesda

Why did Jesus question the man when He could see his problem? _____

_____

_____

How did the man answer? Was it in faith? _____

_____

_____

Why did Jesus have the man pick up his bed and walk? ___

_____

_____

What effect did the healing have on the man himself? On others? _____

_____

_____

What sin had this man committed? (See verse 14) _____

_____

_____

Luke 5:17-26; Mark 2:1-12 The man with the palsy

Who was seemingly more desirous of the healing, the man or his friends? _____

_____

_____

What did the four men have to do to bring their friend before the Master? What does this tell us about intercession for others? _____

_____

What need did Jesus first see in the sick man? _____

_____

_____

What relationship is there between forgiveness and healing?

_____

_____

What result did the miracle have on the man, the four friends, and the crowd? _____

_____

_____

John 9:1-41 The Blind man

What is the relationship between sin and sickness? Does God punish us by sending illness? _____

_____

_____

What part does Satan have in illness? _____

_____

_____

What was Jesus' unique method of healing this man? _____

_____

_____

What was the reaction of the Pharisees, the parents, the man himself? _____

_____

_____

Mark 3:1-5; Matthew 12:9-13; Luke 6:6-10 The man with the withered hand

How were the Scribes and Pharisees trying to trap Jesus?

_____

_____

What did Jesus command the man to do? _____

_____

_____

Is one type of healing harder to obtain than another? Compare, for instance, acquired illnesses over against birth defects

256

(such as this man apparently had). _____

_____

_____

Matthew 8:5-13; Luke 7:1-10 The Centurion's sick servant

What was the job of a Centurion? _____

_____

_____

What good trait did Jesus see in him that helped the healing miracle to take place? _____

_____

_____

What is the relationship between our acceptance of authority and our faith for healing? _____

_____

_____

John 8:1-11 Woman caught in adultery (Inner Healing)

What was the attitude of the accusers toward the woman, toward Jesus, and toward themselves? _____

_____

_____

What did Jesus do? How did she respond? _____

_____

_____

How did this incident help her be inwardly healed of her past? _____

_____

_____

John 4:46-54 The nobleman's son

In this second miracle healing by Jesus in Galilee, how did the noble man know it was Jesus who healed his son? _____

_____

_____

What was the result of the son's healing on the nobleman and his family? _____

_____

_____

Do miracles, signs and wonders always lead to belief in Jesus?

_____

_____

Luke 17:11-19 Ten lepers

What is significant about where this miracle took place? ___

_____

_____

What means did Jesus use to bring about their healing? ___

_____

_____

Who recognized the true source of the healing? What did he do? _____

_____

_____

Matthew 8:14-17; Mark 1:29-34; Luke 4:38-41 Peter's mother-in-law

How did Jesus heal her? How long did it take for her to be well? _____

_____

_____

Does a healing have to be instantaneous to be from the Lord?

_____

_____

Mark 9:14-29 The child with epilepsy

What was the father's perception of his child's problem? ___

_____

_____

Why couldn't the disciples heal this boy? _____

_____

_____

What did Jesus say was the key to this healing and deliverance? _____

_____

_____

Luke 13:11-17 Woman with an infirmity

What was this woman's problem? _____

258

_____

_____

How is Satan involved in illness? _____

_____

_____

Why was Jesus reprimanded for healing her? _____

_____

_____

There are other incidents of Jesus' healing which we won't consider now. But, if you're interested in further study, you might look up: *Matthew 9:23-26* for the healing of Jairus' daughter; *Matthew 9:27-30,* for the healing of two blind men; and *Luke 14:1-6,* for the healing of the man with dropsy.

How Do We Receive Healing for Ourselves?

Psalm 107:20 We must believe the Word of God, for _____

_____

_____

Matthew 8:8 The Centurion knew his servant could be healed by Jesus because _____

Thus, we know that we need _____

_____

_____

Proverbs 4:20-22 We are to _____

for God's Word _____

_____

_____

Jeremiah 30:17 Here, we learn that _____ _____

_____

_____

Mark 16:18 The fifth *sign* to follow believers is _____

_____

_____

James 1:6 and 7 When we ask anything of the Lord, we are to

_____

_____

James 5:13-16 If we're sick, we're to _____

_____

_____

Romans 8:11 We can claim the Word that _____

_____

_____

Hebrews 4:2 The way to profit from the Scriptural promises is to _____

_____

_____

James 1:22 We must not only hear the Word, but _____

_____

_____

SUMMARY

The woman with the issue of blood exemplifies but one miracle of healing which Jesus performed during His ministry. The Gospels not only contain specific accounts of individual healings, but often say that He healed people wherever He went. As believers in the Lord Jesus Christ, we have the promise of healing, too. As we know God's Word, believe it, and accept it for ourselves, we can also have healing manifested in our bodies.

MODERN EXAMPLE

When our daughter Laurie was home for Christmas vacation, we noticed she was very tired. We weren't unduly concerned. December had been a busy month with Christmas activities in the Christian school where she was teaching. But when she returned to school she realized she was still exhausted, so she made an appointment to see the doctor. Meanwhile, at three different times, II Corinthians 4:7-18, *"Our bodies are constantly facing death...we know that the same God who brought Jesus back to life will also bring us back to life...these troubles are small and will not last long...yet this short time of distress will result in God's richest blessing,"* came to her in unusual ways. Not realizing how God had been preparing her, she received the result of the tests. Not only was she suffering from a very acute attack of mononucleosis, but she had a tumor the size of a large orange on one ovary. The doctor was very concerned. He wanted to operate immediately, but couldn't, because of the mono. He then informed her of the possibility of malignancy and all this would mean—hard news for a 24-year-old woman. He scheduled surgery two weeks later and sent her home to bed.

Since she lived about 100 miles from us, I made arrangements to stay with her. We spent the time immersing ourselves in God's Word as much as possible—reading the Bible, listening to tapes of Scripture songs, reading a book telling of how Jesus healed all who came to Him in His earthly ministry—as well as praying and doing spiritual battle. From hearing all this Word, our faith increased. It grew even more when we realized we were totally at the mercy of God. The doctor had said he could do nothing. Of course, we were also encouraged to hear that others were praying, and enjoyed the visits of concerned friends

Since my husband was coming for the weekend, we made arrangments with Laurie's pastor to have him, a couple of elders from her church, her school principal, and her father come together for a time of prayer, anointing Laurie with oil according to the Scripture. Afterwards, since Laurie was feeling better and had roommates to watch after her, we returned home.

Though God had given us faith to claim Laurie's healing, we were surprised when we received her telephone call later that week after her visit to the doctor. He had taken another ultrasound and was completely baffled. The tumor had completely disappeared, and her mono was gone—a very unusual occurance for a disease that usually takes weeks to run its course. Needless to say, She was one happy young woman with two very grateful parents.

But one of the best expressions of glory to God for what He had done, came at a school assembly the next week when Laurie was asked to share what had happened. The children all sat on the edges of their seats as they listened to her tell why she had been absent. When she finished her story, there was silence—and then a spontaneous cheer. Simultaneously, all the children shot their fists up into the air and yelled, "Yea, God!" No doubt, many went home that night to tell their families how God had supernaturally healed one of their teachers.

WHAT DO YOU THINK?

1. Have you ever experienced a supernatural healing? _____

_____

_____

2. What role do doctors and drugs play in healing? _____

_____

_____

3. How do you claim health and healing for yourself and/or your loved ones? _____

_____

_____

What are some of the things you can do to help in the process?

_____

_____

_____

WOMEN
IN THE BIBLE

4. Do you share the availability of God's healing with others?

_____

_____

EVAULATE YOURSELF

1. In what ways are you implementing the principles learned from this woman? _____

_____

_____

2. In what ways are you failing to implement the principles learned from her? _____

_____

_____

3. What do you need to do to change? _____

_____

_____

4. How will you do it? _____

_____

_____

Lesson 27
Herodias & Pilate's Wife

An Example of Revenge—Dreams

"Vengeance belongeth unto me, I will recompense, saith the Lord."

Hebrews 10:30

"As a dream comes when there are many cares, so the speech of a fool when there are many words."

Ecclesiastes 5:3 (NIV)

SETTING THE STAGE

A wife, especially the wife of a ruler, is in a very strategic position. Her relationship with her husband often has far-reaching effects on the lives of others. This was true in the case of Herod and Herodias, as well as Pilate and his wife. A look at both of these couples will bring to light some interesting facts, but will also teach us concerning two other subjects—revenge and dreams. Though they may seem entirely unrelated, both revenge and dreams often dictate our actions.

Herodias wanted to do away with John the Baptist for pointing up her sin of living unlawfully with Herod. Revenge motivated her to ask for John's head when her husband offered to do her daughter a favor. Herod complied and John was put to death.

Pilates' wife, on the other hand, tried to influence her husband to do what was necessary to keep Jesus from being killed. Because of a dream which she had, she warned her husband against condemning Jesus to death. Pilate didn't comply and Jesus was crucified.

THE COUNTERFEIT SUCCESS
OF HERODIAS

(Based on Matthew 14:1-12; Mark 6:14-29; Luke 3:19 and 20)

According to historians, Herodias was the daughter of Aristobulus, who was son of Herod the Great, and Mariamne, who was daughter of Hyrcanus. Herodias' first husband was Philip I, the son of Herod the Great and Mariamne; so she married her uncle, by whom she had a daughter, Salome.

When Herod Antipas (one of the succession of Herods who ruled in Palestine on behalf of Rome) visited Rome, he was entertained by Philip and Herodias. He abducted his royal brother's wife, divorced his own wife, and made Herodias queen in her place.

When John the Baptist told him it was wrong to be living

with Herodias, Herod had him imprisoned. Herodias hated the man who had so disturbed her husband, and on Herod's birthday she got her chance for revenge. Salome, Herodias' daughter, was asked to dance before the men invited to the festive occasion. She so thrilled the audience that Herod vowed to give her anything she wanted. She consulted her mother who, connivingly, told her to ask for the head of John the Baptist.

Herod was immediately sorry, but he had to keep his word. So he sent one of his bodyguards to the prison to behead John and then bring his head to them on a platter. Thus, Heroidas' revenge at last did away with John.

What happened to her? According to the historian Josephus, her ambition was the ruin of Herod. Jealous of the power of Agrippa, her brother, she prodded Herod to demand of Caligula, the emperor, the title of king. Agrippa saw to it that this demand was refused, and Herod was banished in shame and exile. Herodias' pride forced her to be faithful to Herod, even in the disgrace and misfortune she had caused partly, through revenge.

LESSONS FROM HERODIAS
Revenge

Dictionaries define *revenge* as inflicting harm in return for an injury; taking vengeance.

Man's natural instinct (his old nature) wants revenge when he has been hurt in any way. He wants to even the score and return evil for evil.

Herodias was one who wanted to take revenge. When John the Baptist pointed out Herod's sin of living unlawfully with another man's wife, it was for the purpose of calling him to repentance. Herodias, however, felt guilty. To justify her relationship, she sought to get even with John.

She isn't the only one in Scripture who took revenge. Read the following and summarize these questions. Who took revenge? Why? How did they do it?

Genesis 34:1-31 _____

_____

_____

Judges 16:23-30 _____

_____

_____

I Kings 19:1-3 _____

_____

_____

Esther 3:1-15 _____

_____

_____

The need for revenge is born out of a desire to be the judge. It comes from lack of repentance and unforgiveness in one's own life. Thus, one sets himself up as God, to whom judgment and vengeance truly belong.

God Is Judge

Genesis 18:25 God is judge of _____

_____

_____

Deuteronomy 32:36 The Lord shall judge _____

_____

_____

Psalm 9:8 He shall judge the world _____

God's judgment includes qualities that ours does not. ____

_____

_____

Romans 2:2 _____

_____

_____

Romans 2:6 _____

_____

_____

Romans 2:11 _____

_____

_____

Romans 2:16 _____

_____

_____

According to I Corinthians 3:12-15, *"every man's work shall be made manifest."* God will allow our works to be judged by fire to see whether they're of gold, silver, precious stones, or of wood, hay, and stubble.

Since God is Judge, it's also His prerogative to take vengeance (to mete out the appropriate consequences for sin). Hebrews 10:30 (a quote from Deuteronomy 32) says, *"For we know him that hath said, Vengeance belongeth unto me, I will recompense, saith the Lord. And again, the Lord shall judge his people."* David recognized God's prerogative when he said, in Psalm 94:1, *"O Lord God, to whom vengeance belongeth; O God, to whom vengeance belongeth, show thyself."*

Though individuals have been the recipients of God's judgment (such as Ananias and Sapphira in Acts 5), there are also large groups of people who have known the result of His vengeance.

Genesis 6:1-8 The first display of God's wrath occurred in the time of Noah. This was due to _____

_____

_____

Genesis 6:17; 7:10-12 God _____

_____

_____

Genesis 11:1-9 Here, we find God displeased because ____

_____

_____

so He _____

_____

_____

Genesis 18:20; 19:12, 13, 24 and 25; Ezekiel 16:49; Jude 7 God destroyed Sodom and Gomorrah because _____

_____

_____

He did this by _____

_____

_____

Jeremiah 15:6 and 14 Through this prophet (and others), God declared that He would _____

_____

_____

because _____

_____

_____

II Chronicles 36:16-21 This was fulfilled when _____

_____

_____

Along with vengeance, God also gave a promise which, according to *Isaiah 35:4-10* was _____

_____

_____

Luke 21:6-28 Jesus tells of a time of God's wrath to come. This

includes _____

_____

_____

This will be because _____

_____

_____

Though we may, indeed, go through much trial and persecution, how can we escape the final wrath of God?

According to I Peter 1:17, judgment of all men is plainly the office of God the Father. However, in John 5:22 and 23, Christ reveals that the Father has chosen to commit all judgment to the Son. We find that Jesus Christ transferred the final authority of judgment from His own person to the Word of God. He says in John 12:47 and 48, *"And if any man hear my words, and believe not, I judge him not; for I came not to judge the world, but to save the world. He that rejected me, and receiveth not my words, hath one that judgeth him: the word that I have spoken, the same shall judge him in the last day."* Therefore, if we allow God's Word to judge us now, if we accept it, believe it, and act upon it, we will, as those who have been *born again*, take part in the first of three final judgments which the Bible describes. This is the judgment seat of Christ, as mentioned in Romans 14:10 and better described in II Corinthians 5:10, which says, *"For we (believers) must all appear before the judgment seat of Christ, that every one may receive the things done in his body, according to that he hath done, whether it be good or bad."* At this time, our *works* will be made manifest, and *rewards* (or crowns) given accordingly. Therefore, as we allow God's Word to judge us now, we will escape the ultimate wrath of God, needing only to stand before the judgment seat of Christ for judgment of works, not for eternal salvation.

Those who don't allow the Word of God to judge them in this life have a judgment awaiting them. It's the *great white throne* judgment of Revelation 20:11-15. There we find those whose names are not written in the Lamb's Book of Life being judged and then cast into the lake of fire.

If We Leave Vengeance to God, What Are We to Do?

Luke 6:35-38 _____

_____

_____

Matthew 5:38-48 _____

_____

_____

Matthew 5:11 and 12 _____

I Peter 3:8-11 _____

_____

_____

Ephesians 4:31 and 32 _____

_____

_____

I Corinthians 5:11-13 _____

_____

_____

I Corinthians 4:3-5 _____

_____

_____

Romans 14:4; 10-13 _____

_____

_____

THE FAILURE OF PILATE'S WIFE
(Matthew 27:15-30)

While the Bible doesn't tell us who the wife of Pilate was, the Apocryphal book, The Gospel of Nicodemus, identifies her as Claudia Procula, a granddaughter of the Emperor Augustus. The book also says that she was a proselyte to Judaism, being among the women of higher classes over whom the Jewish religion exercised considerable influence. In the only verse of Scripture concerning her, we find that she'd had a dream and begged her husband not to condemn the prisoner who was before him. No one knows what she dreamed, nor why such a dream wasn't given to Pilate himself.

When Pilate asked Jesus if He were the King of the Jews, Jesus didn't respond as expected. Pilate decided to give the crowd a choice between releasing Jesus or another prisoner, Barabbas. As he sat down on the judgment seat, Pilate received the message from his wife who warned him to have nothing to do with this *just man (Jesus).*

But the chief priests and elders persuaded the multitude that they should ask for Barabbas. When Pilate asked what he should do with Jesus, called the Christ, the crowd demanded His crucifixion. Pilate saw that this was what they wanted. He took water and, symbolically, washed his hands of the whole affair. Pilate's wife had done what she could, though she failed in her attempt to fulfill the message she had received in a dream.

268

LESSONS FROM PILATE'S WIFE
Dreams

From Genesis to Revelation, God used dreams and visions as a means of communicating with man. Only once do we have record of a dream being given to a woman, and all we know about this dream is contained in one verse, Matthew 27:19. Whatever the dream was, its message was not taken to heart by the one who could have done something about it.

We're told that in the last days, dreams and visions will occur as God pours out His Spirit upon all flesh (Acts 2:17). We must realize, however, that not all dreams contain messages from God.

Dreams can be triggered by an incident during the day, or even by a bedtime snack. Satan can also influence our dreams—especially if they produce fear, which is not of God.

How do we know when our dreams are from God? As with any message from the Lord (such as prophecy), they should be tested. God doesn't give one message and contradict Himself in another. Does the dream agree with God's Word? How do other believers witness to it? Have we asked God for His gifts of discernment, wisdom, and knowledge? Does it turn us to the Lord (such as in prayer)? God rarely gives specific instructions without preparing the hearer previously.

Finally, we don't need to *make* a dream come to pass. If it's of God, *He* will do it.

We should be open to God's direction through dreams, but they should never be our only source of guidance. If, like Pilate's wife, we feel that we've heard from God though a dream, and it passes all the tests of a true message, we can pass it on to those concerned. If they don't heed the message, then that's their responsibility. God warned Pilate through a dream given to his wife. Certain history was made because Pilate chose not to listen.

Job 33:14-17 In dreams, God can _____

_____

_____

Acts 2:17 and 18 In the last days, _____

_____

_____

Jude 8 (KJV) Some dreamers are described as _____

_____

_____

Deuteronomy 13:1-5 We're warned concerning interpretations of dreams that _____

_____

_____

I Samuel 28:6 God evidently answered men by _____

_____

_____

as well as by Urim and the Prophets.

Jeremiah 23:25-32 Some prophets who have dreams are ___

_____

_____

Jeremiah 27:9 and 10 We aren't to always hearken to _____

_____

_____

for _____

_____

_____

II Timothy 1:7 God doesn't give _____

_____

_____

but _____

_____

_____

II Corinthians 13:1 In the mouth of _____

_____

_____

shall God's Word be established.

Jeremiah 23:16 We need to determine if the message is ___

_____

_____

or _____

_____

_____

See Chart 27A

SUMMARY

These two unlikely subjects, Herodias (wife of Herod), and Pilates's wife (named Claudia by some commentators), come together only because we are considering the wives of two rulers. One ruler was prominent at the beginning of Jesus' ministry; the other at the end. Because John the Baptist accused Herod of unlawful marriage to Herodias, she sought

DREAMS IN SCRIPTURE

Match the person to the dream.

Example—Pharoah	He was told to restore a wife to her husband.
Daniel	He saw a ladder of angels reaching from earth to heaven.
Nebuchadnezzer	He dreamed of ring-streaked, speckled, and spotted rams.
Solomon	He saw several sheaves bowing down to one sheaf of grain.
Joseph (Jesus' father)	Grapes from three vine branches were pressed into a cup, and birds ate out of a basket upon a man's head.
Joseph (Old Testament)	Seven lean cows ate up seven fat cows. Seven thin ears of corn devoured seven full ears of corn.
Butler and Baker	A huge loaf of barley bread came tumbling down, hit a tent, and knocked it flat.
Wise Men	God asked this man what he would like most in the world.
Abimelech	He saw a great image. Parts of the body were made of gold, silver, grass, iron and clay.
A Man	A tall, flourishing tree was cut down and only a stump remained.
Nebuchadnezzer	He saw four great, strange-looking beasts come up from the sea.
Jacob	He was told to flee into another country.
Joseph (Jesus' father)	He was told when and where to travel.
Jacob	Warning was given not to see a particular person.

revenge and saw that he died. Pilate's wife had a dream whereby she tried to warn Pilate.

MODERN EXAMPLE

A woman living in Israel had a dream which the Lord used to save the life of a man. Beverly worked for the Christian Broadcasting Network in Israel, where she taught the children of the Middle East Television staff.

She awoke from her disturbing dream the morning of March 10, 1985. At first, she couldn't recall many of the details of the dream—only that she kept seeing the face of Ken, a young TV producer for the network. The staff, including Ken's family and hers, lived near the Lebanon border, one of the most volatile places in the world. Beverly began to pray for her family, for the staff, and especially, for Ken. She even went to a neighbor, who agreed with her in prayer specifically for Ken's safety.

Early that afternoon, Ken abruptly changed his plans to go across the border to the Middle East Television station in Lebanon, and instead, sat down to lunch.

Meanwhile, an Israeli troop carrier crossed the border. A terrorist, in an act of suicide, rammed his car full of explosives into the carrier. Twelve Israeli soldiers died and many others were wounded.

When she later learned what had happened Beverly had real reason to rejoice. If Ken hadn't changed his plans, he would have been on the border at the exact time of the explosion.

Through a dream, a woman felt the urgent need to pray that the Lord might protect a fellow worker and save his very life.

WHAT DO YOU THINK?

1. Have you ever felt like seeking revenge? What did you do?

_____

_____

2. How can you describe God's vengeance? _____

_____

_____

3. Have you ever had a significant dream? What did you do about it? _____

_____

_____

4. What precautions should you take in interpreting dreams—yours or others? _____

_____

_____

EVALUATE YOURSELF

1. In what ways are you inplementing the principles learned

272

from Herodias and Pilate's wife? _____

_____

_____

2. In what ways are you failing to inplement the principles learned from them? _____

_____

_____

3. What do you need to do to change? _____

_____

_____

4. How will you do it? _____

_____

_____

Lesson 28
Mary Magdalene, Joanna, & the Other Mary

An Example of Women Who Ministered with Jesus

"And many women were there beholding afar off, which followed Jesus from Galilee, ministering with him."

Matthew 27:55

SETTING THE STAGE

Though many other women may have been present at Calvary and witnessed the crucifixion of Jesus, the Bible names only five—Mary, the mother of Jesus; Mary Magdalene; the "other" Mary; Joanna, and Salome. Other lessons present Mary, the mother of Jesus, and Salome. In this lesson, we'll consider the remaining three—Mary Magdalene, the "other" Mary, and Joanna—as we look at the functions of these women in this greatest event of history. We'll discover, as well, the ministries God provides for women today.

The three women of this lesson are included in the oft-used phrase, *the women of Galilee.* They're the ones from that area who followed and ministered with Jesus. Each of them received personal ministry *from* Him, just as they ministered *with* and *to* Him. Note the prominent role given to women at the time of Jesus' crucifixion, as well as on resurrection morning. They were the first to spread the good news that Jesus was Risen.

THE WOMEN OF CALVARY

(Based on Matthew 27:55, 56 and 61; 28:1; Mark 15:40 and 47; 16:1-13; Luke 8:1-3; 23:55; 24:10; John 19:25; 20:1-18)

Instead of thinking of these women as failures or successes at this time, we'll simply listen to what may have been their thoughts as they witnessed the crucifixion of the One whom they had served—their fears, disillusionment and then, supreme joy when, at the tomb, they discovered that their Lord had risen as He said He would.

Joanna stands as part of the crowd who lines the way as Jesus bears His cross to Calvary. The "other Mary" stands beneath the cross where a select five gather. Mary Magdalene is on the way to the tomb on Resurrection morning.

Joanna "I can't understand this. What has happened anyway? First Jesus speaks of His own death. Now He talks of judgment still to come. He tells us not to weep for Him, but for ourselves. I can't help myself. I can only weep for Him today.

"It seems only a short time ago that I was healed by Jesus and committed myself to following Him. Before very long, I joined the other women in serving Him and His disciples, as we ministered from place to place. He so wanted to reach the lost. He even performed miracles of healing and deliverance so people might see the power of God. Why would anyone want to reject Him, much less crucify Him?

"Yet, I know rejection does take place. I remember when my husband, Chuza, lost his job as Herod's steward because I'd become a follower of Jesus and shared with others in the household there. Herod was not only willing to have Jesus' cousin, John the Baptist, beheaded as a favor to his wife, but now he has joined Pilate in allowing Jesus to be put to death!

"Now my heart is broken—not only for my friends and others who have already rejected my beloved Jesus, but also for Him in His suffering today. Oh God, where is your mercy? Where is your justice?"

The "other" Mary "Oh, my God! Oh, my Beloved Jesus! Oh, Mary, my poor sister and mother of my Lord. Mary, Mary Magdalene, what can we do? I'm so broken-hearted; so angry; so perplexed. I'm nearly as confused as my identity. Some call me Mary, the sister of Jesus' mother; that I am. Some call me the wife of Clopas or Alphaeus; that I am. Some call me the mother of James the Less and John; that I am. Others simply call me the "other" Mary. All I know is that I want to be called a follower of Jesus, even though I don't understand what that means now. What are we to do? How can His work continue with Him hanging dead upon a cross?"

Mary Magdalene "I remember the first time I saw Jesus. I was afraid of Him. I, who was so mentally and emotionally disturbed, must have been quite a sight to Him as well. My disheveled hair, my glaring eyes, and my sunken cheeks must have broadcast to everyone the complete demonic possession I was in bondage to. But, glory to God, Jesus brought me deliverance and peace of mind and heart. I can never thank Him enough. No, never!

"The years I spent ministering with Him weren't enough. I must attend to His needs, even now.

"Those hours beneath the cross were sheer agony. To see His mother grieving so and know that our Heavenly Father must have been suffering as well. How could He bear to see His own Son die in such a dreadful way?

"Will Jesus be alive? Will He rise from the dead as He said He would? No matter. I'll go to the tomb. Nothing else is as important as being as close to Him as I can."

Mary Magdalene was one of the first at the tomb on Resurrection morning. She stood outside the tomb, crying. As she wept, she bent over to look into the tomb and saw two angels in white, seated where Jesus' body had been, one at the head and the other at the foot.

They asked her, "Woman, why are you crying?" And she replied that they had taken her Lord away, though she didn't

276

know where they had put Him. Then she turned around and saw Jesus standing there, but she didn't recognize Him. Thinking He was the gardener, she said, "Sir, if you have carried him away, tell me where you have put him, and I will get him."

Jesus said to her, "Mary." She turned toward Him and cried out, "Rabboni!" (which means Teacher)

Jesus replied, "Do not hold on to me, for I have not yet returned to the Father. Go instead to my brothers and tell them I am returning to my Father and your Father, to my God and your God."

So, Mary Magdalene, with the other women, ran to tell the disciples of the joyful event which had taken place. Jesus was alive! He had, indeed, risen from the dead!

LESSONS FROM JOANNA, MARY MAGDALENE AND THE "OTHER" MARY
Calvary

When we speak of *Calvary*, we usually mean the experience of Jesus' suffering and death upon the cross as He was sacrificed as the Lamb of God for our sin.

The site of Calvary isn't far from the walls of Jerusalem where Christ was crucified and near which He was buried. The Latin word *calvaria* is a rendering of the Greek word *kranion*, meaning *skull*. The common explanation is that the name was due to the cranial shape of the hill.

The exact site of Calvary is a matter of dispute. Two sites contend for acceptance, both are visited by tourists to the Holy Land. One is the Church of the Holy Sepulchre. Within the walls of the present *old city*; the other is just outside the Damascus Gate and is better known as the *Garden Tomb*, or *Gordon's Calvary*.

The place of Jesus' agony and arrest is the Garden of Gethsemane, also outside the old city, but across the Kidron Valley on the Mt. of Olives. Within this Garden, today, eight ancient olive trees remain standing. The word *Gethsemane* means *oilpress*. This is significant in that Jesus was "pressed" as He spent the night in agonizing prayer just prior to His arrest.

It's most difficult for us, as finite man, to comprehend the suffering of Jesus, God-incarnate. We'll never know what it meant for God to contain Himself in an earthly body. It was only because of His agape love for us that God could so humble Himself. Yet Hebrews 12:2 reminds us that it was for the *joy* that was set before Him that He endured the cross, despising the shame. He loved us so much He was willing to give His life to atone for our sins.

Part of His suffering must have come from being with the disciples who didn't seem to understand why He had come and what was going to happen. And, though He knew that His Father hadn't forsaken Him, Jesus knew it would be very difficult to do His will. No doubt Satan tormented Him as well. Yet the long night in the Garden was but a prelude to the three hours of excruciating physical pain He endured upon the cross until He gave up His Spirit.

Isaiah 52:13-53:10 Name some of the ways, foretold here, that

Jesus would suffer. _____

_____

_____

Matthew 16:21-23 Jesus, Himself, told of some of the things He would suffer. _____

_____

_____

Mark 10:42-45 Jesus came to _____

_____

_____

Matthew 26:1-4 After Jesus spoke of judgment and the events to come, the chief priests, scribes and elders _____

_____

_____

Matthew 26:14-16 and 47-50 Even one of His twelve disciples, Judas, _____

_____

_____

Matthew 26:56 Then all of His disciples _____

_____

_____

Matthew 26:69-75 Peter _____

_____

_____

Matthew 27:1 and 2 Jesus was _____

_____

_____

Matthew 27:22-31 Here, before Pilate, He was sentenced to death and _____

_____

_____

Mark 11:18 When Jesus cleansed the temple, the Scribes and chief priests _____

_____

_____

Mark 14:32-42 Even though He asked to be released from the

278

cup of suffering, He was willing to _____

_____

_____

Mark 14:60-65 When Jesus told of His coming again, the response was _____

_____

_____

Luke 11:53 and 54 When Jesus denounced the Scribes and Pharisees, they _____

_____

_____

I Peter 3:18 Christ suffered for sin that _____

_____

_____

Hebrews 5:7 and 8 Through trials and suffering, Jesus learned

_____

_____

Matthew 27:32-50 Some of the suffering of Jesus described here: _____

_____

_____

What the Crucifixion of Jesus Accomplished

I Corinthians 2:2 Like Paul, the most important thing we should want to know is _____

_____

_____

Romans 3:23 _____

_____

have sinned and come short of the glory of God.

Romans 6:23 The wages of sin is _____

_____

_____

I Corinthians 15:3 Christ died _____

_____

_____

Isaiah 53:8 He was punished for _____

_____

_____

I Peter 2:24 He bore our sins upon the cross that _____

_____

_____

Ephesians 2:1-7 Through Jesus' death upon the cross, _____

_____

_____

II Corinthians 5:14 and 15 Because Christ died _____

_____

_____

Galatians 2:20 We were _____

so that _____

_____

_____

Romans 6:4-11 Because of Christ's death and resurrection,

_____

_____

Colossians 1:12-14 Because of Jesus' death, we have _____

_____

_____

Colossians 1:20-23 Through the blood of Jesus, _____

_____

_____

Colossians 2:13-15 At the cross, Jesus _____

_____

_____

Ephesians 2:13-18 Through Jesus' shed blood, _____

_____

_____

Galatians 6:14 We can glory in the cross of Jesus because

_____

_____

280

Philippians 3:8-10 The most important thing we can know is

_____

_____

The Women of Calvary

Though Scripture doesn't mention these women (except for Mary, the mother of Jesus) again, we can assume that they became active participants in the life of the early Church.

They do, however, show us the prominent part women had in the events surrounding, Jesus' death, burial, and resurrection—the greatest event in all history.

Women were:

1) recipients of the only recorded words spoken by Jesus on His way to crucifixion. (Luke 23:28-31)
2) the only persons *named* (except for John) as standing beneath the cross of Jesus.
3) the first to witness Jesus' resurrection from the tomb.
4) the ones who bore the good news of His resurrection to the other disciples.

Praise the Lord for the women of Calvary!

Ministries for Women Today

Throughout this study, we've seen various Bible women involved in ministry to others because of their love of God. In review, let's look at women and the ministry in which they participated (whether they recognized it as such or not):

Jochebed—raised her children in the fear of the Lord

Miriam—led God's people in worship and praise

Deborah—held a position of leadership, anointed by God

Abigail—ministered peace in a crisis situation

Widow of Zarephath—took a needy person into her home

Naaman's wife's maid—shared the good news with another person

Huldah—shared God's Word in prophecy

Anna—ministered to the Lord in prayers and fasting

Martha—opened her home in hospitality

Woman of Samaria—became the first missionary

Widow with two mites—gave of her finances

Dorcas—used her ability as a seamstress to clothe the needy

Phoebe—served as a deaconness in her church

Priscilla—taught the Word of God

In which of these ministries have you been involved?
To what ministry do you believe God is calling you?

Virtuous Woman

Interwoven in 22 verses of Scripture are the qualities that, in God's sight, make a woman worthy of praise. Read Proverbs 31:10-31 and consider the following.

Her character traits:

Diligent _____

_____

Industrious _____

_____

Compassionate _____

_____

Beautiful inside _____

_____

Her attributes as a wife:

Verse 11 _____

_____

Verse 12 _____

_____

Verse 23 _____

_____

Her attributes as a mother:

Verse 15 _____

_____

Verses 18 and 19 _____

_____

Verses 21 and 25 _____

_____

Verse 27 _____

_____

Her rewards:

Her children will _____

_____

Her husband will _____

_____

Her works will _____

_____

Her Lord will _____

_____

SUMMARY

Women played a prominant role at the time of Jesus' crucifixion. Some stood beneath the cross as Jesus hung upon it. Some watched from afar. Some went to the tomb to prepare His body for burial. Some were the first to witness to the resurrection. In fact, few men are named in each of these instances; we are specifically told that the disciples fled. Women seem drawn to the crises of life and can, thus, come close to the heart of God.

MODERN EXAMPLE

Velma Barfield, the first woman in 22 years to be executed in the United States, came to understand the true meaning of the cross of Jesus Christ while in a jail cell. She then spent the rest of her life serving Him in a very unique ministry.

Velma was born in North Carolina, into a family of nine children. Hers was not a happy childhood. Her father often beat his family while he was drunk.

At age 16, she joined a Baptist church through the influence of some friends. When she was 17, she eloped. Though she left her childhood home because of ill-treatment and a desire to be loved, Velma lived most of the rest of her life blaming herself for much of the hurt and pain suffered by others.

She and her husband had two children. They also had many problems, including accidents, poor health, increased drinking on his part, and unemployment. Finally, Velma collapsed with a nervous breakdown. It was then that she took her first tranquilizer. Soon she was hooked.

Before long, her husband died in a fire which started because he was smoking in bed while drunk. Velma remarried, but by this time drugs and stealing money to support her habit consumed her life.

During this time she poisoned four people, including her new husband and her mother. From then on, Velma was in and out of jails, at the same time, attending church when she could.

One Saturday night while she was in jail, Velma lay on her cot listening to the guard's radio, which was tuned to a gospel station. At 11 p.m., a new program came on. She was intrigued by the music. Suddenly it stopped, and a preacher declared, "Wherever you are tonight, God loves you!" Velma felt as though God was speaking directly to her and, after listening to the radio preacher present the gospel and explain the plan of salvation, she broke down and wept for nearly two hours. She knew, without a doubt, that Jesus had paid the price for *her* sin no matter how bad a person she had been.

After her trial, she was sent to prison. There, pastors, Christian friends, and the prison Chaplain ministered to her.

Through the help of the Lord, and a drug withdrawal program, she became free of drugs. Extremely grateful for what Jesus' death and resurrection had accomplished for her, she began to show the love of God to all around her. She prayed, held Bible Studies, and ministered to fellow prisoners.

The original date set for her execution was in 1979, but God extended it so that she might minister in His name. When Velma was executed on November 2, 1984, two groups of

WOMEN IN THE BIBLE

people gathered outside Raleigh Central Prison. A small group broke out into cheers upon hearing the announcement of her death. A larger group, about 200, kept a vigil of lighted candles, then sang the hymn "Amazing Grace" before disbanding. With tears in their eyes, they remembered a woman with a very unique ministry on behalf of her Lord Jesus Christ.

WHAT DO YOU THINK?

1. Are you beginning to better appreciate the role of women throughout Scripture, especially in the life of Jesus? ____

_____

_____

2. What unique functions of women seem to make us more sensitive to the heart of God? _____

_____

_____

3. What is your response in seeing others having to suffer?

_____

_____

4. What does Jesus' crucifixion mean to you? _____

_____

_____

EVALUATE YOURSELF

1. In what ways are you implementing the principles learned from the women of Calvary? _____

_____

_____

2. In what ways are you failing to implement the principles learned from these women? _____

_____

_____

3. What do you need to do to change? _____

_____

_____

4. How will you do it? _____

_____

_____

Lesson 29
Salome & Rhoda

An Example of Suffering, Persecution and Rejection

Yea, and all that will live godly in Christ Jesus shall suffer persecution."

II Timothy 3:12

SETTING THE STAGE

Jesus asked the mother of James and John (otherwise known as Salome) the question He eventually asks of each of His disciples. "Are you able to drink of the cup that I shall drink of, and be baptized with the baptism that I am baptized with?" In other words, are we able to partake of His suffering as part of our commitment to Him?

For the joy that was set before Him, Jesus endured the cross and the shame. To truly know Jesus, we must experience the power of His resurrection, as well as the fellowship of His sufferings. If we suffer with Christ, we shall also reign with Him. We must be crucified with Christ, so that he can live in us. That is death to self.

We must be prepared to suffer as Christians, just as we must expect persecution on the part of the world. Harder to take, sometimes, is the rejection we experience from other believers when we must stand alone, as did Rhoda.

Though God doesn't delight in man's suffering, man sinned and has to live in this world with the consequences of his sin. But since God can work all things together for good, He can use whatever suffering we experience, for His good. It's part of the refining process of the Church, that makes her a fit Bride for His son, Jesus Christ. Whatever suffering or persecution we may endure will one day be worth it all.

THE FAILURE OF SALOME
(Based on Matthew 20:20-24; 27:56; Mark 15:40 and 41; 16:1 and 2)

Salome was the wife of Zebedee, a prosperous fisherman on the Sea of Galilee. The only glimpse we have of him is in his boat, mending the nets, when Jesus came and called his two sons to follow Him. There was no action on Zebedee's part to detain them.

Reading between the lines, one can see agreement in this Capernaum family concerning their response to the call of Jesus.

Salome, one of the saintly women who followed and ministered to Jesus, appears to have been one of His disciples from the outset of His public ministry. She had no doubt as to His Messiahship.

She remained a faithful disciple of Jesus' up to the very end.

She was present at the crucifixion, when her sons had withdrawn. She was also among the women who went to the tomb and found that Jesus has risen from the dead.

Yet, Salome didn't understand what Jesus meant by the Kingdom of God. So, As a very ambitious mother, she asked for her sons to be placed at His right and left hands when the earthly kingdom she expected came into being. Jesus explained that these positions weren't His to give. He also questioned her as to whether she and her sons would be able to endure the suffering that would be required. In effect, Jesus asked if her sons were prepared to drink the cup of martyrdom, which in the end, they did. James was the first apostle to be martyred, and John, the last. This mother sought instant position for her sons. But by losing their lives for Christ's sake, they gained greater honor in heaven.

LESSONS FROM SALOME
The Sufferings of the Apostles

All of the apostles were persecuted by the enemies of their Master. They all died the death of a martyr. See what history and tradition says:

Matthew suffered martyrdom by being slain with a sword in Ethiopia.

Mark died in Alexandria, Egypt, after being dragged through the streets and drawn into a fire.

Luke was hanged upon an olive tree in Greece.

John was put in a caldron of boiling oil. He escaped death in a miraculous manner, and was afterward banished to Patmos (where he received the Revelation).

Peter was crucified at Rome with his head downward.

James, the greater was beheaded in Jerusalem.

James, the less was thrown from a lofty pinnacle of the temple and then beaten to death.

Bartholomew was flayed alive.

Andrew was bound to a cross, from whence he continued to preach until he died.

Thomas was impaled with a lance in the East Indies.

Jude was shot to death with arrows.

Matthias was first stoned, then beheaded.

Barnabas was stoned to death at Salonica.

Paul, after various tortures and persecutions, was eventually beheaded in Rome by Nero.

Persecution of the Church

From its very beginning, the Church underwent suffering and persecution. Even on the Day of Pentecost, when it was born, the disciples were mocked and accused of being drunk as God poured out the fullness of the Holy Spirit upon them to empower them for their work. Because Rome was in power and unsympathetic to their cause, Christians were greatly persecuted.

The Roman government feared that it would be overthrown. Romans hated Christians because Christians despised Rome's false gods. They blamed the Christians for the disasters that occurred, such as earthquakes, famines, wars, and droughts. During the time of the Emperors, the Coliseum was built in Rome for entertainment. People went there as a recreational sport, to see gladiators slay beasts and wild animals.

Before long, Christians were thrown to the lions. The spectators reveled in seeing hundreds of them mauled to death.

Foxe's *Book of Martyrs*, contains stories of many who gave their lives through the centuries for their faith and belief in Jesus. Ignatius, a bishop of Antioch, was sent to Rome because he professed Christ, and was given to wild beasts to be devoured. Polycarp, the bishop of Smyrna, was burned alive for Christ's sake. Such persecution continued until the time of Constantine.

Constantine the Great was emperor of Rome from 312 to 337 A.D. His reign was marked by two great events—a tremendous growth of Christianty and the moving of the capital of the empire from Rome to Constantinople (now Istanbul, Turkey).

The former occurred because Constantine was converted to Christianity and proclaimed religious tolerance for Christians. Constantine so established the peace of the Church that, for the space of a thousand years, there was no set persecution against the Christians (until the time of John Wycliffe).

During the intervening years, religion became corrupted. Christ became only a name, even to many Christians. The Christian world, which had forsaken the lively power of God's Word, was blind in its outward ceremonies and human traditions. Wycliffe perceived what had happened and protested publicly. John Wycliffe, a teacher at Oxford, England, began to translate the Bible into English so that it could be read by the laity and not only the Church hierarchy. Since there were no printing presses, he enlisted 100 scribes to make copies of the New Testament, which he'd translated by himself. He tried to call the Church back from her idolatry, especially in the matter of the sacrament of the body and blood of Christ. He was persecuted until his death, at which time his body was burned and his ashes scattered.

Foxe lists other martyrs—Sir John Oldcastle, John Huss and William Tyndale, to name a few—all of whom gave their lives for their faith in Christ Jesus. One of the most notable was Martin Luther, who nailed 95 objections to indulgences on the door of a church so clergy, citizens, and students might read of his protest against the then-ruling Catholic Church. Needless to say, he underwent great persecution and was excommunicated by the Pope. As a result, we have what has come to be known as the Protestant Church. About this time, the printing press also came into being and the Word was made available to the common people. As people began to read the Word for themselves, more were forced to give their lives for their belief in Jesus.

Many of us are unaware of the suffering and persecution of Christians in many parts of our world today. Perhaps many of us began to be more aware of this when, following World War II, we heard of the annihilation of six million Jews in Germany. Stories such as that of Corrie ten Boom's *Hiding Place* tell of Christians who tried to protect the Jews and were, themselves, thrown into concentration camps. Constantly there are stories of torture in Communist labor camps and other persecutions behind the Iron Curtain and in China. Many books are available on this subject. They help us appreciate the faith and strength the Lord gives in time of great suffering and persecution.

The Mystery of Suffering

As has been mentioned throughout this study, God is calling and preparing an eternal companion called the *Bride* who is to sit with His son on His throne and rule with Him in the ages to come. In order to qualify for this exalted position, the Bride must be as nearly like the Son as possible. If they are to rule together, they must share the nature of God. Because there is no maturing of godly character without suffering, suffering is a necessary preparation for rulership.

Sinful man is very self-centered, and, self-centeredness is the opposite of sacrifical love of others (including God). To bring man into the likeness of His son, God must *decentralize* him. This begins at the salvation experience and continues, as man allows it, through the process of sanctification. Phillippians 1:6 (LB) says, *"And I am sure that God who began the good work within you will keep right on helping you grow in his grace until his task within you is finally finished on that day when Jesus Christ returns."*

We learn from Scripture that sorrow, suffering, tribulation, and pain which come to the believer are not primarily for punishment, but preparation for rulership.

The history of Israel illustrates this point. In prosperity, she forsook Jehovah for idolatry. Only by chastisement was she led to repent and return to Jehovah. For centuries, while God sought to obtain a pure remnant through whom He could bring the Messiah, it was the same routine—prosperity, backsliding and apostasy, chastisement, repentance, return to God.

What's even more amazing is that it was part of God's plan to have His Son, Jesus, suffer. Hebrews 2:10 says, *"For it became him, for whom are all things, and by whom are all things, in bringing many sons to glory, to make the captain of their salvation perfect through sufferings."* And, *"Though he were a son, yet learned he obedience by the things which he suffered"* (Hebrews 5:8). Because He suffered, He is now fully qualified to serve as captain of man's salvation.

Christ's suffering only matured and perfected His human experience. It purged nothing from Him because He had no sin. But with man, sin is purged through suffering, as well as a Christ-like nature being formed. The Church must suffer to be conformed to the likeness of Jesus that she, as His Bride, may reign with Him. (see I Peter 4:1 and 2).

Let's consider what the Scripture says concerning suffering and persecution.

Matthew 5:10-12 When persecuted for righteousness sake,

288

we're to _____

_____

_____

Matthew 5:38-47 To love our enemies, we're to _____

_____

_____

Matthew 13:19-21 When persecution comes and one falls away, it may be because _____

_____

_____

Matthew 10:17-20 We're to _____

because _____

_____

_____

Matthew 10:22 We'll be _____,

but _____

_____

_____

Matthew 10:24-36 We're to fear only _____

_____

_____

Mark 10:28-30 Wholehearted commitment to Jesus may bring
_____

_____

_____

Luke 9:23 and 24 If anyone follows Jesus, _____

_____

_____

Luke 12:49-53 Jesus came to bring _____

_____

_____

John 15:18-20 We'll be hated because _____

_____

_____

John 16:33 In the world, we'll have _____

_____

_____

Acts 5:41 The apostles rejoiced because _____

_____

_____

Acts 14:22 We enter the kingdom of God by _____

_____

_____

II Corinthians 4:11-17 We may be _____

_____

but our light affliction _____

_____

II Corinthians 11:23-28 Paul suffered through _____

_____

_____

II Thessalonians 1:4 It's assumed that believers will _____

_____

_____

II Timothy 3:12 All that live godly in Christ Jesus will _____

_____

_____

I Peter 1:6 and 7 The trial of our faith should bring _____

_____

_____

I Peter 2:18-24 The difference between suffering for our faults
and suffering for Christ is _____

_____

_____

I Peter 3:13-18 The result of suffering for righteousness' sake is

_____

_____

Revelation 2:10 It's assumed that we _____

_____

but, _____

_____

290

THE SUCCESS OF RHODA

(Based on Acts 12:1-19)

Most of the time, when we think of persecution we think of it coming from unbelievers. We suffer mainly because they don't understand.

Another type of persecution, however, and one probably harder to take, is that which comes from other Christians. Sometimes our brothers and sisters in the faith don't understand us and reject what we say. Perhaps they don't see God alive today and ridicule us when we speak of miracles. Rhoda, a servant girl, had the experience of being rejected by believers when she was telling them the truth. But she stood alone for what she knew to be true.

During the days of terrible persecution, the saints of Jerusalem gathered regularly in Mary's home to read the Word of God and pray for the afflicted saints. One particular night, their prayers concentrated on Peter, whom Herod had put in jail and decreed would be the next apostle to die.

As the believers spent the night in intercession, God heard their prayers and supernaturally freed Peter by sending an angel to undo his chains. The angel took him out of the prison and through the streets without anyone seeing what was happening. Suddenly, the angel disappeared and Peter found himself standing at Mary's door.

As he knocked, Rhoda, the servant girl, ran to open the door. But when she heard Peter's voice, she forgot all about opening the door and ran back to tell those in the house who it was. With unbounding joy, she tried to explain that Peter was now at the door. But to her surprise, they replied that she must be mad. She continued to affirm the truth, and they continued to disbelieve her. All the while, Peter kept knocking. When they finally decided to open the door, they were astonished. At first they thought it was his angel. But Peter beckoned to them with his hand, indicating that they were to be quiet, as he told them how the Lord had delivered him from prison.

Though praying fervently, the saints couldn't believe God supernaturally answered their prayers, and so, when Rhoda brought them the news, they mocked her. Though Rhoda's rejection and persecution was short-lived, it must have been, nevertheless, difficult to bear.

LESSONS FROM RHODA
Standing Alone

We must be prepared to stand alone whenever we must choose what God says over what others even fellow Christians, say. How do each of the following Scriptures guide us in making these choices?

Proverbs 1:7-19 _____

_____

_____

Daniel 1:1-17 _____

_____

Colossians 2:8 _____

_____

_____

Proverbs 19:27 _____

_____

_____

Proverbs 14:7 _____

_____

_____

II Thessalonians 3:14 and 15 _____

_____

_____

Romans 12:2 _____

_____

_____

II Corinthians 6:14 _____

_____

_____

Ephesians 5:11 and 12 _____

_____

_____

SUMMARY

In the last lesson, we considered the suffering of Jesus. In this one, we looked at the suffering and persecution His followers should expect and will endure. Salome was confronted by Jesus when He asked if she was able to drink of the cup and be baptized with the same baptism He would undergo (meaning suffering).

Rhoda, a servant girl, was mocked by believers when she tried to tell them of a miracle God had performed. Suffering and persecution have been the lot of Christians since the time of Jesus, and will probably increase until He comes again.

MODERN EXAMPLE

Eighteen-year-old Julie was excited as she took Bob's letter from the mailbox. Having been introduced by a mutual friend, they'd been writing for quite some time, though they'd never met. Soon he would be out of the Navy and she could meet him at last. She opened the letter, and yes, he

292

asked her out.

Though he had to travel some distance to see her, they met for dinner and had lots of fun reviewing the things they'd learned about each other through their correspondance. However, Bob seemed to think it gave him license to be quite affectionate. Julie realized that he wanted to go much further, much faster than she did. Suddenly, the dream man she had lived with via letters was real. And she was scared. So she told him she wasn't ready to get serious, and he dropped out of her life.

Thus began a series of relationships with young men. Ten long years of wondering who the Lord had in store for her, all the while trying to stand for what she believed. Julie had been active in her church's youth program during her high school days. Not only had she received Scriptural teaching, but she had dedicated herself to the Lord at this time.

During the years of her struggle, her parents were rather silent, mainly because they had married young themselves and never faced the situations she encountered. Two of her brothers told her that they thought most boys wanted more than mere friendship from a girl. Her younger sister made her feel abnormal for not being able to find a man. When she overheard her youngest brother tell her mother that he "didn't want to be an old-maid like Julie," she was really hurt.

As Julie finished college and began teaching, she found fewer men in her life. She joined a single's club in her church, but the first person she dated there took her to his apartment and showed her his bed.

She met Bill. She was really attracted to him and dated him for quite a while. But when she discovered that he'd been married before, she began to feel uneasy and terminated their relationship.

By this time, Julie had decided that, perhaps the Lord wanted her to remain single the rest of her life. So she determined to forget about men and concentrate on her career. She signed up for a teaching job overseas when, at the last minute, she accepted a friend's invitation to attend a "Tall Person's Club." Her 5'10" height had often been a problem, but she had stayed away from such clubs because she assumed that mostly worldly men attended them. That was true—except for one special young man who ended up becoming her husband.

Was all the waiting worth it? Was all the standing alone for what she believed in worth it? Was taking all the hurtful experiences worth it? Was keeping herself sexually pure worth it? Sixteen years and five children later, Julie responds, in no uncertain terms, "Yes, indeed it was!"

WHAT DO YOU THINK?

1. Have you ever undergone any kind of persecution for what you believe? If so, why and how? _____

_____

_____

2. Do you know anyone who has had to endure much suffering for their faith? _____

_____

_____

3. Are you willing to suffer for Jesus' sake? _____

_____

_____

4. Have you ever felt mocked by fellow believers? If so, when and how? _____

_____

_____

EVALUATE YOURSELF

1. In what ways are you implementing the principles learned from Salome and Rhoda? _____

_____

_____

2. In what ways are you failing to implement the principles learned from Salome and Rhoda? _____

_____

_____

3. What do you need to do to change? _____

_____

_____

4. How will you do it? _____

_____

_____

Lesson 30
The Widow with Two Mites & Sapphira

An Example of Stewardship

"But seek ye first the kingdom of God, and his righteousness, and all these things shall be added unto you."

Matthew 6:33

SETTING THE STAGE

As we look at the widow with two mites, and Sapphira, we find an interesting contrast in the attitudes and responsibilities one can have concerning possessions. The first woman, a poor widow, sacrificially gave all, with no thought of herself. The second, Sapphira, seemingly gave what was required but secretly tried to benefit herself.

When God created the earth, He gave Adam and Eve dominion over every living thing, as well as supplying their every need. Because of sin, man lost what he had been given and was forced to labor for his daily bread. In God's own time, He gave a most valuable gift, His only-begotten Son, as a sacrifice for sin so man might, once again, have his full inheritance and become joint-heirs with Jesus Christ.

As we become His children (through the blood of Jesus), we realize that *all things* belong to Him, including our lives and possessions (Psalm 24:1). Out of gratitude for what God has done for us we then *want* to change our attitudes and reorder our priorities concerning the things we possess. We see them as a loan from God to accomplish His purpose, as well as to benefit His work in the world. We fulfill our desire by giving back to God, through tithes and offerings (the first-fruits of what He has already given us) of our time, talents, and possessions. It's our attitude and responsibility concerning our possessions that we'll consider in this lesson.

THE SUCCESS OF THE WIDOW WITH TWO MITES

(Based on Mark 12:41-44; Matthew 6:1-4)

Jesus had spent the day teaching in the temple and He was weary. He sat down across the room from where the people placed their offerings in receptacles that lined the walls, and watched them file by. Some put in large amounts, others, only a little.

As He sat, He thought about the events of the morning. The

Pharisees had tried to catch Him concerning His teaching on submission to the government. Then the Saducees had raised the questions of resurrection and marriage in heaven. The scribes had joined the discussion with their questions. Everything He had shared that morning seemed to have disturbed someone.

It was Pascal Week. People from everywhere were streaming to the temple with their offerings. Many of the wealthy made no attempt to conceal the amount of their offerings.

As Jesus watched, a little old woman hobbled up to the box and dropped two mites in. He knew of her sacrifice. These two coins represented all she had—one hundred percent.

No doubt He thought back to how, earlier in His ministry, a rich young ruler came to Him, wanting to know how to obtain eternal life. He was a devout young man, having obeyed all the commandments. But when Jesus told him that he needed to sell all that he had, take up his cross and follow Him, the young man went away sorrowfully.

Yet today, He'd seen one willing to do just that. He saw a poor widow give all she had to her God.

LESSONS FROM THE WIDOW WITH TWO MITES
God Wants to Bless His Children

God has given us, His children, many promises in His Word concerning prosperity. He desires that we not only have our needs met, but that we be abundantly blessed, so we can pass on material blessings to others as well. Some of these promises are:

Deuteronomy 14:22 _____

_____

_____

Deuteronomy 15:4-6 _____

_____

_____

Deuteronomy 28:8 _____

_____

_____

Deuteronomy 28:11-13 _____

_____

_____

Joshua 1:8 _____

_____

_____

Deuteronomy 29:9 _____

I Chronicles 29:11 and 12 _____

_____

Philippians 4:19 _____

_____

Matthew 6:33 _____

_____

III John 2 _____

_____

Psalm 23:1 _____

_____

_____

Psalm 34:10 _____

_____

_____

Psalm 84:11 _____

_____

_____

Psalm 37:4 _____

_____

_____

Proverbs 3:9 and 10 _____

_____

_____

Our Attitude Toward Our Possessions

Even though God made provisions for our prosperity, He also made some demands of us. For instance, in Deuteronomy 28, we're given several promises concerning the abundance of possessions that the Lord desires for us. Yet, these are conditional. Verses 1 and 2 say: _____

_____

In the New Testament, this is reaffirmed in Matthew 6:33. We are given the condition: _____

_____

The rich young ruler is an example of one who was unwilling to put his submission to Jesus above his material possessions. The result was (Matthew 19:16-24) _____

_____

Likewise, in a parable, Jesus tells of a rich young fool (Luke 12:16-21) The point of the story is _____

_____

In another of Jesus' parables, "The Sower" (Matthew 13:3-9; 18-23), we find that thorns choke out the Word of God, resulting in unfruitfulness. These thorns represent _____

_____

In I Corinthians 7:34, Paul says that even marriage can be a hindrance to our commitment to the Lord because _____

_____

It's interesting to note that Solomon, according to I Kings 10:23, *"exceeded all the kings of the earth for riches and for wisdom."* Yet, he lost it all because (I Kings 11:1-11) _____

_____

Jesus, on the other hand, created all things (Colossians 1:16). Everything is His. Yet, in this earthly life, He chose to (Matthew 8:20) _____

Coveteousness

One of the problems with possessions is that we're tempted to covet them. We develop an insatiable desire for worldly gain. We aren't satisfied with what we have; the more we have, the more we seem to want. Or, we want what others have.

According to God's Word, coveteousness produces the following:

Theft	Joshua 7:21	Falsehood	Acts 5:1-10
Lying	II Kings 5:20-27	Lust	I Timothy 6:8, 9
Murder	Proverbs 1:18, 19	Apostasy	I Timothy 6:10

Ezekiel 33:31 We can show love with our mouth and, at the same time, _____

298

Ephesians 5:1-5 Coveteousness excludes one from _____

_____

Luke 12:15-21 We're to beware of coveteousness, for _____

_____

Colossians 3:2-5 We're to set our affection on _____

_____

and put to death _____

_____

THE FAILURE OF SAPPHIRA

(Based on Acts 4:32 - 5:11)

Sapphira was one of the Christians of the early Church. After the Holy Spirit had been poured out upon the 120 men and women in the upper room, the Lord moved mightily through miracles, signs and wonders. Over 3,000 came to the Lord in just one day after hearing Peter preach under the power and anointing of the Holy Spirit.

The first converts were so totally committed to God that they sold their possessions and held all things in common. They brought all their own material resources and laid them at the apostles' feet, so that those who lacked would be provided for.

Luke notes that these early Christians were of one heart and one soul; they were in complete agreement in this arrangement of sharing with each other. This oneness of heart and soul had to have come from the Lord, for only He could bring about such unity.

One day, Ananias and his wife, Sapphira, sold some property and brought part of the money to the apostles. They pretended that what they brought was the full price, though they both knew it wasn't.

But Peter was given a word of knowledge and asked them why they were allowing Satan to fill their hearts, and why they were lying to the Holy Spirit. As soon as Ananias heard the accusation, he fell to the floor, dead. Everyone was frightened. Some young men covered him up, carried him out, and buried him.

Three hours later, Sapphira came before the same group unaware of what had happened to Ananias. When Peter asked her if they had sold the land for a certain price, she replied that they had. Then Peter told her what had happened to her husband and *she* fell instantly to the floor, also dead. She was carried out and buried beside her husband, while terror gripped all who saw and heard what happened.

The amount of money this couple kept back for themselves was inconsequential; it was their reluctance to be truthful that grieved the Lord. Their possessions were of more value to them than trusting Him to supply their need. We don't know why God meted out such severe punishment. But we can be sure that no one else tried to do the same thing very soon after that!

LESSONS FROM SAPPHIRA
Our Responsibility Toward Our Possessions

As the Church began to grow and spread, Paul made missionary journeys to establish new churches. Giving was encouraged among all Believers. It not only helped them to become less selfish, but also helped those who truly were in need. It also strengthened the family ties as they became "sisters and brothers" in the Lord.

We can note a significant contrast between two of the churches Paul helped found—the church in Philippi and the one in Corinth. Paul wrote the Philippian church from prison, saying that he thanked his God for the remembrance of them (Philippians 1:3-5). He goes on (in 3:15) to tell them they were the only church to send him offerings from time to time. The Philippian church, though made up of slaves and the lower classes, had abundant joy—because of what the Lord had done to set them free from idolatry and because they were loved by Him. They wanted to express this love to others; it was their way of thanking Paul for his part in bringing the good news to them.

The Corinthian church, on the other hand, was located in a city of wealth. It's members had not yet learned the joy of giving. In Paul's second letter to the Corinthians, chapter 8, he tells them that the churches of Macedonia (where Philippi was), gave to him, with great liberality even through their great trial of affliction. He also tells the Corinthian church that they need to learn to give, and do it *cheerfully*. He reminds them that as they give, God is able to give them everything they need and more, so that there will not only be enough for their own needs, but plenty left over to give joyfully to others. Then two good things would result—those in need would be helped, and God would be praised.

Though we in the Church today may not have all things in common, we do have a responsibility to give (again, that we may grow in unselfishness and to benefit the work of the Lord in the lives of others).

Giving is commanded in Scripture. It's part of our obedience to the Lord.

I Corinthians 16:1 and 2 _____

_____

_____

II Corinthians 9:7 _____

_____

_____

Malachi 3:10 _____

_____

Leviticus 27:30 _____

_____

_____

Stewardship

The Word has specific things to say concerning the stewardship of our possessions—how we obtain them, our attitude toward them, our use of them, and the benefit they're to be to us and others.

I Corinthians 6:19 and 20 We're not our own; we were ____

_____

Therefore, _____

_____

I Corinthians 4:2 It's required of stewards that _____

_____

_____

James 4:1-3 We don't have what we need because _____

_____

_____

I Timothy 6:6-10 We're reminded that we're to be _____

_____

_____

Philippians 4:11 and 12 We're reminded that _____

_____

_____

II Corinthians 8:1-9 From this, we learn concerning our giving that _____

_____

Paul reminds us that Jesus _____

_____

so that _____

_____

_____

Luke 16:1-13 From this parable of the dishonest steward, we learn that _____

_____

_____

Luke 16:19-31 The relationship of our riches in this life with eternal life is _____

_____

_____

Psalm 49:16 and 17 Here, we're told _____

_____

_____

II Corinthians 9:6-9 As we give _____

_____

_____

I Timothy 5:17 and 18 The laborer is worthy of _____

_____

_____

Acts 20:35 Regarding giving, Jesus said, _____

_____

_____

Tithing

Tithe means *tenth*. History reveals that the practice of making the *tenth* the rate to pay tribute to rulers, and offer gifts as a religious duty, existed in ancient Babylon, Persia, Egypt, and China. It's quite certain that Abraham knew of this principle when he migrated from Ur of Chaldees. He's the first one recorded in Scripture to give a tithe to a priest of the Most High (Genesis 14:17-20).

It was a long time before definite legal requirements were set concerning tithing, so customs in paying tithes varied. At first, the tither was commanded to tithe to the Levites (Deuteronomy 14:22-29). If a Hebrew lived too far from the temple to make taking his tithes practical, he could sell them and use the money gained to buy substitutes at the temple (Deuteronomy 14:24-26). This permit eventually led to gross abuses by the priests, as we see happening in the time of Jesus (Matthew 21:12 and 13).

The methods developed for paying tithes became somewhat complicated when the firstlings of the flocks were added to the tithes of the firstfruits (Exodus 13:12 and 13). When the Levitical system was established, provision for the upkeep of the sons of Levi was made through tithes (Numbers 18:21-24). The Levites, in turn, gave a tenth to provide for the priests (Numbers 18:25-32). Rules and regulations varied until, by the time of Christ, Roman rule had greatly affected the economic life of Judea. Hence it was difficult for people to tithe, though the laws of tithing were still observed when possible (Luke 18:9-14).

Jesus commended giving of a portion of one's income, in Luke 11:41 and 42; He even told the manner in which to give them in Matthew 6:1-6.

302

Actually, the word *alms* is used more in the New Testament than the word *tithe*. *Almsgiving* was of two kinds: alms of food and money received daily for distribution, and alms of the chest (coins received on the Sabbath for widows, orphans, strangers, and the poor). A primary function of deacons was to distribute these alms (Acts 6:1-3).

In the early church, giving *alms* is not named as such. Rather, a spirit of sacrificial sharing with others was encouraged. More important than tithes is the total commitment of one's self and possessions to the Lord for His use, whatever the need.

SUMMARY

A study of two women points out an interesting contrast in the attitude and responsibility one can have concerning the stewardship of possessions. The first, a poor widow, sacrificially gave her all with no thought to her own needs. The second, Sapphira, seemingly gave what was required, but secretly tried to benefit herself. All things belong to God; we're only His stewards. Out of gratitude, we should be willing to give back to Him, cheerfully, at least the first part of what He has given us.

MODERN EXAMPLE

The murky dishwater reflected Susan's dismal mood. She plopped another dish into the suds and sighed as she surveyed the rest of the kitchen cupboards, as well as the sticky floor beneath her feet. The whole apartment was a mess, and she was angry.

Susan and Jim had been away on a short-term outreach with Youth With a Mission. It was a rewarding experience, leading several teams of young people in a summer of service. God had provided their finances, good health, and even a friend to house-sit while they were gone.

As Susan opened kitchen drawers her anger flared even more. From one she pulled out her assorted sets of placemats and napkins. Parts of each set were missing. She banged that drawer shut and opened another, Her white tablecloth, a wedding gift, was stained with tea. "Oh, God," Susan moaned, "Why did You let these things happen? We thought You'd provided so well in arranging for someone to house-sit. Now I've come home to find all my things in shambles! Is this what I get for serving You?"

Susan continued to open drawers. She found an apron stuck in the back corner of one. Pulling it out, she held it up for examination. It had never been used, but the once-white lace was now a bit ivory. The bright pink print had faded. Suddenly she realized that even when things haven't been used, they sometimes lose their newness anyway.

She put on the apron and began to work on the stained tablecloth. As she worked, God began to tug at her heart and thoughts began to surface to her mind. Hadn't she asked the Lord for a home that would be open to people? Hadn't she committed her possessions, as well as her life, to the Lord? What about the poor they had served that summer? Did her feeling of frustration over some missing napkins and a stained tablecloth outweigh their problems of hunger, disease, and poverty?

Susan unplugged the sink and watched the water disappear. She felt her anger and resentments go gurgling down the drain with the suds. Then she smiled and went to the phone. She wanted to call Peggy and thank her for house-sitting the apartment all summer.

WHAT DO YOU THINK?

1. What is your attitude towards your possessions? Are you a good steward of what you have been given? _____

_____

_____

2. Do you covet anything? If so, what? _____

_____

_____

3. Are you responsible with money? _____

_____

_____

4. Do you tithe? Why or why not? _____

_____

_____

5. Are you willing to share what you have with others? ___

_____

_____

EVALUATE YOURSELF

1. In what ways are you implementing the principles learned from Salome and Rhoda? _____

_____

_____

2. In what ways are you failing to implement the principles learned from these two women? _____

_____

_____

3. What do you need to do to change? _____

_____

_____

4. How will you do it? _____

_____

_____

Lesson 31
Dorcas, Lydia, Phoebe & Priscilla

An Example of Servants

"If any man serve me, let him follow me; and where I am, there shall also my servant be; if any man serves me, him will my Father honor."

John 12:26

SETTING THE STAGE

Through the four women of this lesson—Dorcas, Lydia, Phoebe, and Priscilla—we have a glimpse of the faith and commitment of the believers of the early Church. Each, in her unique way, contributed to the welfare and function of the Body of Christ. All were women who had servant hearts. They rendered service to others. By doing so, they exemplified a living faith in a living Lord.

Though Dorcas has the distinction of being a woman raised from the dead, she was also well-known for the works which she did. Even at her deathbed, women gathered around and showed Peter the many garments which she had made to clothe those in need.

Lydia was a business-woman, a seller of purple, in Philippi. When she heard the good news from Paul, she was baptized. She then invited Paul to her home, where, it's believed, the Philippian church came into being.

In the only two Scripture verses we have about Phoebe, we find that she was a deaconness in the church of Cenchrea. Paul recommended her to the church in Rome as one who had been of great help to many, including himself.

Priscilla and her husband accompanied Paul on his missionary journeys. They also worked with him in the tentmaking business. They were fellow-laborers together as they all served the risen Christ.

In the Body of Christ today, we have many opportunities for service. Each member has a different function so that the whole body can do the work it has been called to do. Thus, it behooves each of us to receive the gifts which God gives us, through His grace, and allow them to be used to minister to others. In this way, He can edify His Church, as well as conform His Bride to His own image. It's also the means He has of bringing the good news of Jesus Christ to a lost and dying world. As we now take a look at each of these four women, we will also consider the unique and successful ways they served the Church and their Lord.

THE SUCCESS OF DORCAS
(Based on Acts 9:36-42)

Dorcas (also called Tabitha) lived in Joppa, a town on the Mediterranean coast where there was a group of believers.

One day Dorcas died, and many women came to mourn her. They sent for Peter, who was in a nearby town, and he came to minister to them. The women showed Peter the garments Dorcas had made and left the room while he knelt down and prayed. Turning to Dorcas' body, Peter said, "Tabitha, arise!" Then, Dorcas opened her eyes and sat up.

Naturally, there was much rejoicing when Peter presented the live woman to those who had been mourning her death. The news spread throughout Joppa, and many believed because of this miracle.

Dorcas was a woman who met practical needs by using her physical abilities and talents. God has said the *"pure religion and undefiled before God and the Father is this, to visit the fatherless and widows in their affliction"* (James 1:27). James 2:14-17 goes on to say, *"What doth it profit, my brethren, though a man say he hath faith, and have not works? Can faith save him? If a brother or sister be naked, and destitute of daily food, And one of you say unto them, Depart in peace, be ye warmed and filled; notwithstanding ye give them not those things which are needful to the body; what doth it profit? Even so faith, if it hath not works, is dead, being alone."* Matthew 25:35-46 also tells us that judgement will be based upon whether or not we have fed the hungry, clothed the naked, and visited those who are sick and in prison. God needed Dorcas in her day so much that He extended her life. God still needs Dorcases in His Church today.

THE SUCCESS OF LYDIA
(Based on Acts 16:12-15 and 40)

Scripture doesn't supply us with any information regarding Lydia's background apart from the fact that she lived in Philippi. While it isn't certain whether she was of Jewish descent, it is evident that she was, at least, a Jewish proselyte; we're told that she worshipped God. In spite of her secular obligations, she made her way daily, to the riverside where prayers were being said.

Although sincerely religious, Lydia wasn't a Christian. However, she did seem to have a deep spiritual hunger, for when Paul came to the riverside to minister to those gathered there, she heard his message and wanted to be baptized. Her conversion led her to witness to many others. Thus she became Paul's first European convert.

Lydia's transformation was evidenced by her eagerness to give the missionaries hospitality in her fine home, which also became a center of Christian fellowship in Philippi.

Thyatira, Lydia's native city in Asia Minor, was known for the unique purple dye it produced. When she came to Philippi, Lydia began a thriving business as a seller of purple. Lydia was, first of all, a consecrated Christian, then a conscientious business-woman who sold her purple dyes.

THE SUCCESS OF PHOEBE

(Based on Romans 16:1 and 2)

Phoebe is mentioned in only two sentences in Scripture. She is called our sister, and a servant of the Church.

Phoebe lived in the city of Cenchrea, a seaport town nine miles east of Corinth. It was said that she was a *succorer* of many. The expression translated *succorer* comes from a verb with a double meaning of *to lead* and *to care for.* Both were obligations of the leading members of the early Church. This implies that Phoebe was a woman of responsibility whose duty was to care for others. She is also called a servant of the church. This word, *diakonos,* comes from the verb which basically means *to serve,* such as a waiter at a meal. It appears that, by Phoebe's time, the gift had become an office. Her ministry, bearing responsibility and caring for others, wasn't merely a private effort, but was sanctioned by the congregation at Cenchrea. In her position, she probably watched over the women converts, visited the sick and those in prison, as well as performed some of the functional duties in preparation for worship services. In our day, she would probably be called a deaconness.

Phoebe served as a courier of a letter Paul sent to the church in Rome. At the close of this letter, Paul reminded the believers in Rome that Phoebe was a fellow sister in the Lord. He commended her to them and asked that they help her in any way they could. Phoebe was willing to do what she could, for she had a servant's heart.

THE SUCCESS OF PRISCILLA

(Based on Acts 18:1-3; 18-26; Romans 16:3 and 4; I Corinthians 16:19; II Timothy 4:19)

Priscilla and Aquila (her husband) were a courageous couple who seemed to be very successful in their trade of tent-making. They were able to afford houses large enough to be used as churches in both Rome and Corinth (and, perhaps, in Ephesus as well). Apparently they traveled extensively, spending at least 18 months in Corinth, the center of commerce for all Achaia. They eventually settled in Ephesus. As a tentmaker himself, Paul often joined them in their trade, even living with them for a while.

Both Priscilla and her husband appear to have been active teachers in the early Church. It's of special significance that Priscilla's name is mentioned before that of her husband in their instruction of Apollos. The things that Priscilla heard from Paul, she committed to Apollos, also a faithful teacher.

It was unusual that eloquent Apollos should be instructed by a woman. But because she was under the authority of both her husband and Paul, she was allowed to do so. And God blessed them all. She was an exceptionally learned woman, and the Holy Spirit provided her with the gift of teaching.

Priscilla was flexible. She was willing to give up her rights and go where the Lord called. Paul admonished Christians to comfort and edify one another (I Thessalonians 5:11). As a woman who opened her home to others and taught them well, Priscilla carried out her tasks as a servant in the Early Church.

WOMEN IN THE BIBLE

LESSONS FROM DORCAS, LYDIA, PHOEBE AND PRISCILLA

The Church—The Body of Christ

In Scripture, the Church is the *ecclesia*, the *called-out* ones—those who are blood washed, born again, and Spirit-baptized. The Church is called:

1) **a body**—*"Now ye are the body of Christ, and members in particular."* (I Corinthians 12-27)
2) **a building** (a Holy Temple)—*"In whom all the building fitly framed together groweth unto a holy temple in the Lord; In whom ye also are builded together for a habitation of God through the Spirit."* (Ephesians 2:21-22)
3) **a Bride**—*"...that I may present you as a chaste virgin to Christ."* (II Corinthians 11:2; Ephesians 5:23-27)

The Foundation When Peter replied to Jesus' question, in Matthew 16:16, that *"Thou are the Christ, the Son of the Living God,"* Jesus responded, *"Thou art Peter* (Petros, a pebble) *and upon this rock* (Petra, a big rock, not Peter) *I will build my church."* Here Jesus declares that He will build His church with Himself (the true rock, the confession of Peter) as the foundation. Peter later describes this Church, in I Peter 2:1-10, and says that Jesus is the *cornerstone*. The believers are living stones Christ is the foundation. See also:

I Corinthians 3:11 _____

_____

_____

Isaiah 28:16 _____

_____

_____

The Head of the Church Christ is not only the foundation; He is the cornerstone and the Head of the Church (See Colossians 1:18). This Church is more than an organization; it's an organism with Christ as the living Head. It's alive with the life of Christ in each member. These members, according to I Corinthians 12:1-31, function in various ways, yet are important to one another. God set ministries in the Church, and the Holy Spirit gives it gifts.

The Organization There is Scriptural evidence of some organization in the early Church, but not as we commonly know it today. In Ephesians 4:1-13, we find that God has called some as apostles, prophets, evangelists, pastors and teachers for the perfecting of the saints, for the work of the ministry, for the edifying of the body of Christ. We find that some will be elders, as described in I Timothy 3:1-7 and some will be deacons, as described in I Timothy 3:8-13. But, it is the *Lord* who adds to the Church daily those who should be saved (Acts 2:47).

The church's ordinances include baptism (Romans 6:3-6), which identifies the believer with Christ in His death, burial and resurrection and, the Lord's Supper (I Corinthians 11:23-26) a reminder of Jesus' death and resurrection.

Discipline The Church is to purge any evil in its member-

308

ship. The motive for doing so is to discipline one another in love. The goal is to restore one who has sinned to fellowship with His Lord and the Church. (See Matthew 18:15-17 for procedure in doing this.)

Worship and Work To worship is to bow down in awe, to pay honor to God in humble, reverent homage. The worship of the Church must be in Spirit and in Truth (John 4:24). The main work of the Church is to share God's Word and love with one another, and its faith and hope with the lost. The following Scriptures tell how this is to be done:

Matthew 28:18-20 _____

_____

_____

Mark 16:15-18 _____

_____

_____

II Corinthians 5:1-9 _____

_____

_____

I Corinthians 3:5-10 _____

_____

_____

Romans 12:3-21 _____

_____

_____

Its Power On the day of Pentecost, the Church received power to evangelize the world. The outpouring of the Holy Spirit resulted in conviction of sin, repentance towards God, and faith in the Lord Jesus Christ. Some were empowered with special service, but all received power to witness. A Spirit-empowered Church will evangelize (II Timothy 4:5), reproduce itself (I Peter 1:23), change people (Acts 2:37-41), and turn the world upside down (Acts 17:6). In the power of the Holy Spirit, the Church is also to wage war (Ephesians 6:10-18), run a race (Hebrews 12:1 and 2) and labor in love (I Corinthians 3:9).

The Future The true Church has a glorious, victorious future in the world, in the air, in the kingdom, and in eternity. The church will emerge triumphant for *"we are more than conquerors through Him that loved us"* (Romans 8:35-39). The church cannot fail because Christ is its Head; the Holy Spirit, its power; and the Word of God, its guide. Someday, the Church will reign as Christ's Bride.

A Servant-Heart

The nature of God, which He wants to conform in us through service, is that of a servant. John 12:26 says, *"If any man serve me, let him follow me; and where I am, there shall also my servant be: if any man serves me, him will my Father honor."* (See also Luke 22:27)

Where is Jesus? He's everywhere that there is a need. Jesus serves man, but He wants to do it through us. As we become His servant, we become more like Him!

Charles Swindoll, in his book *Improving Your Serve*, gives a portrait of a servant. He (or she) is a giver, a forgiver, and a forgetter. He puts the welfare of others before his own. He must be willing to do God's will above his own. *"The Son of Man did not come to be served, but to serve"* (Matthew 20:28). To be a servant of God, one must be a servant of people.

There are consequences and rewards in service, as we can see in Scripture. Paul was, perhaps, one of God's greatest servants. Yet, in II Corinthians 11:23-28, we find that he paid some consequences for all that he did. Some of these were:

_____

_____

Service to God also has great rewards. Ultimately, we will spend eternity with God in the place He has prepared for us. In anticipation of this, we also know that He has promised rewards to His servants for a job well done (Matthew 25:21). However, Scripture not only tells us of eternal rewards, but of specific rewards we can receive as we serve in His Body now:

Isaiah 41:10 _____

_____

_____

II Corinthians 4:16-18 _____

_____

_____

Philippians 4:13 and 19 _____

_____

_____

Galatians 6:9 and 10 _____

_____

_____

Luke 17:7-10 _____

_____

_____

The Woman's Role in the Church

As we become part of the Body of Christ and begin to follow Jesus, we grow in appreciation of who He is and what He has done for us. As a result, we want to please Him, to serve Him in whatever way we can. Our service is the outgrowth of our faith and love, not the means to earn acceptance from Him. As we serve and love others, we benefit as well, for we conform more to Jesus' nature.

Jesus submitted as a servant to the will of His Father. We've

310

already seen how woman was placed in a submissive position. Thus is she designed for the role of servant.

In a previous lesson, we considered some of the ministries available to women, patterned after the women found in the Bible. In this lesson, we've seen how four women served in various capacities in the Early Church.

God said that in the last days He will pour out His Spirit upon *daughters* and *handmaids* (see Acts 2:17 and 18), thus equipping us, too, for service in His Body. Furthermore, He designed the woman's role to be symbolic of that of the Bride of Jesus Christ. What a privilege He bestowed upon His female children, and what a responsibility to minister in His Name as His servant.

SUMMARY

Through the four women of this lesson, we gain a glimpse of the faith and commitment of the believers in the early Church. Each of these had true servant-hearts. They contributed to the welfare and function of the body of Believers as fellow-laborers with God. In order to understand how to function and serve in the Church, we will consider what the Church is, as well as women's role in it.

MODERN EXAMPLE

From a mission for AIDS victims in New York City, to a center for lepers near Calcutta, India, to a soup kitchen for the hungry in France, the service of Mother Teresa for her Lord Jesus Christ reaches around the world.

Born in 1910 of well-to-do Albanian parents in what is now Yugoslavia, Agnes Gonxha Bojaxhiu (now known as Mother Teresa) knew, at age 18 that she was called to serve the poor of the world. After study in Ireland, she was sent to India's Himalayan foothills where she began her novitiate as a Catholic nun. The school in which she taught overlooked a terrible slum. She would often go there after school, to minister to the people. After a few years, she obtained permission to be a free nun outside the cloister and went to the slums of Calcutta to work among the poorest of the poor. There she was joined by a former student. Then others came. They lived on the top floor of a large house offered by a Christian, and they begged for food, medicine, land, and schools for the poor.

The Order which she founded began in October 1950. Workers now associated with it have grown to over 3 million people in 70 countries.

They visit the elderly and sick and work in soup kitchens and homes for the destitute providing food, clothing, and medicine for those in need.

Winner of the 1979 Nobel Peace Prize, Mother Teresa heads an organization which feeds 126,000 families, teaches 14,000 children, cares for 186,000 victims of leprosy and 22,000 dying destitutes. Having personally cared for many of the world's poor herself, this living saint spends the early hours of every morning in prayer, for it is to God she brings her needs and it is from Him she receives the love she gives.

That Mother Teresa sees her service as a command of God can be seen from one of her remarks. A volunteer once sent a note to Mother Teresa saying that she couldn't perform her duty that day because she was running a fever. Mother Teresa returned the note, replying that she too, had a fever, but thought it was better to burn in this world than the next.

It makes one want to be present when, one day, Jesus says to Mother Teresa, "Well done, thou good and faithful servant."

WHAT DO YOU THINK?

1. What do you see as your function in the Body of Christ?

_____

_____

2. How do you serve in your church? _____

_____

3. In what other ways would you like to serve the Lord? (something that you aren't doing now) _____

_____

_____

4. Do you have a servant's heart? If not, how can you have one? _____

_____

_____

5. What are some of the rewards of service? _____

_____

_____

EVALUATE YOURSELF

1. In what ways are you implementing the principles learned from these four women? _____

_____

_____

2. In what ways are you failing to implement the principles learned from them? _____

_____

_____

3. What do you need to do to change? _____

_____

_____

4. How will you do it? _____

_____

_____

Lesson 32
Euodias & Syntyche, Lois & Eunice, & the Elect Lady

An Example of Relationships in the Body of Christ

"And as we have opportunity, let us do good unto all men, especially unto them who are of the household of faith."

Galatians 6:10

SETTING THE STAGE

In the last lesson, we looked at four women who gave themselves in service as part of the Body of Christ. We saw that this Body, also called the Church, has many members, each of which has a unique function. Jesus Christ is its Head and we are its hands, feet, eyes, ears, etc. All parts work together to accomplish God's purpose. This includes reaching the lost as well as being a means through which God may conform the Bride to the nature of His Son, Jesus Christ.

We'll now look at another five women and consider the relationships God wants for us as we are *"builded together for a habitation of God through the Spirit"* (Ephesians 2:22). This symbolism of the Church found in I Peter 2:5 is that of a spiritual house, its members being lively stones, and Jesus, the cornerstone. II Corinthians 6:16 also tells us that we are the temple of the living God, a dwelling place for Him. Euodias and Syntyche exemplify the conflicts that arise in working together. Lois and Eunice show the family relationships we are to have as believers. The Elect Lady makes us aware of the relationships we are *not* to have, particularly with false teachers.

Let's begin with an understanding of how we're to be a habitation for God and rightly-related to Him. We'll then see what He desires for our relationships with one another.

A Dwelling Place for God

God created Adam and Eve for the pleasure of having fellowship with them, (Revelation 4:11) but this relationship was broken by sin. From that time on, the only way to be reconciled to God was through a system of sacrifices and, eventually, the ultimate sacrifice—Jesus.

That God wanted to dwell with man became evident as He

brought His people out of Egypt and led them through the wilderness on the way to the Promised Land. He gave them a cloud to follow by day and a pillar of fire by night as a sign that He would lead them. Then He ordered Moses to build a tabernacle, a place where He could actually dwell among the people. We find the details of this tabernacle, constructed according to very specific instructions, in Exodus 25-30 and 37-40. Exodus 40:33-38 gives the account of the finished work. Exodus 40:34 and 35 says, *"Then a cloud covered the tent of the congregation, and the glory of the Lord filled the tabernacle. And Moses was not able to enter into the tent of the congregation because the cloud abode therein, and the glory of the Lord filled the tabernacle."* Though the tabernacle was first set up at Sinai, it stood at Kadesh for over 35 years. Under Joshua, the first site of the tabernacle in Canaan was probably at Gilgal, though there is no direct mention of this. During Joshua's lifetime, the tabernacle was moved to Shiloh to avoid disputes and jealousy among the tribes. Perhaps the degree of permanence associated with this site led to the designation of the structure as a temple, (I Samuel 1:9; 3:3). It may indicate that the fabric had become worn and was replaced by a more substantial building. Whatever the case, Shiloh was the central sanctuary until the ark was captured by the Philistines.

The subsequent history of the tabernacle is somewhat obscure. When David wished to institute tabernacle religion in his capital city of Jerusalem, he prepared a place for the ark and pitched a tent in the tradition of the Gibeon tabernacle (II Samuel 6:17). The altar of the tabernacle at Gibeon was used for sacrifical worship until the time of Solomon, when both it and the Davidic tabernacle were superseded by the building of the temple. The new edifice incorporated all that remained of earlier tabernacle worship (I Kings 8:4). The Temple then became the place where people met God as they made sacrifices to atone for sin and sang their praises to Him.

Actually, three successive temples stood on Mt Moriah (II Chronicles 3:1) in Jerusalem. These included Solomon's temple, the temple restored by Zerubbabel and the Jews following their captivity, and the one built by Herod the Great (in use at the time of Jesus). This last temple was destroyed when Jerusalem fell to the Roman armies in A.D. 70. This destruction made complete and final the break between the Temple and the Church. Since then, God hasn't allowed any Temple to take its place, for He now dwells in His believers, the Church of Jesus Christ.

See Chart 32A

God's People as His Dwelling Place

With the death of Christ and the birth of the Church, God's dwelling place changed. He no longer put Himself within a specific building, but in the hearts of men. In I Corinthians 6:19 and 20, Paul reminds the believers that they are temples of the Holy Spirit, therefore, they're not their own; they were bought with the price of Jesus' shed blood, and need to allow the Holy Spirit to do His work in conviction of sin so that they might be cleansed and become a holy people unto God.

314

TABERNACLE

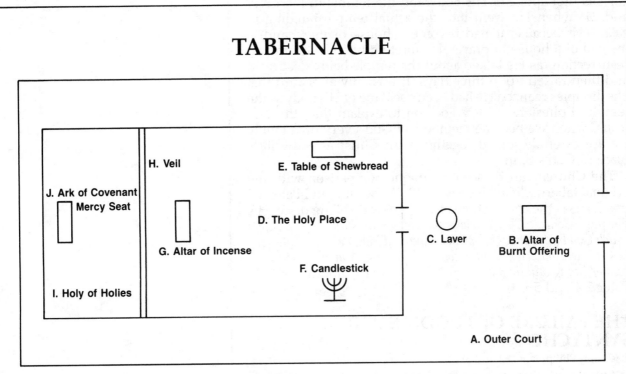

H. Veil

E. Table of Shewbread

J. Ark of Covenant
Mercy Seat

D. The Holy Place

G. Altar of Incense

C. Laver

B. Altar of Burnt Offering

F. Candlestick

I. Holy of Holies

A. Outer Court

Exodus 25-27 Description of the tabernacle as given by God to Moses

II Chronicles 3-5 Description of temple as built by Solomon

Hebrews 9-10 Description of Jesus as High Priest of a more perfect tabernacle

I Corinthians 6:19 and 20; 12:12 Description of the Body of Christ with each believer as a temple of the Holy Spirit

Seven articles of furniture: Altar—Blood
Laver—Water
Table of Shewbread—Bread
Golden Lampstand—Oil
Altar of Incense—Prayer
Ark of the Covenant—Law
Mercy Seat—Grace

A. *Outer Court* Place of the Gentiles (Exodus 27:9-19; 38:9-20)
Christian Parallel—Most of Jesus' ministry took place among the Gentiles

B. *Altar of Burnt Offering* (Exodus 27:1-8)
As one comes in the only door, he is confronted with the need of a sacrifice
Christian parallel—Jesus is the door (John 10:9), the only way to the Father. He is also the Lamb of God, sacrificed for us

C. *Laver* (Exodus 30:17-21) Place of cleansing
Christian Parallel—Our need of cleansing (Psalm 51:2). The command to cleanse ourselves (II Corinthians 7:1); way of cleansing (I John 1:7 and 9; Ephesians 5:25-27)

D. *The Holy Place* Where God's people are. (Exodus 40)
Christian Parallel—The anointed body of believers and the articles of furnishings available to them (fellowship, ministry, communication with God) (John 14:23)

E. *Table of Shewbread* (Exodus 25:23-30; Levitius 24:5-9) Elevated table containing the bread which represented God's presence among his people.
Christian Parallel—Jesus was lifted up (John 12:32); Jesus is the Bread of Life (John 6:32-36)

F. *Golden Lampstand* (Exodus 25:31-40; Leviticus 24:1-4)
Christian Parallel—Jesus is the light of the world (John 8:12);
Believers are lights (Matthew 5:14-16)

G. *Altar of Incense* (Exodus 30:1-10)
Christian Parallel—Prayer is as incense (Psalm 141:2) Incense represents the prayers of the saints (Revelation 8:3-5)

H. *Veil* (Exodus 26:31 and 32) Separated holy place from the most holy place (Exod··s 26:33);
Only High Priest could go through it, then only on the day of atonement (Hebrews 9:6 and 7);
Torn at Jesus' death (Matthew 27:51)
Believers can now enter God's presence because of Jesus' shed blood (Hebrews 10:19-22)

I. *Holy of Holies* (Exodus 28:29; 26:33) Place where God dwells Contained:

J. *Ark of Covenant* (Exodus 26:33) *& Mercy Seat* (Exodus 26:34; Hebrews 9:5-12) (Ark of Covenant contained 10 commandments, Aaron's rod, pot of manna) Symbolizes God's law and provision—place of His atonement

The Church as the Temple

Jesus first spoke of His Body and the temple in John 2:19 and 21, when He went into the actual temple building to cleanse it because it had become a house of merchandise instead of a house of prayer. He foretold his own death and resurrection, as He talked about the temple being destroyed and then raised up in three days. It was only afterward that His disciples realized He had been speaking of His body as the temple. Ephesians 2:13-22 goes on to explain that, through Jesus, when we become members of God's very own family we are carefully joined together with Christ as a dwelling place of God's Spirit.

The Church can be seen in unique comparison with the original tabernacle in Hebrews 7-10. We see too, in I Peter 2:7 that Jesus is the cornerstone of God's new dwelling place, His people. *"Come to Christ, who is the living Foundation of Rock upon which God builds though men have spurned him, he is very precious to God who has chosen him above all others. And now you have become living building stones for God's use in building his house"* (I Peter 2:4 and 5 LB).

THE FAILURE OF EUODIAS AND SYNTYCHE

(Based on Philippians 4:2 and 3)

At Philippi, women were the first to respond to the Gospel. We saw this to be the case when Paul brought the Good News to Lydia when he found her down by the riverside praying to Jehovah.

Believers at Philippi then began to meet in Lydia's house; perhaps Euodias and Syntyche were workers in the local church that came into being. In some way, they were fellow laborers with Paul in that city. We don't know what caused the rift between these two; we don't even know the outcome. It's only certain that they had some kind of conflict, which Paul saw as a hindrance to the work of the Lord and that he urged them to be reconciled and live in peace.

LESSONS FROM EUODIAS AND SYNTYCHE

Relationships in the Family of God

Though we were created by God, we don't become His *children* until we receive Jesus as our Savior and Lord. We must be *born again* (John 3:5-8) and translated from the kingdom of darkness to the kingdom of His dear Son (Colossians 1:13). *"And, if children, then heirs, heirs of God, and joint-heirs with Christ"* (Romans 8:17).

In this new relationship, with God as our Father and Jesus Christ as our *brother,* we find ourselves part of a new family. As with human families, there must be a working out of relationships. As children, we need instruction as well as correction, for if we endure discipline God deals with us as with sons (Hebrews 12:7 and 8).

Paul had problems with quarrelsome women in his day. Women in the Church, today, still need to learn to love one another and to relate to one another as part of the same body.

316

Like Euodias and Syntyche, we are laborers together with God. Each person has a function in His Body. We're to know our place and be in submission to authority. Only as we fill our minds with God's Word can we come into the same mind, for then we'll have the mind of Christ. It's the oneness in His mind that brings us into real unity and accord.

I Corinthians 3:1-4 Division and strife come from having a mind that is _____

_____

This means _____

_____

I Corinthians 2:16 We're to have the _____

_____

_____

John 16:13-15 The _____

helps us come into one mind by _____

_____

_____

I Corinthians 1:10 Believers are exhorted to _____

_____

_____

I Peter 3:8 and 9 As Believers, we're to _____

_____

We are called to _____

not _____

_____

_____

Philippians 2:2-8 To have the mind which was in Christ Jesus,

we _____

_____

_____

Psalm 133:1 We're to dwell together in _____

_____

_____

James 3:16 Where there is _____

_____

there is _____

I Corinthians 12:25 There should be no _____

_____

but rather _____

_____

Ephesians 4:1-13 We come into unity of the faith by _____

_____

_____

Ephesians 4:14-32 As we come into a mature relationship with God and with each other, we will _____

_____

_____

THE SUCCESS OF LOIS AND EUNICE
(Based on II Timothy 1:1-8; Acts 16:1-3)

Though grandmothers are referred to in Scripture, the term _grandmother_ is used only once. This is in reference to Lois, mother of Eunice, and grandmother of Timothy.

Lois was a devout Jewess who had instructed her beloved daughter and grandson in the Old Testament Scriptures. She was a living example of Joel 1:3, which says, _"Tell ye your children of it, and let your children tell their children, and their children another generation."_ Hers was a family which passed the Word of God from generation to generation.

The family lived in Lystra, it's possible that Paul, during a visit there, had the joy of leading Lois and Eunice and Timothy to Christ (Acts 14:6 and 7; 16:1). He then wrote of the unfeigned faith that dwelt in all three. We have no record of Timothy's father, apart from the fact that he was a Gentile.

The Bible tells us that Eunice and Lois had great spiritual influence upon Timothy. These godly women trained him up in the way he should go. How grateful they must have been when Paul chose Timothy as his companion in missionary work. To Timothy, Paul seemed to say, "You have always been schooled in the Scriptures. This represents God's grace to you. So be thankful."

After Paul's reference to Lois and Eunice, they aren't mentioned again. They may, however, have been the ones he alluded to in I Timothy 5:4 and 5: _"But if any widow have children or nephews, let them learn first to show piety at home, and to requite their parents; for that is good and acceptable before God. Now she that is a widow indeed, and desolate, trusteth in God, and continueth in supplications and prayers night and day."_

LESSONS FROM LOIS AND EUNICE
Relationships Between Generations in the Family of God

God's desire is that whole families be saved so the Church

318

will be composed of people of all generations. What is the prayer of Psalm 71, particularly verses 17 and 18? _____

_____

_____

Describe the salvation of the following whole families:

Rahab's (Joshua 2:17-19; 6:25) _____

_____

_____

Cornelius' (Acts 10:21-44) _____

_____

_____

The Philippian Jailer's (Acts 16:31-34) _____

_____

_____

THE SUCCESS OF THE ELECT LADY
(Based on II John 1:1-13)

Though the Elect Lady can be called a success, what we read about her contains a warning lest she fail. Who was she?

First, she was a *lady*, implying that she was a woman possessing dignity. She was *elect*, meaning she was chosen of the Lord. Not only was this lady elect in the sense of character, but also in being elect or chosen of God according to His eternal purpose. This elect lady was probably a convert of John's ministry. He extols her for her devotion to the Lord.

It's evident that she was well-known to John. Since no husband is mentioned, she was probably a rich widow with ample means to care for the saints of God who came her way. It was because she was so given to hospitality that John warns her about welcoming false teachers who denied that Jesus came as God manifest in the flesh. John urged the elect lady to not be deceive or lose what she already had. He told her not to entertain these deceivers in her home. And, to be safeguarded against such, she must be obedient to the truth.

Her children, following her faith, walked in the truth and were also praised by John for this.

LESSONS FROM THE ELECT LADY
Relationships We Are Not to Have As Part of God's Family

While we're told to come into unity with fellow believers we're also warned not to have relationships with those who will deceive and lead us astray.

I John 4:1-6 Here we're warned concerning _____

_____

because _____

WOMEN IN THE BIBLE

II Peter 2:1-22 We're warned against false teachers and prophets who _____

_____

_____

Matthew 10:5-15 When Jesus sent out His disciples, He warned them to _____

_____

_____

II Corinthians 6:16-18 Here, we're warned to _____

_____

_____

II Thessalonians 3:14 and 15 Here, Paul is warning _____

_____

He said, in this case, to _____

_____

_____

Matthew 18:15-17 Concerning church discipline, Jesus says

_____

_____

II Timothy 4:1-4 Those living in the last days are warned

_____

_____

SUMMARY

Using the concept of the church as a spiritual house, we consider the relationships God wants us to have with one another as we are "builded together for a habitation of God through the Spirit" (Ephesians 2:22). Euodias and Syntyche exemplify conflicts that often arise in working together. Lois and Eunice lift up the family relationships we're to have as believers.

The Elect Lady makes us aware of the relationships we're *not* to have, particularly with false teachers. We can learn from each of these how to be better sisters in the Lord.

MODERN EXAMPLE

As a recent widow Ruth found much time on her hands, so she volunteered to help an inter-church ministry which maintained a center where the needy came for food and other emergency needs. Several days a week she could be found interviewing clients, stocking the pantry, updating records—whatever needed to be done. She was not only capable, but she liked to keep busy. The more involved she became the more she saw things that needed to be done. So on various occasions, she suggested changes to the leadership. Often, procedures were altered or new policies were made because of Ruth's insights. However, the longer she worked and the more her suggestions were heeded, the more domineering she became toward the other volunteers.

When Pamela, a young mother, volunteered to help with the Christmas project, she was unaware of the situation. She only knew that she was excited about special ways to decorate the baskets, messages to put into them, and the possibility of adding toys to the supply of food. She even talked with the director, who approved her new and fresh ideas.

But when Ruth discovered what Pamela was doing, she took her aside and explained that the baskets had never been done that way before. Then she subtly discredited Pamela's ideas whenever she was talking with other volunteers. Pamela was hurt, but she didn't know what to do. She was already very involved in the project and wanted to see it through, so she prayed.

The center's leadership became very concerned about the toll the situation was taking on their already stressed volunteers. This season of "goodwill to men" was fast becoming one of "bad will in the ministry." The whole purpose of their Christmas outreach was being lost amidst hurt feelings.

Tension was high as the volunteers gathered for their regular monthly meeting. They clustered into small groups instead of mingling with each other as usual.

To begin on a more positive note, the director announced that business would be discussed at the end of the meeting. He then introduced a pastor, who began to read the Christmas story. Following the Scripture reading, the pastor discussed the uniqueness of each of the gifts of the wise men He talked about how each person, today, has a unique gift of service which he can bring before the Lord.

In closing, he asked that heads be bowed in prayer, and that each person give the Lord his or her own unique gift—the special service he was performing this Christmas season.

While all was very still, Pamela got up out of her chair and crossed the room. She put her arms around Ruth, giving her a hug as she whispered in her ear. Soon, the others could hear Ruth's soft weeping—but they dared not look up because of the tears in their own misty eyes. Now, thinking about their own unique gifts seemed quite inappropriate. They had just witnessed what the Lord's unique gift to man had done. Jesus, whose birth they were remembering through the giving of Christmas baskets, came to bring God's love. For Ruth and Pamela, this love brought forgiveness and reconciliation. What greater gift was there to remember at Christmas time?

WHAT DO YOU THINK?

1. What is your concept of the true Church? _____

WOMEN IN THE BIBLE

_____

2. How do we, as believers, come into unity, one accord, or one mind? What hinders this? _____

_____

_____

3. How do you express love and concern toward your fellow sisters in the Lord? _____

_____

_____

4. What is your attitude to be toward those you don't agree with? _____

_____

_____

5. What is the Scriptural warning concerning false teachers and prophets? _____

_____

_____

EVALUATE YOURSELF

1. In what ways are you implementing the principles learned from these five women? _____

_____

_____

2. In what ways are you failing to implement the principles learned from them? _____

_____

_____

3. What do you need to do to change? _____

_____

_____

4. How will you do it? _____

_____

_____

Lesson 33
The Bride of the Lamb of God

An Example of The Glorious Church

"That he might present it to himself a glorious church...For we are members of his body, of his flesh, and of his bones. For this cause shall a man leave his father and mother, and shall be joined unto his wife, and they two shall be one flesh. This is a great mystery: but I speak concerning Christ and the church."
Ephesians 5:27a, 30-32

SETTING THE STAGE

As we come to the last lesson of this course of study, we'll take a deeper look at the ultimate woman in the Bible—the Bride of Jesus Christ. She isn't a single person, nor even a composite of many persons, but a new creation of all those whose names are written in the Lamb's Book of Life. She's the Church, the true born-again believers, the Body of Jesus Christ. She's the culmination of God's desire and plan for man—people with whom He can have intimate fellowship throughout eternity.

In the first lesson, we introduced the Bride as the one whom God is, even now, preparing to reign with Jesus. Throughout this study, we've seen how each woman in the Bible teaches us something which helps us conform to the nature of Jesus. By allowing the Holy Spirit to work these truths in our lives, we'll become the Bride with all the splendor and beauty that God desires.

We'll learn that God has the ultimate responsibility for bringing this Bride into being, but that we also have a part. We must accept what God accomplished through Jesus, obey His Word and yield to the work of the Holy Spirit in our lives.

The Bride of Jesus Christ

According to God's Word, the Church is both the Body of Christ and the Bride of Christ. These two concepts have to do with a difference in time. Today, the Church is the Body of Christ manifesting the life of Christ in the world. One day in the future, God will present the Church to Jesus Christ as His Bride.

Adam and Eve show us a type of Jesus and the Church (as was pointed out in the lesson on Eve). Eve was the *first Adam's* wife, taken from his side while he was asleep, and made from Adam's rib; she was of the body of Adam. God brought her to Adam and she became his wife.

In like manner, the Church, the *last Adam's* wife, came from

Christ. As Jesus hung upon the cross, His side was pierced; and blood and water flowed out. These represent Christ imparting his life to us. As we accept what His blood did in atoning for our sin, and drink of the water of life which He freely offers, we become of His Body. Then, as Eve was presented to Adam, God will present us to Jesus as His Bride. Thus, those who receive eternal life from Christ will someday, be brought to Him.

Ephesians 5:28 and 29 speaks of the relationship of Christ and the Church by comparing it to a marriage relationship. As the Bridegroom-to-be, Jesus loves His Church, sanctifies it, makes it holy (without spot and blemish), and cleanses it, preparing it to be presented unto Himself as glorious Bride.

Genesis 1:27 and 28 The Bride can be compared to the first woman God created in that she _____

_____

_____

I Corinthians 15:45-49 Adam was the _____

_____

The Lord from heaven (Jesus) is the _____

_____

_____

Hosea 2:19 and 20 God says of Himself _____

_____

_____

Isaiah 54:5-7 Israel's husband is _____

_____

_____

Colossians 1:18-22 Jesus is the _____

_____

_____

Ephesians 2:1-7 Because of our acceptance of what Jesus has done for us, we _____

_____

_____

Ephesians 5:22-32 Christ is the _____

_____

The Church's relationship to Christ is compared to _____

_____

_____

324

Revelation 3:21 The ultimate position of the Bride (the Overcomers) is _____

_____

_____

Making Ourselves Ready

Though it's ultimately God who makes the entire provision for the glorious Bride of Jesus Christ, we find (in Revelation 19:7), that she also "hath made herself ready." How does she do this? By accepting the provision God made for her redemption through the blood of Jesus Christ, obeying His Word, and yielding to the work of the Holy Spirit in her life.

What part do you have in becoming part of the Bride?
(See John 3:3-8; Romans 10:17; II Corinthians 5:17; Revelation 19:7)

_____

_____

What is your part in being made clean, pure and white?
(See I John 1:9; I John 2:1 and 2; Ephesians 5:26; Revelation 7:14)

_____

_____

What can you do to help separate yourself unto God?
(See I John 2:6 and 15-17; Hebrews 9-14; John 17:17; Romans 8:14-18)

_____

_____

What part does prayer have in bringing about the fulfillment of God's divine plan?
(See Ezekiel 22:30 and 31; Matthew 9:38; Matthew 16:18 and 19; Luke 10:19; John 20:21-23)

_____

_____

How can you begin to rule, even now?
(See Ephesians 6:10-18; II Corinthians 10:3-5)

_____

_____

What does Matthew 25:1-13 teach you concerning being prepared for the coming wedding?

_____

_____

"Beloved, now are we the sons of God, and it doth not yet appear what we shall be; but we know that, when he shall appear, we shall be like him; for we shall see him as he is" (I John 3:2).

Thus, the Bride of Christ will be one who:
* has accepted what Jesus did to redeem her
* loves Jesus and is committed to Him with her whole heart
* fully obeys God's Word
* diligently prays that His Kingdom come
* intercedes in prayer so others might know Him
* participates in spiritual warfare
* lives by faith in Him and claims His Word for her own
* gives worship and praise to Him, having pleasure in intimate fellowship with Him
* is an overcomer in this life
* is willing to suffer for and with Him
* always seeks to do His will
* gives Him glory for all good that happens
* knows that He is in complete control of everything
* testifies of Him whenever possible
* separates herself unto Him
* allows the Holy Spirit to conform her to His nature

The Marriage of the Bride and Groom

Understanding marriage customs of Bible times gives insight to the coming together of the Church and Jesus Christ.

The bridegroom traveled from his father's house to the home of his intended bride. (Sometimes the father sent a servant.)

Jesus left His Father and came to earth to get His Bride. (Ephesians 5:25-28; John 1:14; Matthew 10:40; John 20:21)

The father of the bride-to-be negotiated with the bridegroom as to the price he must pay to purchase his bride.

Jesus paid the price of redemption with His own blood. (I Corinthians 6:19 and 20)

When the price was paid, the marriage covenant came into being. At that point, the man and woman were regarded as husband and wife, even though they had not consummated the marriage. (Such was the case of Joseph and Mary before Jesus' birth.)

The Church has been set apart (sanctified) for the bridegroom, Jesus Christ. (Ephesians 5:25-27)

As soon as the covenant was made, the bride was declared to be set apart for the bridegroom. The couple then drank from a cup over which the betrothal benediction had been pronounced.

Jesus symbolized this marriage covenant during the Passover supper with his disciples. The Church shares it by partaking of the Last Supper in remembrance of Him. (I Corinthains 11:25)

The bridegroom then left the home of the bride and returned to his father's house. There, separated from his bride, he remained for twelve months.

326

Jesus ascended back to the Father after paying the purchase price for His bride. (John 6:62; Acts 1:9-11)

During the separation, the bride gathered her wedding trousseau. The bridegroom prepared future living accommodations for his bride.

Jesus is now preparing a place for His Bride. The Holy Spirit has also given gifts as part of this preparation. (John 14:2; Ephesians 4:11-13)

After the period of separation, the groom and his groomsmen left the house of the groom's father—usually at night—and conducted a torchlight procession to the home of the bride.

Jesus will soon come again from His Father's house accompanied by a heavenly host. (John 14:3; Matthew 24:30; 25:31)

Though the bride expected the bridegroom, she never knew when he would come. So, she must be prepared at any time—day or night. As he drew near, he would give a shout! *We don't know the day or hour of Jesus' return. But, are told it will be preceded by a shout. (I Thessalonians 5:2; 4:16; Matthew 24:36)*

The bridegroom took his bride, and her servants, and returned to his father's house.

The Bride will be caught up in the air to be with the Lord. (I Thessalonians 4:14-17)

The bride and bridegroom entered into the bridal chamber and consummated their marriage in physical union.

Jesus' union with the Church will take place in heaven for all eternity. (I Thessalonians 4:14-17; Revelation 19:7-9; Revelation 22:5)

Let's look at additional Scriptures which tell us of some of the marriage customs:

Genesis 24 What similarities do you see between Rebekah becoming the bride of Isaac and the Church becoming the Bride of Jesus Christ?

_____

_____

What do the following tell us of the betrothal period?

Genesis 24:58-61 _____

_____

_____

I Samuel 18:17-27 _____

_____

_____

Matthew 1:18 and 19 _____

_____

_____

Matthew 25:1-13 What do we learn about the procession to

the bride's house? _____

WOMEN IN THE BIBLE

_____

_____

Genesis 24:65 What did the bride wear? _____

_____

Isaiah 61:10 How was the bridegroom bedecked? _____

_____

_____

Matthew 22:11 and 12 What was the distinctive clothing of the guests? _____

_____

_____

John 2:1-11 How did the guests celebrate the occasion? _____

_____

_____

Revelation 19:1-9 What insights do you gain from reading about the Marriage Supper of the Lamb? _____

_____

_____

Song of Solomon From this book, which is full of imagery and symbolism, do you see anything of the love relationship between Jesus and His Bride? If so, what? _____

_____

_____

SUMMARY

The Bride of Jesus Christ is the Church, the true born-again believers of Jesus Christ. She's the culmination of God's desire and plan for man—a people with whom He can share intimate fellowship throughout eternity.

WHAT DO YOU THINK?

1. Have you ever thought of yourself as part of the *Bride* of Jesus Christ? Do you now? How does this change your thinking and present relationship to Him? _____

_____

_____

2. Are you eagerly anticipating the marriage supper of the Lamb? How can you make yourself ready? _____

328

3. Do you now see how all the women in God's Word help you be conformed to the nature of Jesus, so that you truly can be a "glorious church?" _____

ENERGIZE, REVITALIZE, REVOLUTIONIZE
YOUR BIBLE STUDY WITH ANOTHER SELECTION
FROM HENSLEY PUBLISHING

Through the Bible in One Year
Alan B. Stringfellow • ISBN 1-56322-014-8

Christian Discipleship
Steven Collins • ISBN 1-56322-022-9

God's Great & Precious Promises
Connie Witter • ISBN 1-56322-063-6

Couples in the Bible — Examples To Live By
Sylvia Charles • ISBN 1-56322-062-8

Preparing for Marriage God's Way
Wayne Mack • ISBN 1-56322-019-9

Men in the Bible — Examples To Live By
Don Charles • ISBN 1-56322-067-9

Becoming the Noble Woman
Anita Young • ISBN 1-56322-020-2

7 Steps to Bible Skills
Dorothy Hellstern • ISBN 1-56322-029-6

Women in the Bible — Examples To Live By
Sylvia Charles • ISBN 1-56322-021-0

Great Characters of the Bible
Alan B. Stringfellow • ISBN 1-56322-046-6

Pathways to Spiritual Understanding
Richard Powers • ISBN 1-56322-023-7

Great Truths of the Bible
Alan B. Stringfellow • ISBN 1-56322-047-4

Inspirational Study Journals
A FRESH APPROACH
TO INDIVIDUAL AND SMALL-GROUP STUDY

In His Hand
Patti Becklund • ISBN 1-56322-068-7

Rare & Beautiful Treasures
Nolene Niles • ISBN 1-56322-071-7

In Everything You Do
Sheri Stout • ISBN 1-56322-069-5

Love's Got Everything To Do With It
Rosemarie Karlebach • ISBN 1-56322-070-9

AÑADE ENERGIA, REVITALIZA Y REVOLUCIONA
TU ESTUDIO BIBLICO CON OTRAS SELECCIONES
DE PUBLICACIONES HENSLEY

A Traves De La Biblia En Un Año
Alan B. Stringfellow • ISBN 1-56322-061-X

Mujeres En La Biblia
Sylvia Charles • ISBN 1-56322-072-5

Preparando El Matrimonio
En El Camino De Dios
Wayne Mack • ISBN 1-56322-066-0